TREATING
SEXUAL DISORDERS

THE JOSSEY-BASS LIBRARY OF
CURRENT CLINICAL TECHNIQUE
IRVIN D. YALOM, GENERAL EDITOR

NOW AVAILABLE

Treating Alcoholism
Stephanie Brown, Editor

Treating Schizophrenia
Sophia Vinogradov, Editor

Treating Women Molested in Childhood
Catherine Classen, Editor

Treating Depression
Ira D. Glick, Editor

Treating Eating Disorders
Joellen Werne, Editor

Treating Dissociative Identity Disorder
James L. Spira, Editor

Treating Couples
Hilda Kessler, Editor

Treating Adolescents
Hans Steiner, Editor

Treating the Elderly
Javaid I. Sheikh, Editor

Treating Sexual Disorders
Randolph S. Charlton, Editor

Treating Difficult Personality Disorders
Michael Rosenbluth, Editor

Treating Anxiety Disorders
Walton T. Roth, Editor

Treating the Psychological Consequences of HIV
Michael F. O'Connor, Editor

FORTHCOMING

Treating Children
Hans Steiner, Editor

TREATING SEXUAL DISORDERS

A VOLUME IN THE JOSSEY-BASS
LIBRARY OF CURRENT CLINICAL TECHNIQUE

Randolph S. Charlton, EDITOR

Irvin D. Yalom, GENERAL EDITOR

Jossey-Bass Publishers • San Francisco

Substantial discounts on bulk quantities of Jossey-Bass books are available to corporations, professional associations, and other organizations. For details and discount information, contact the special sales department at Jossey-Bass Inc., Publishers (415) 433–1740; Fax (800) 605–2665.

For sales outside the United States, please contact your local Simon & Schuster International Office.

Manufactured in the United States of America on Lyons Falls Pathfinder Tradebook. This paper is acid-free and 100 percent totally chlorine-free.

Library of Congress Cataloging-in-Publication Data

Treating sexual disorders/Randolph S. Charlton, editor.
   p.   cm.—(Jossey-Bass library of current clinical technique)
   Includes bibliographical references and index.
   ISBN 0-7879-0311-6 (alk. paper)
   1. Sex therapy. I. Charlton, Randolph S., date. II. Series.
RC557.T73 1996
616.6'906—dc20

96-8762
CIP

FIRST EDITION
PB Printing 10 9 8 7 6 5 4 3 2 1

CONTENTS

FOREWORD

At a recent meeting of clinical practitioners, a senior practitioner declared that more change had occurred in his practice of psychotherapy in the past year than in the twenty preceding years. Nodding assent, the others all agreed.

And was that a good thing for their practice? A resounding "No!" Again, unanimous concurrence—too much interference from managed care; too much bureaucracy; too much paper work; too many limits set on fees, length, and format of therapy; too much competition from new psychotherapy professions.

Were these changes a good or a bad thing for the general public? Less unanimity on this question. Some pointed to recent positive developments. Psychotherapy was becoming more mainstream, more available, and more acceptable to larger segments of the American public. It was being subjected to closer scrutiny and accountability—uncomfortable for the practitioner but, if done properly, of potential benefit to the quality and efficiency of behavioral health care delivery.

But without dissent this discussion group agreed—and every aggregate of therapists would concur—that astounding changes are looming for our profession: changes in the reasons that clients request therapy; changes in the perception and practice of mental health care; changes in therapeutic theory and technique; and changes in the training, certification, and supervision of professional therapists.

From the perspective of the clientele, several important currents are apparent. A major development is the de-stigmatization of psychotherapy. No longer is psychotherapy invariably a hush-hush affair, laced with shame and conducted in offices with separate entrance and exit doors to prevent the uncomfortable possibility of clients meeting one another.

Today such shame and secrecy have been exploded. Television talk shows—Oprah, Geraldo, Donahue—have normalized psychopathology and psychotherapy by presenting a continuous public parade of dysfunctional human situations: hardly a day passes without television fare of confessions and audience interactions with deadbeat fathers, sex addicts, adult children of alcoholics, battering husbands and abused wives, drug dealers and substance abusers, food bingers and purgers, thieving children, abusing parents, victimized children suing parents.

The implications of such de-stigmatization have not been lost on professionals who no longer concentrate their efforts on the increasingly elusive analytically suitable neurotic patient. Clinics everywhere are dealing with a far broader spectrum of problem areas and must be prepared to offer help to substance abusers and their families, to patients with a wide variety of eating disorders, adult survivors of incest, victims and perpetrators of domestic abuse. No longer do trauma victims or substance abusers furtively seek counseling. Public awareness of the noxious long-term effects of trauma has been so sensitized that there is an increasing call for public counseling facilities and a growing demand, as well, for adequate counseling provisions in health care plans.

The mental health profession is changing as well. No longer is there such automatic adoration of lengthy "depth" psychotherapy where "deep" or "profound" is equated with a focus on the earliest years of the patient's life. The contemporary field is more pluralistic: many diverse approaches have proven therapeutically effective and the therapist of today is more apt to tailor the therapy to fit the particular clinical needs of each patient.

In past years there was an unproductive emphasis on territoriality and on the maintaining of hierarchy and status—with the more prestigious professions like psychiatry and doctoral-level psychology expending considerable energy toward excluding master's level therapists. But those battles belong more to the psychotherapists of yesterday; today there is a significant shift toward a more collaborative interdisciplinary climate.

Managed care and cost containment is driving some of these changes. The role of the psychiatrist has been particularly affected as cost efficiency has decreed that psychiatrists will less frequently deliver psychotherapy personally but, instead, limit their activities to supervision and to psychopharmacological treatment.

In its efforts to contain costs, managed care has asked therapists to deliver a briefer, focused therapy. But gradually managed care is realizing that the bulk of mental health treatment cost is consumed by inpatient care and that outpatient treatment, even long-term therapy, is not only salubrious for the patient but far less costly. Another looming change is that the field is turning more frequently toward the group therapies. How much longer can we ignore the many comparative research studies demonstrating that the group therapy format is equally or more effective than higher cost individual therapies?

Some of these cost-driven edicts may prove to be good for the patients; but many of the changes that issue from medical model mimicry—for example, efforts at extreme brevity and overly precise treatment plans and goals that are inappropriate to the therapy endeavor and provide only the illusion of efficiency—can hamper the therapeutic work. Consequently, it is of paramount importance that therapists gain control of their field and that managed care administrators not be permitted to dictate how psychotherapy or, for that matter, any other form of health care be conducted. That is one of the goals of this series of texts: to provide mental health professionals with such a deep grounding in theory and such a clear vision of effective therapeutic technique that they will be empowered to fight confidently for the highest standards of patient care.

∽

The Jossey-Bass Library of Current Clinical Technique is directed and dedicated to the front-line therapist—to master's and doctoral-level clinicians who personally provide the great bulk of mental health care. The purpose of this entire series is to offer state-of-the-art instruction in treatment techniques for the most commonly encountered clinical conditions. Each volume offers a focused theoretical background as a foundation for practice and then dedicates itself to the practical task of what to do for the patient—how to assess, diagnose, and treat.

I have selected volume editors who are either nationally recognized experts or are rising young stars. In either case, they possess a comprehensive view of their specialty field and have selected leading therapists of a variety of persuasions to describe their therapeutic approaches.

Although all the contributors have incorporated the most recent and relevant clinical research in their chapters, the emphasis in these volumes is the practical technique of therapy. We shall offer specific therapeutic guidelines, and augment concrete suggestions with the liberal use of clinical vignettes and detailed case histories. Our intention is not to impress or to awe the reader, and not to add footnotes to arcane academic debates. Instead, each chapter is designed to communicate guidelines of immediate pragmatic value to the practicing clinician. In fact, the general editor, the volume editors, and the chapter contributors have all accepted our assignments for that very reason: a rare opportunity to make a significant, immediate, and concrete contribution to the lives of our patients.

Irvin D. Yalom, M.D.
Professor Emeritus of Psychiatry
Stanford University

INTRODUCTION

Randolph S. Charlton

There have been thousands of different drawings of the world,
many maps made of reality. Each puts the gods, the good, the false
and the true in a different place. They cannot each be correct—
there are too many counterclaims—yet society after society has
sailed to greatness (not simply the doom they also doomed
themselves to) following these false charts, these fictions that have
been projected on the planet. And the planet, like the great screen
of a drive-in movie, accepts them all, lighted by the illusions of
passion, for as long as the passions last. If so, then our lives are
made of fictions, beliefs we construct and then dwell in like a beach
house in Malibu.

WILLIAM H. GASS

This book appears at a time when there is no shortage of books about sex and sex therapy. On the shelves of the public library down the street from my house are volumes describing sex on the Internet, melatonin and its effect on sexual desire, the nature of sexual perversions, female masturbation, what women really want, how to be your own sex therapist, how to spice up a marriage, and one that I think should be in the fiction section about how to have a two-hour orgasm. A collection of the best erotic short stories of the year is displayed prominently by the cash register at our local bookstore. A textbook, two journals devoted to the scientific study of sexual issues, and *Yellowsilk*, a magazine of erotic poems and stories, are stacked on the corner of my desk, silently waiting their turn to be read.

Two shelves in the bookcase behind me are devoted to sex. That amounts to eight feet, four inches of words, tables, and pictures about the erotic side of our lives. One of my favorites is an old, well-worn paperback entitled *Is Sex Necessary?* Although written at the tail end of the roaring twenties, E. B. White and James Thurber captured something timeless about human nature. While the stock market was getting ready to crash, Elliot Ness was working his way up in the FBI, and Prohibition was only a whisper of an idea in the electorate's mind, America's intelligentsia was thinking about sex. According to the authors,

> The problem in this case was to make sex seem more compli- cated and dangerous. This task was taken up by sociologists, analysts, gynecologists, psychologists, and authors; they approached it with a good deal of scientific knowledge and an immense zeal. They joined forces and made the whole matter of sex complicated beyond the wildest dreams of our fathers. The country became flooded with books. Sex, which had hith- erto been a physical expression, became largely mental. The whole order of things changed. To prepare for marriage, young girls no longer assembled a hope chest—they read books on abnormal psychology. If they finally did marry, they found themselves with a large number of sex books on hand, but almost no pretty underwear. Most of them, luckily, never married at all—just continued to read.

It appears that history is repeating itself. If I were to read all the sex books that came my way, I wouldn't be able to find the time to have any sex at all.

So, before you get lost in the pages of this book, go out and get yourself or your partner something sexy to wear, light a fire in the grate, and spend an evening making love. It's probably the best thing you can do for yourself and the best thing you can do to learn about sex and sex therapy. Having good sex counts. Hey, having bad sex counts. Bad sex isn't much fun, of course, but if you pay attention, it might help you understand something about people whose sex lives aren't working for them.

That said, I want to encourage you to interrupt your sex life now and then to read this book. You will find it helpful when you want to treat individuals with sexual problems. If you are just beginning to work in the sexual arena, you will find ample material to get you started and take you through evaluation and treatment of all the major sexual disorders. If you are already familiar with the techniques of sex therapy, you'll find that this book will help you organize your thinking and augment your therapeutic abilities.

∽

Evaluating another person's sexual experience is a risky business. For the most part, people do not want their sexual desire, function, and fantasy to see the light of their own consciousness, much less that of a relative stranger. Think about it for a moment. How many times have you told the intimate details of your sexual life to someone else—your erotic daydreams, your sexual failures, your most private pleasures? Once? Maybe a couple of times? More likely, never. At least not all of it.

Even in the relatively nonjudgmental context of a loving relationship, people do not feel comfortable revealing their deepest sexual passions. There's too much at stake. Our most vulnerable and precious sense of self is contained in our sexuality, and it is no small task to share this with another, especially another who might judge our actions and desires as normal or deviant. And yet, patients do bring their sexuality into therapy—reluctantly, fearfully, sometimes hopefully.

Understandably, the details of sex are concealed behind masks of social propriety and are only brought forward after patient and therapist have formed a safe and trusting relationship. And even then there is anxiety.

"Am I normal?"

"What do you think about me knowing I masturbate?"

"Are you disgusted that I fantasize about having sex in a public place?"

I think almost everyone has had at least an experience or two in which sex simply didn't work. Erections that didn't erect. Lubrication that wasn't there to lubricate. Lots of thrusting, signifying nothing, ending in frustration and dismay. As an infrequent occurrence, such failures of our bodies and our expectations are tolerable. But what happens when failure is the norm, rather than the exception?

Throw a pebble into a small, quiet pond, and gentle ripples will extend out from the spot where the pebble disappeared. Drop a truck in the same pond, and the resulting waves will spill over the bank; the quiet will disappear, and the once lovely pond may never return to normal. A crude metaphor perhaps, but it's one a patient of mine used to describe his lifelong struggle with an erectile disorder.

∾

Let me tell you about the year I spent working as a medical intern at a large university hospital. As a student I'd been taught how to take a medical history. In theory, you begin with the patient's presenting symptoms and ask questions pertinent to the development of the problem, be it chest pain, nausea, or double vision. With that information in hand, you move on to past medical history, family history, and the review of systems. To do a review of systems, you start at the top of the patient's head and ask questions about the function of everything you come to on the way down. Do you have headaches? Have you ever fainted? How's your hearing? Do you ever see spots in front of your eyes? And so on, taking each vital organ system one by one until you reach the far end of the patient. It's actually a pretty good way of remembering questions you might otherwise forget.

During my first week as a "real doctor," Mr. Rogoff, a retired businessman forty years my senior, was admitted to the ward for evaluation of gastrointestinal bleeding. I still remember his Russian accent, wide smile, and white mustache. Just looking at him told you something was terribly wrong. His eyes had a yellowish cast. He'd lost thirty pounds, and his skin hung on him as if it had been made for someone else.

I sat in the hardbacked chair next to the bed and asked about the development of his symptoms. Mr. Rogoff was polite and cooperative. We progressed rapidly to the review of symptoms. I was doing fine, moving down his body, asking things that would help me understand the condition of his eyes, ears, lungs, heart, liver, and kidneys.

Then I got to his genitals.

Sexual function is supposed to be part of the review of systems. It comes right after bladder function.

"Do you have any trouble urinating?"

"No."

"Have you had any sexually transmitted diseases?"

"No."

Now what? The questions I'd learned to ask about actual sex were general, vague even.

"How is your sex life?"

"OK."

Almost everyone said, "OK" or "Pretty good."

Most interns let it go at that.

Could I expect a man who looked deathly ill, whom I'd just met, to tell me the intimate details of his sex life? How could I, a twenty-five-year-old still wet behind the ears, ask a man old enough to be my father what he did or didn't do in bed?

I guess some people could, but I couldn't. Several barriers were in the way, perhaps the same barriers that obstruct many professionals in their efforts to communicate about sex.

- Aside from my small arsenal of a few general questions, I didn't know what to ask.

- I experienced Mr. Rogoff as an authority figure, making it very difficult for me to relax and ask him about his private life.

- I felt sorry for Mr. Rogoff. Although this is understandable, it contributed to my reluctance to "bother" him with intimate questions.

- I didn't have a secure sense of self from which to ask about his sexual experience. I would have been too embarrassed and too uncomfortable even if I had known what to ask.

- I incorrectly believed that Mr. Rogoff didn't want to talk
  about sex. After all, I thought, he was in the hospital so that
  we could find out what was wrong with him and do something
  about it. Although this was true, it was a very limited vision of
  what it means to be human.

As it turned out, Mr. Rogoff had cancer of the colon and was transferred to the surgical ward, where he underwent an operation to remove the tumor. I bumped into him on the way to radiology one morning, and we chatted. He was hopeful that they'd gotten all the cancer and that he'd be OK.

Unfortunately, it didn't turn out that way. I saw Mr. Rogoff again when he was admitted to a medical floor for management of metastatic lesions in his liver.

We developed a relationship, a kind of friendship really. Eventually, we did talk about sex. Mr. Rogoff brought it up. He asked me if he would be able to make love to his wife again. He'd been impotent since the new cancerous lesions were discovered.

We began a discussion that ranged from the fatigue he felt, to his fear that he was unattractive to his wife because he'd lost all his hair, to his yearning to be held that went far beyond sexual excitement and orgasm.

I didn't know how to do psychotherapy at that time, so mostly I listened. I told him what I knew about his medical condition and what little I knew about sexual function. I told him that I thought he was a brave man. I asked him if he was scared to die; he asked me if I was scared to grow old. In retrospect, it turned out that I pretty much did the right thing.

I enjoyed my conversations with Mr. Rogoff. They were difficult, certainly, but they were real, and they were quite human. I spent most of my day rushing from one bedside to another—drawing blood, doing spinal taps, listening to heart sounds—hardly having enough time to think, much less feel anything. It was a relief to slow down and sit down. I was drawn into Mr. Rogoff's experience. I didn't know what empathy was at the time, at least not intellectually, but somehow I figured it out.

Mr. Rogoff did make love with his wife again. And she did hold him.

I think I helped.

I know Mr. Rogoff helped me. He helped me decide to go into psychiatry. I wanted to learn how to talk to people about what matters and what is difficult to say. He helped me see that with tact and grace and perseverance you can talk about almost anything.

And he helped me understand that sex is a part of life that carries with it the very seeds of our identity.

When we first began to treat sexual disorders at Stanford, a group of about twenty professionals met several times a week to share information from our various specialties. We worked together to understand and treat patients referred to the medical center with a wide variety of sexual problems. Those of us trained to do psychotherapy did the initial interviewing and the majority of the therapy. Clinical psychologists administered objective and projective tests. Medical specialists did physical exams, obtained necessary lab tests, and participated in the formulation and planning stages of therapy. This was back in the days when teaching hospitals had money, clinicians had time, and patients had an abundance of motivation and hope that therapy could improve their sexual experience. Masters and Johnson had recently published their ground-breaking works on sexual physiology and the treatment of sexual dysfunction. They described in detail how sex worked, or at least how it was supposed to work. The Stanford Clinic was receiving two or three calls a day from individuals and couples wanting information about the treatment of sexual difficulties.

Times have changed, and even medical schools don't have the resources to support a sex clinic where twenty professionals confer leisurely on a case. So what are you, the reader, to do? You can't be an experienced sexologist, psychiatrist, clinical psychologist, marriage and family therapist, nurse practitioner, internist, urologist, gynecologist, and sociologist all rolled into one.

I've tried to create a book that I hope will help solve this problem. I've learned that one way to compensate for lack of experience is to borrow it from someone else. If you choose well, you end up with a mentor whose wisdom is greater than your own, one who not only offers you factual information but also helps you to discover new and useful ways to understand and experience the world. This book will put the services of a urologist, a nurse practitioner specializing in gynecology, two experts in the use of the sleep lab to evaluate male erectile disorders, and several psychiatrists, sex therapists, and clinical psychologists at your disposal. Each will describe the elements that are unique to his or her specialty.

You'll be able to share the ideas and experiences of seasoned professionals. They are people who know from long experience how to treat sexual disorders, but that's not the only reason I asked them to contribute to the book. I picked individuals who have a sense of humor, enjoy reading, and know how to write well. I haven't asked them, but I have the suspicion that most of them would not be above taking time out to buy pretty underwear.

Together we'll review the physical substrate of sexual physiology, including information to help you understand the nature of the diseases and medications that alter sexual function. We'll go over the evaluation of sexual disorders in detail, so that you know what to ask and how to ask it. You'll learn how and when to refer a patient for medical evaluation and psychological testing.

Most important, you'll learn how to treat sexual disorders. We'll cover each of the diagnostic categories of the *DSM-IV* and help you understand what brings them about and what you can do to help a patient resolve them. Experts in the use of short-term focused sex therapy, preorgasmic women's groups, and individual and couple psychotherapy will give specific examples so that you can understand not only what to say but how to think about clinical situations.

∾

I've been seeing patients with sexual symptoms and teaching human sexuality and sex therapy for over twenty years now. In the beginning, I would often find myself getting a headache before seeing an individual or couple, or before teaching a class. I was younger and understandably anxious because I didn't have much experience, but that's only a small part of the story. I think the headaches were painful announcements of my fear that I didn't know enough about sex.

Oh, I conscientiously reviewed the anatomy and physiology of sex. I avidly read the psychiatric literature. I read Masters and Johnson's *Human Sexual Response* and *Human Sexual Inadequacy* cover to cover. Helen Kaplan's *The New Sex Therapy* was the first textbook I used to teach the techniques of sex therapy. I don't know how many times I read through it, and yet I still felt unsure of my ability to teach and to treat sexual matters.

I don't get headaches when I teach classes on sexuality or see patients with sexual disorders anymore. What's changed?

My knees, for one. The clicks and creaks they create are daily reminders that I'm older. Life experience is invaluable to all psychotherapists. It offers us a richer ground from which to understand and empathize. In terms of sexuality, growing older offers a perspective on how the stages of life influence sexual interest, function, and intimacy.

When I was a young man, I knew about a young man's sexuality. I could have told you that the textbook said that as a man ages, the period during which he is unable to reach a second orgasm increases in length, but I wouldn't have had the least idea what that felt like. Before I had a family, I understood that having young children running around the house alters the space within which a couple can comfortably be sexual, but I'm not sure I would have realized how limiting that experience can be.

When I finished my residency training and started practicing, I could still play rugby and run marathons. It made perfect sense that arthritis, low back pain, and fatigue could interfere with sexual desire, but this was a notion pertinent only to other people. Unfortunately, I now know more about this subject than I ever wanted to.

Do you have to have gray hair to treat sexual disorders? Certainly not, though it can offer a semblance of authority. My point is intended to encourage you to honor your own experience while remembering that there is more in heaven and earth than you've probably imagined. Curiosity may have killed the cat, but it won't kill *you*. It's a vital part of what makes psychotherapy for sexual disorders work.

It's your job to make evaluations and draw conclusions, but judgments made outside of an empathic connection to a patient are fraught with the dangers of arbitrariness, personal bias, and countertransference distortion.

Sex is the meeting place of mind and body. It involves issues of meaning, value, and emotional nuance—love, dependency, trust, need, desire, excitement, family patterns, cultural norms, religious beliefs—everything that makes us human can, and does, become part of the psychological experience of sex.

Sex cannot be separated from meaning. Even meaningless sex has a meaning: despair, disconnection, anger, frustration, to name a few possibilities. The same sexual act can have dramatically different consequences depending on whether it is experienced as an intrusion, a submission, a loving encounter, or a waste of time.

Experience has helped me to see more of the possible meanings that we human beings put into sex. It has also helped me to realize that I don't need to know all the answers for my students and patients. Experience has taught me that not knowing the answer is sometimes more important than knowing it.

When I thought I was supposed to know all the answers and be able to tell a patient what to do and how to do it, I got headaches. When I realized that my job was to help my patients figure out what to do and how to do it, I relaxed, and my work improved.

I firmly believe that once you know the basics behind sexual function and sex therapy, your patients will tell you the rest of what you need to know. This book will provide you with those basics and, one hopes, instill a sense of wonder and curiosity about the multiplicity of ways in which we humans express our sexuality.

ACKNOWLEDGMENTS

A book is the sum of many experiences. It rests on the shoulders of all those whose ideas are contained in it, all those whose sweat, blood and tears have made it happen, all those who have supported the authors and allowed them the space and time to reach into their souls to find the words to say what they know.

Without patients, we folks who call ourselves therapists are little more than people with an inordinate interest in suffering. With patients, we are what we most need to be: alive, relevant, and helpful. I think that the very existence of good therapists is predicated on their patients, for their patients are the ones who teach them. I understand only what my patients have taught me.

Our editor at Jossey-Bass, Alan Rinzler, a therapist himself, is one of the few individuals who knows enough about both writing and psychotherapy to have guided this project between the shoals of despair and the turbulent waters of chaotic writing. His advice, support, and hard work are what hold this book together. It seems to me that the inside front cover of the book should have a watermark saying "This book was read and reread by Alan Rinzler." You won't be able to tell where Alan suggested changes, but trust me: this is a much better book because of his labors.

Irv Yalom is the grandfather of this volume. He asked me to organize and edit it. I've known Irv for many years. He was one of my first, and best, teachers at Stanford. Like Alan, he's one of those Renaissance men who can do excellent psychotherapy, write a stirring story or a touching paragraph, and, in Irv's case, play a mean game of tennis.

There are many therapists whose ideas fill the pages that follow. They all deserve thanks and credit. I apologize for being a bit of a wise guy, but I simply can't stop myself from what I'm about to do: Freudjungkohutfairbairnstollerwinnicotschaferkaplanmastersandjohnsonschnarchoffitwheelissprueillgoldbergglobitzandmyanalystallubin.

Without friends and colleagues, a therapist—and an author more so—lives in a vacuum. Let me thank each and every author who has contributed to this book. Without their hard work, this book would not exist.

Finally, there's my family. Putting up with someone who has pretty much disappeared into the computer is not an easy task. Without my family's support and encouragement I would have fallen into apoplexy months ago. Without my son's periodic urging to shut off the word processor and come outside to throw a football, my muscles might have withered away. Without my daughter's laughing request to join her for a cup of coffee and a chat, my mind might have been lost on a dangling participle. Without my wife's loving presence, I would certainly have forgotten that without each other, words don't mean a thing.

Thank you all.

Notes

P. xiii, *There have been thousands:* Gass, W. (1987, January 4). Deciding to do the impossible. *The New York Times Book Review,* p. 1. Copyright © 1987 by The New York Times Co. Reprinted by permission.

P. xiv, *The problem in this case:* Thurber, J., & White, E. B. (1984). *Is sex necessary?* New York: HarperCollins, p. 1.

TREATING
SEXUAL DISORDERS

For Louise, Genevieve, and Blake
With love

I

TALKING AND THINKING ABOUT SEXUALITY

Teri Quatman

We Americans—therapists and clients alike—are typically not provided safe passage into our adult sexuality by the prior generation. As a result, few of us ever get beyond our adolescence with respect to our sexuality. We step into our sexual experience furtively, stealing it in surreptitious sips. The media says yes to our emerging sexuality; our peer group gleams with admiration at our contraband; but the parents within never really change their initial message. "Don't touch yourself there" never completely fades from our experiential memory bank. We are, most of us, people in sexual conflict.

Recently, a guest speaker in my master's level human sexuality class was relating to us how "naturally" he and his father had once communicated about the vast mysteries of male sexuality. My speaker was twelve at the time, and he was accompanying his father on a business trip through eastern Connecticut. The Connecticut Women's Penal Facility had just come into and passed from their view. His father was driving the family Chrysler, and, as though inspired somehow by the sight of the women's prison, he interrupted their silence without moving his eyes from the road: "So, son, have you had any nocturnal emissions yet?"

The speaker felt completely wrong-footed. He knew in that irrevocable instant that he and his father were about to have

THE TALK, and he knew he was trapped. He couldn't leap from the car on the Connecticut highway . . . or maybe he could. He pressed himself as tightly as possible against the door of the car and hurled forth with the one defensive weapon at his disposal.

"Daaaad! I already know all about that stuff. We don't need to talk about it."

To his enormous shock and unspeakable relief, that was enough to quell the enemy advance. He held his position for quite some time, pasted up against the passenger-side escape hatch, and neither spoke of it, or anything else, until they stopped for dinner in New Jersey.

The class laughed heartily at the story. Each of those soon-to-be therapists could empathize—could draw on his or her own experience and feel the awkwardness of the moments described. A tale for Everyman, because nearly every one of the thirty-four students gathered there that afternoon had had his or her experience of THE TALK. For some, it was the spontaneous appearance of sanitized sex-ed reading materials on the dresser; for some, a manly fishing trip; for some, a question-and-answer session that left them only slightly more confused than they had been before; for some, the preempting of the parental "duty" by the teenage rite de slumber party. With rare exception, we all resonate. Time passes. Sexual mores change. But some things are changeless. Why?

OUR CULTURAL NEUROSIS

Why has discomfort become the medium of sexual exchange from one generation to the next? Why is our experience of ourselves as sexual beings stitched so intricately to the fabric of that discomfort? These questions are the beginning of our journey together as we consider the treatment of sexual disorders. Much as it is inconvenient to the task, it seems that an honest approach to treatment issues around sexual disorders must include first and foremost the "treatment" of the therapist—not for erectile dysfunction or vaginismus, although those problems may indeed be present—but for our commonly shared cultural neurosis about being sexual human beings: the stuff that makes us laugh with extra gusto when the jokes are sexual, the stuff that makes the human sexuality course the most enrolled course in the curriculum. Throughout our training as psychotherapists, we learn over and over again that we are not issue-free. We are not parent-free. And, especially in the realm of our sexuality, we are not culture-free.

Learning from Our Parents

What is the nature of our cultural neurosis? From Freudians to social learning theorists, students of human development agree that what we experience with our parents becomes in one way or another incorporated into our patterns of behavior and personality. Our parents are our primary objects, our primary models. From them we learn the parameters of our potential as human beings, the vast repertoire of ways we should and should not be. We observe with utmost astuteness what words to say, in what tone of voice, with what volume, under what conditions; how to think, how to act, how to aspire. We learn emotional valences as well as physical realities. We know somehow not to ask Mom about Uncle Frank. We know when we can jump on Dad and when we can't. And, in those moments when our knowing fails us, we get powerful doses of feedback.

What were the "knowings" we received from our parents about our sexuality? Certainly one has to allow for wide variation in individual experience in order to answer such a question, but I will be so bold as to pose some generalities, based on my years of teaching postgraduate, master's level students as well as on the reported experiences of my client sample for the last decade.

What knowings did we receive? The modal answer is simply this: none. We knew nothing. We had *no* knowings! We had a dad (if we had a dad at home) who dressed out of our view and went to work in the morning, and a mom who did the same and perhaps stayed home to care for the kids or also went to work. We saw Dad or Step-Dad peck Mom on the cheek or the lips on the way in and out the door. We saw them sit in separate chairs and watch TV at night. If they were particularly bonded as a couple, we might have seen them hold hands on occasion. They might have dressed up for an occasional evening out. They might have danced in the kitchen while the chicken was frying. If they were modal, they never talked about their sexual relationship. If they were modal, there would be nothing we could observe as children that might lead us to suspect that they had a special way of relating to one another. If they were modal, they were asexual, as far as we could tell. Closed bedroom doors don't in and of themselves lead children to imagine penises and vaginas or, for that matter, romance and affection. Witness the shock of most kids when they first hear the act of sexual intercourse described.

The patterns of our culture cause most children to spend their younger years completely unaware of Mom and Dad's physical and emotional relating. There is, however, a substantial percentage of children who encounter not asexuality but a sort of dangerous and predatory aura around a parent's sexuality. For some, Mom has many boyfriends who come for a while and spend the night, and it feels unsafe. For some, Daddy viewed and fondled them in uncomfortable ways from the time they were little.

The Power of Silence and Secrecy

Regardless of whether the environment is hermetically sealed from all sexual expression or grossly overtly sexual, two commonalties mark the American experience: silence and secrecy. Whatever else may be true, there are no words. Erections don't have names; arousal doesn't happen. Penises are pee-pees; vaginas are tinklers (both refer to urinary function). Parents' doors get shut and opened again without words. Children are instructed not to touch themselves "down there." And, God forbid, if they are discovered to be touching some other child "down there," the whole thing is put to rest as discreetly and quietly as possible. Kids get ogled and kissed inappropriately by relatives and in-laws—all without any ways to describe what is happening. It is a studied exercise in cultural denial: if we don't really speak of it, perhaps it doesn't exist. And if it doesn't exist, then we're all safe (presumably) from its abuses.

The trouble with silence and secrecy is that if we pretend something doesn't exist, but in fact it does exist, we operate outside the boundaries of reality. We participate in one big, shared cultural thought disorder, and thereby open ourselves to psychological anxieties whose influence is vast. As in any denial-based system, that to which we cannot refer wields enormous psychological power. If I cannot have my anger, if I cannot name it in the interactive space between myself and another, then it silently leaks into the pores of the relationship, stultifying and suffocating the integrity of the relational field. So too with sexuality: that which cannot be handled symbolically (in words) must be expressed in other, more primitive ways.

So, if parental models indeed shroud in silence and secrecy the legitimate expressions of sexual intimacy, how then do children acquire the permission to be and to do what they from birth have already been and done? (Boys have erections from birth; girls experience vaginal lubrication from birth.) How do children learn to identify sexual feelings and impulses, to own such feelings (rather than cutting them off)? We behave in this culture as though these things happen quite naturally as a function of high school pre-registration. But such psychologists as Winnicott and Kohut, and more recently Greenspan, have elucidated the pivotal role of parental mirroring in the stable acquisition of aspects of the self. If an incipient aspect of the self, such as sexuality, is left unmirrored in children, it is forced to develop without essential parental support. Instead of being fully experienced and thus accessible for ongoing development, sexual feelings can then become alloyed to feelings of shame or estrangement, or become in some ways repressed or cut off. For many—probably most—that which was literally part of their birthright becomes conflicted and furtive to them as children. And when finally the irrepressible forces of biology eventuate in the sexualization of the often unsuspecting preadolescent, this process occurs, as has everything that preceded it, on the shroud of silence and secrecy. Paradoxically, when parents who have been silent throughout their child's developing years finally do attempt to break the silence with their adolescent, the youngster, who has by that time internalized her parents' proscriptions finds THE TALK a ludicrous and intrusive venture.

Another guest speaker for my human sexuality class told us of her children's day-to-day experiences of their sexuality. She related that the day before, her seven-year-old, Tina, had been masturbating in the back seat of the van while her older sister and nanny occupied the front seat. The nanny had brought the information back to my speaker. She waited for the next moment when she and Tina were alone together at home.

"Tina, honey, Janet tells me that you were touching yourself around your vagina yesterday in the van. You know, Sweetie, we all touch ourselves there because it feels good to do that. Daddy does, Mommy does, you do. But it's probably best if you only do it when there's no one else around—like in your bedroom or in the bathroom—in a private place. That's where Mommy and Daddy do it. Would that be OK with you?"

"Yeah, Mom, that would be OK."

"Do you have any questions about that, Honey?"

"Yeah, well—I don't like the way it smells."

"Well, Hon, how does it smell?" [Tina quickly proffers the first two fingers of her right hand and waves them under her Mom's nose.]

"Like that." [Mom pulls her daughter's fingers up to her nose for a closer whiff.]

"Well, Honey, it smells just like mine. That's how it's supposed to smell. I like it!"

Tina responds, "Oh." End of conversation.

Unfortunately, this kind of support for a child's sexual development is the rare exception. The cultural norm is that by the time a child moves into puberty, he is in a singularly untenable place. He has no quarter of sexual legitimacy in his own family. Furthermore, he has none in the larger culture. There are no "compensatory" institutions of permission in our culture wherein the adults of the culture recognize and welcome the adolescent's passage into sexual adulthood—no rites of passage, no initiation ceremonies, no clear and unambiguous markers to transit the young person from sexual dys-permission to sexual permission (unless you count sex-ed films). There is, of course, the American media, which extends its often lurid "permissions" ubiquitously. But the media in no way functions in loco parentis, and the modal adolescent knows it.

Thus, the sexually developing adolescent—if she is to develop sexually—has to "steal" sexual knowledge and experience. She learns the tricks of the trade from both the media and the more experienced teens who have preceded her. The players get together in locker rooms and late-night talk sessions to compare contraband. The "baddest" kids have the most to teach. But the game is understood to be at least slightly illicit. How could it be otherwise? The problem is, that which is acquired by illegal means is always somewhat tainted. It cannot be freely explored or fully embraced; it cannot be brought out into the light of day. And so it is disconnected from its spiritual moorings. Our kids cannot receive the grace and power of their sexuality from those who have gone before them, nor can they benefit from the collected wisdom of the grandmothers and grandfathers. They are constrained to be introduced into the (conflicted) joy of their sexual heritage by other adolescents—truly the blind leading the blind. In my human sexuality classes, I'm benignly amused that it is most often the youngest students—the twenty-three- to twenty-eight-year-olds—who feel that they have the most to teach about human sexuality. They often argue passionately about issues of sexual experience with those in the class twice their age.

We accept our cultural neurosis as though it were normative for the species. We accept the silence and secrecy model of parenting our children's sexual development. We accept adolescent knowledge of sexuality. Why? Because most of us were recipients of the same model, and so, at some level, our options are limited. We do silence and secrecy as a default; anything else would require the work of consciousness and, of course, the attendant anxiety.

CLINICAL IMPLICATIONS

How does our cultural neurosis affect the practice of psychotherapy? How does our participation in the culture constrain us as therapists? What is the nature of our sexual countertransference? How can we function freely as clinicians if our own roots drink from the soil of silence, secrecy, shame, and repression?

We do nothing as clinicians if we fail to confront the truth of where we ourselves are. Otherwise we work daily as purveyors of authenticity in others while failing to pursue it in ourselves. All other implications aside, our therapeutic effectiveness is apt to suffer. Especially in the realm of sexual issues, my degree of comfort with my own sexual issues will define the limits of the therapeutic comfort I can extend to another human being. In this most delicate of territories, I can't fake it! I may pretend very well that it is no big deal to talk with clients about their sexual issues, but if I am not at ease with my own issues around sexuality, it will be communicated to them. I will bring my discomfort to the sexual dialogue as countertransference. Nonverbally, unconsciously, through look and tone and expression, my discomfort will make its presence felt. I, human being, must "defend" threatened territory somehow; whether it's through compromise of my emotional presence, subtle voyeurism, or out-and-out discomfort, I will cloud the field. And so, some issues will just not come up; others will be quietly truncated. And I as therapist may never know what has been foreclosed.

It is essential to understand the influences of our own personal and familial culture on us as developing sexual human beings.

The understanding may well yield a sense of freedom. But suppose, instead, you as clinician are just normal—modal. Then to some extent the dys-permissions involved in our cultural neurosis are yours as well. The slowly accumulated and emotionally constraining experiences around your own sexuality as a developing child may make the work in sexual issues tacitly conflicted.

Breaking the Silence

One of the tasks of therapy in general is to promote symbolization—to move feelings and experiences from unconscious to conscious, from nonverbal to verbal. The rationale is that as we are able to put thoughts, feelings, and experiences into words, we gain freedom and flexibility as human beings. We are not limited to acting out what we feel. We can say what hurts or angers us; we can ask for what we might need; we can give meaning and substance to parts of us that would otherwise go unknown or unshared. Surely, then, in the context of sexuality, one of our tasks as therapists is to free up our own sexual symbolization—to move our own sexual experience and expression from nonverbal to verbal.

How might such movement take place? In a culture of silence and secrecy, how do we find safe ways to break our own silence? Perhaps as a first step, it is essential that we, the therapists, step away from all the "good" reasons why we might otherwise stay silent in the sexual domain: "To me, it's private—very personal." "It's not meant to be talked about." "I'm a better listener than I am a talker." "I could talk about it if I wanted to, I just don't have the need. You may have the need. . . ." These may not be your reasons, but you know what yours are. The reasons may well be valid, but these "reasons" keep us from being fully present to our clients.

As a second step, we need a kind of therapeutic humility and openness with ourselves. Because as we struggle to put into words—out loud—what for a lifetime has remained wholly or partially silent, we will bump into the anxiety that has surrounded our sexuality since we were little—the anxiety that is the "why" behind the silence. And often we will at first have no more than a little person's command of language with which to express ourselves. This is embarrassing and distressing, because although everybody is awkward talking about sexuality, no one wants to appear awkward. In fact, it's natural to struggle when bringing any realm of experience from the nonverbal to the verbal. We watch our clients struggle regularly to say what has never been said or to put into words what has been forever locked in indescribable feeling. We walk first, then we stumble, then we run, then we stumble some more.

And, of course, we need an audience—a therapist, a spouse, a friend, a therapy group—whose stance is to support us rather than to silence us. One of the most important features of my human sexuality classes is the small groups in which students gather to speak to one another about their sexual experience. Recently, one of my students related to me that just one day after participating in a fairly lengthy small-group session, she was faced with the discovery of a rather alarming pile of child pornography that her thirteen-year-old son had downloaded from the Internet. She said that all the talk—the out-loud, verbal, nonapologetic talk—from class and from the small group gave her a surprising sense of empowerment and verbal facility in dealing with her son. She could engage with him in ways she had not expected, and she felt able to bring her humanness (and her sexuality) to the table in a way that made a potentially disastrous encounter genuine and productive for both son and parents.

Finally, we need to know what to talk about. We need to discover a way to speak about such secrecy-ridden issues as the sexual tone in our own home of origin, our first masturbatory explorations, our feelings about puberty, our comforts and discomforts with our masculinity or femininity. I include for reference three lists of discussion questions we currently use in my human sexuality classes. These questions are in no way meant to be comprehensive, but they may for some provide a point of departure in this difficult-to-navigate territory.

Family/Cultural Background

- Who was in your family/home while you were growing up? What was life like?
- What was Mom like with her sexuality, nudity, verbal expression about sex?
- What was Dad like with his sexuality, nudity, verbal expression about sex?
- What were your earliest spoken sexual messages? From Mom? Dad? What were your earliest unspoken messages? How about nudity? Having babies?
- How sexual were Mom and Dad with one another in your presence? How comfortable was that for you?
- What were your religious/cultural background and messages?
- What early sexual experiences do you remember having? At what age (with self, siblings, pets, others of same gender, opposite gender, mixed groups)? How do you remember feeling about these? What was your role? Were there efforts to be secretive? Were you ever caught? What was the effect? How does it feel to talk out loud about this?
- How "girlish" a girl or "boyish" a boy were you? How conflicted was your experience of your own gender?
- Did you have sexual experiences with adults as a child? Did you ever repress these for a time? Where are you in working through the trauma of those events?
- How did you learn about intercourse? How do you wish you had learned?

Puberty

- Describe your experience of puberty: menstruation, wet/sexual dreams, body changes, pressures, and the emotions you experienced about each. What did you observe in your friends? What questions did you have?
- What were your dating successes and failures?

- Describe your first sexual experience with another person. What effect did it have on you? With whom did you talk about it?

Adulthood

- What do you like and dislike about your body?
- How satisfying have your significant hetero- or homosexual relationships been? What was/were the most positive sexual experience(s) of your life? The most negative sexual experiences(s) of your life?
- Do you have sexual fantasies? What are they?
- What has been your sexual lifestyle/behavior throughout your lifespan, including significant changes? What are your current sexual activities, practices, preferences?
- How do you and your partner talk about your sexual relationship?
- What is your personal theory regarding bi- and homosexuality?
- Have you had medical problems (for example, infertility) that may have affected your sexuality? Do you have sexual problems now? Have you had any in the past? What did you do about them?
- Have there been changes in your sexual activity because of STDs?
- What do you think your sexuality will be like in the future?
- What are the patterns you see as you view your own sexual history over time? Which would you like to change?

The ultimate resting place, of course, is when we find ourselves countertransference-free—able to interact with these questions (or the ones that are relevant to you) without running for the cover of emotional distance or intellectualization. For most, it's a long trek. But then, freeing ourselves from neuroses usually is.

Dealing with Our Clients' Cultural Neurosis

LAURA

One night, the last client I saw after a long day of counseling was a forty-six-year-old woman, the mother of four children. I had seen Laura fairly steadily once a week for the past year or so. She talked rapidly and with animation, as was her usual style. She spoke about her husband, as she often did, but her topic was somewhat different this time.

"We've been having a little more sex lately," she said. "It helps that he's coming to bed at the same time as me. He came home early the other night, and I asked him if there was anything I could do for him. He said he'd like to make love before the kids came home. So, quick as a lick, I was back in the bedroom with my clothes off and ready for him. . . ."

She talked on for awhile about problems between them. "Several years ago, when I was thirty-two, we didn't have sex for two years. I complained to my friend, and she said, 'As I see it, you have three options: first is to do nothing, second is to have an affair, and third is to learn to please yourself.' Well, I was thirty-two, and I never knew a woman could please herself. I didn't know how! Now, I try to wait for Ken, because I think it should come from your husband when you're married. But I can't always. It's frustrating, because he doesn't know how to satisfy me. The other day he came home and wanted to do it, but wouldn't you know, I had already pleased myself just that afternoon. Wouldn't you know! I mean he knows where my spot is and all, but he rubs it like a piece of furniture, you know. Not gentle. I try to tell him but he can't learn."

"Does he rub the tip of his penis like it's a piece of furniture?" I asked.

"No way!" she laughed. "But when it comes to me, he can't learn."

We talked more, and at the end of the session, as she was leaving the office, my client grinned a sort of playful grin, and sighed as if relieved, "Well, now you know how horny I am!"

"How human . . . ," I said.

"Yeah, human," she said with a bigger grin.

"Now we know we're both human," I said as I nodded goodbye.

This excerpt is both timely and important. Here's a woman who, with great courage and all the trust she could muster, revealed to me that (1) she had sexual urges, (2) she had learned to satisfy herself through masturbation, (3) she was conflicted about using this means, (4) she was non-orgasmic with her husband, and (5) they had not found a way to talk about their sexual experience effectively. But more than any of that, she was asking me a question: "Can I bring my sexual self into this office and still retain the right to my dignity before you as a human being?"

This was a funny interchange, really. Here I was with all my potentially very helpful knowledge, beginning to hear for the first time the tentative utterances of this woman whom I had seen for well over a year in therapy, about how she experienced and channeled her sexuality. So what was my job, as Laura began to entrust this very important and vulnerable part of herself to me? What was my goal as therapist in those moments? Was it to assure her that I was OK with what she was saying? Was it to let her know that I teach human sexuality, so she's in good hands? Was it to probe her feelings about sharing what she was sharing? Was it to educate and coach her? All of those options at some level presented themselves. But her real question—her real need—was about dignity and respect. Can I have and share the sexual parts of my being and still retain your respect? Will sharing my experience, my decisions, my practices elicit from you the judgment I fear, the judgment I carry within myself?

Human Respect.   In our talking and thinking about human sexuality with our clients, our culture's neurosis again looms large. Just as most of us grew up with our sexuality outside the purview of parental supervision or parental acceptance, so too have our clients. If I couldn't tell Mommy about touching myself "down there," how can I tell you, therapist? She would tell me I shouldn't, and at some level I still believe her. What will it be like if I tell *you*, therapist, who (according to Freud) actually does stand in loco parentis?

It is the very fact that, in so many ways, we as therapists do reconstellate a sort of parental essence to our clients that such interchanges are powerful. In such moments, we have the opportunity to give to our clients a "parental" acceptance of their sexuality and personhood, which, if administered appropriately over time, can powerfully displace internal sexual dys-permissions. When we offer the grace of respect and approbation for this individual as a sexual being, we reach inside to a place of potential shame and repression—a place that sexual experience, in and of itself, can never quite quench. One's sexual birthright, even in the most sophisticated of us, can at some levels still be abridged. If we, as therapists, ignore the existence of sexual anxiety and go directly to educative or therapeutic concerns, we jump over a central reality.

Respect is the sine qua non of therapy around sexual issues. Without this, there is nothing. There must be respect for the person, for the delicacy of the territory, for the potential traumas suffered, for the defenses the client might have erected over time, for the anxieties they protect, for the vulnerability to shame that is inherent in being sexual in our culture. Like so many other aspects of clinical work, being truly respectful toward another's sexual vulnerabilities is not something one "does"; rather, it is something one "is." Respect emerges from the inside—from one's own work around sexual issues, from one's own painful struggles to bring one's sexuality into words and symbols and feelings that can be communicated in the light of day to another human being. The therapist who rushes in to assure the client of the therapist's acceptance and understanding might well ponder who the rush is for. The hard work around sexual issues is in the acquiring of respect, and that work takes place well before the client walks in the door. Once respect is there, its communication is a non-issue. The therapist who quietly reveres a client's vulnerability cannot help but manifest that reverence.

Beyond Respect. Aside from respect (which we never truly get "beyond"), what other factors ought we to be aware of as we move into the discussion of sexual issues with our clients? Many therapists have been exposed to the PLISSIT model, a helpful guide to handling sexual material in session. *P* stands for *permission*. Some clients need only someone's permission to move through sexual roadblocks. *LI* stands for *limited information*. Sometimes we need to supply clients with information they may be missing. *SS* stands for *specific suggestions*. We may use material from Masters and Johnson's desensitization exercises or from more recent contributors to the realm of sex therapy. *IT* stands for *intensive therapy*. We may need to refer to professional medical or sex therapy specialists in the community. (Refer to Chapter Six for further discussion of the PLISSIT model.)

However, even the PLISSIT model, helpful as it may be, skips over an essential set of interpersonal realities involved in handling sexual material as it emerges in session. The model does not address, for instance, what creates the venue wherein sexual issues can even come up in the first place. And it bypasses the question of how we deal with the anxiety that inevitably appears when we talk about sexual issues. It skips other important questions as well, such as how exactly we should assess for levels of comfort or discomfort. What about trauma? How do we desensitize sexual anxieties with sensitivity?

Sexual issues present themselves in session as cross-products of the client's urgency and the therapist's comfort. If a client is in a great deal of pain, he may bring up issues that are sexual in nature no matter who the therapist is. He will assess the comfort or helpfulness of the therapist in sometimes not-too-subtle ways, and adjust course accordingly. I once saw a young man who, within the first ten minutes of our first session together, asked me how comfortable I would be in helping him explore his possible homosexuality. I was, of course, curious at his rather pressured presentation, and asked what gave rise to that particular question. He spoke to me of his former therapist, a well-seasoned male psychologist, whom this client had found quite helpful in many respects, but who curiously had seemed uninterested or put off by this young man's exploration.

"How did you discern this?" I asked.

"Well, he fell asleep in session the two times I attempted to talk about this issue. He assured me that he had no problem with it, but I couldn't quite trust it."

Clients are constantly picking up cues of safety or nonsafety, and they have a world of nonverbal data to go on, sometimes as unsubtle as the behavior of the aforementioned psychologist. More commonly, clients will move into or veer away from sexual content based on what they perceive to be their comfort, which is often intimately linked to our comfort. Once sexual material is introduced, our ability to contain the anxieties present and to be respectful and honest in the interaction will set the limits of what a client explores with us.

How do we know what levels of anxiety are present? Again, basic cues of safety and security are generally nonverbal. We can watch for autonomic signals of anxiety: dry mouth, tense muscles, sweating, fidgeting, nervous gestures, flushed skin, rapid breathing, pounding pulse. We can watch and listen for subtle changes: eyes, skin tone, vocal tone and cadence, body posture. We can watch process: conversational flow, change of topics, digressions, intellectualizations, attempts to be funny. Perhaps we have a feeling that someone is less than fully present. And if in doubt, it's fair to assume that in the realm of sexual issues, anxiety is present until proven otherwise.

Anxiety and Authenticity. What is the appropriate therapeutic course of action if we sense anxiety in the room? Beyond giving our clients the space of quiet attentiveness and respect, it's

important that we give them authenticity as well. We need to be
aware of and respond honestly to the anxieties that present
themselves along the way.

As an individual or a couple moves through sexual material,
there will be natural times of pause. Sometimes, as in the example of Laura, there is no real pause while the material is coming
forth. The pause only comes at the end of the session. There is
nothing lost by waiting until the next session to process the
process. It might go something like this: "As you left last session,
you expressed relief at having been able to talk about some of
your sexual experiences with Ken. I wonder if you could talk
about what it felt like to share those things with me?" In that
moment, we move from content into process, from narrative
into interpersonal authenticity. Now Laura can tell me about her
anxiety. She can tell me how nervous she felt, how the nervous-
ness expressed itself, and how she experienced me as audience.
As I listen, I might wonder with her what life experiences have
made her anticipations of sharing such material so unsafe. In so
doing, I both acknowledge and authenticate her anxiety. This is
not junior high school, where her social acceptance hinges on
how cool she can appear. Here, at last, she gets to have the whole
of her experience.

In a couple, one person is often more anxious than the other.

KY AND MARILYN

Ky and Marilyn had seen me over the course of five months for
long-standing problems of communication in their marriage. Ky
came in one day and erupted. He could no longer hold down his
anger: "Marilyn and I have no sex life!"

I looked at Ky, then at Marilyn. He appeared angry and tight; she,
white and angular. I prompted Ky to talk more about his frustration.
"If it's not one thing, it's another," he said. "Her back trouble. Her
low desire. I'm overweight. I've got a small penis. She feels
exploited." As the rifts between them had been healing, Ky felt more

and more the incongruity of their sexual arrangement. He came to a pause. The tension in the room was palpable.

"Clearly," I said to Ky, "this is important. You've waited a long time to bring it here. It will be crucial that we give you all the space you need. But I wonder if we could take a minute and check on how we're all doing?"

"Sure," he said, probably not knowing what I meant.

I turned to Marilyn, simply because she looked closer to passing out than anyone else. "How is it for you, Marilyn, that we're beginning to talk about your sexual relationship in here?"

"Oh, it's, it's fine. Ky really needs to talk about it, and I want him to."

"But I wonder what fine means to you, Marilyn. I sense from your paleness that something might feel pretty scary about this exchange."

"Yeah, but it's OK if he talks about it. I don't want him not to."

An important moment. The boundaries of safety would be established as we recognized and authenticated the anxiety.

"Marilyn, is there something about talking about your sexual relationship that feels unsafe to you?"

"Well, yeah! I feel so guilty, but at the same time, I don't know what to do about it. I'm just afraid . . . I don't know why I'm afraid . . . It used to be OK. . . ."

"It will be important that we come to understand what's frightening you. Ky, how about you? You're a little uncomfortable? How do you experience that discomfort? You're shaking? I wonder what it might mean, that you're shaking. . . ."

In these moments, we are doing together the therapeutic work of authenticity—of heading into the anxiety rather than attempting to deny it. By addressing it, we begin to encounter its causes, which will by any measure be germane to the therapy.

As the session continued, I acknowledged my anxiety (which was somehow much higher with these two than is my normal experience) and talked a bit about how normal it is to feel anxious around sexual material. I said that we would acknowledge and not ignore the anxieties that presented themselves, and I asked both of them to keep track of how they were feeling as we talked. The day after the session, Marilyn telephoned me to say that on the previous night, she had for the first time experienced flashbacks to molestation scenes involving her father. The anxiety was authentic. It always is.

We are a culture whose exposure to sexual trauma is by now well catalogued. It is imperative that we be alert to the commonness of such events and their adult sequelae in our clients. But anxieties around sexual touch are not always rooted in molestation. For some of our clients, intimate touch has been compromised in other, more subtle ways. For some, touch evokes the sadness of deprivation—the sheer lack of being held and touched as children. For others, it evokes the anger of mis-attunement, or the fear of being engulfed and taken over by another. These very important aspects of the experience of being touched may need to be elucidated in therapy; their genesis is often poorly understood. How were our clients touched? By whom? Was touch comfortable or somehow forbidden? Paternal or predatory? We must authenticate the anxieties.

Sensitivity and Desensitization. Since the first contributions of Masters and Johnson, issues around sexual anxiety, for better or worse, have been paired with desensitization techniques. The theory goes that because anxiety and relaxation are physiologically incompatible responses to sexual stimuli, one can gradually displace an anxious response to sexual stimuli with a relaxed response, by in essence pitting the two responses in battle against one another and stacking the odds against the anxiety response. The key to desensitization in general is to take small, gradual steps. And most important, the regimen is individualized. It starts with an individual's unique anxiety hierarchy and moves gradually from lower to higher levels of exposure to the feared stimulus.

Desensitization is one aspect of what are often called "exposure therapies." When we are exposed to feared stimuli and can remain in the presence of those stimuli until our intense but fast-twitch fear response expends itself, we will, in subsequent exposures, experience less fear.

For example, several years ago, one of my master's students in a beginning human sexuality class related to me that when she was an undergraduate, her human sexuality professor entered the classroom strewing condoms to the four corners of the classroom. The rationale? Exposure therapy: that which may frighten you today, if you stay with it and prevent yourself from fleeing, will frighten you less tomorrow. Theoretically sound? Yes. But emotional rape nonetheless.

Emotional rape is what happens when one person imposes her standard of comfort or experience on another. Emotional rape happens in classrooms and therapy rooms whenever I use my knowledge, my comfort, my experience as the standard to which you as my charge must submit. I may "expose" you in the service of your growth, but in this culture especially, which has offered so little safety to us as sexual beings, it is important to be gradual and sensitive in our efforts to free people from their sexual anxieties. Whenever by speaking my idiom I cause you to mute yours, I have robbed you of something deeply precious.

MALE CLIENTS, FEMALE CLIENTS: THE EXPERIENTIAL CHASM

If we are to talk and think about what every therapist needs to know about treating sexual problems, we must also be willing to peer into the chasm that separates male from female. In some ways it is a deep and mysterious chasm: dangerous for its depth, enticing for its mystery. But in this culture, the chasm is just plain dizzying. The genders here are a confused lot. They awakened to a childhood of stay-at-home moms and go-to-work dads. Of men who fought wars and women who changed diapers. And halfway through the movie, they watched all the characters change roles. Now she works a sixty-hour week, and he takes Prozac; he helps the kids with homework, and she coaches soccer. Everyone tacitly agrees that it's all moving in the right direction, but what it is to be essentially male or female has become a great mélange. As if to exacerbate the turbulence, popular writers strain to characterize the "true" differences between the sexes, an effort based perhaps more on our craving to know our differences than on anything inherently unique to each gender.

The Gender Gap

There are differences between the genders, but they are not the ones reified in the pop-psych press. Men and women are different in their size and muscle mass and in their primary and secondary sexual characteristics. They also have different brains. While in utero, male and female brain structures are acted upon at two different times by the hormones signaled by the XX or XY status of the fetus. They are again acted upon differentially with the hormone surge of puberty. These neurological differences result in different gender-based experiences across each of the five senses. Men and women have different detection thresholds for a variety of tastes, smells, and sounds (for example, a noise really might seem twice as loud to her and twice as soft to him). They have different visual stimulation and preference patterns, and different patterns of tactile sensitivity. Numerous studies have shown that, although cumulatively equal in intelligence, men have better visual-spatial capacities, and women have better verbal skills. Men have better large-muscle coordination; women have better small-muscle coordination. Men appear across cultures to be the more aggressive gender, women the more nurturant to the young of the species. Women have thicker and more fibrous corpora callosa and thus appear to distribute brain function more evenly across the two hemispheres than do men.

To what extent do these hardware differences destine the two genders to unbridgeable experiential gaps? To what extent do cultures refract and magnify such gender differences as truly are there? To what extent does our culture add on such a complex mix of gender-based experiential differences that men and women wind up feeling as though they come from different planets? These questions are fascinating, of course, but beyond our scope. As therapists, our task is to consider how the combined influence of nature and nurture in this culture affects our experience as sexual beings. Without such understanding, a therapist may well fall into the chasm, and then wonder why the whole business has gotten so dark and mysterious.

Although men and women share in common the sexual dys-permissions that come from our cultural neurosis, they have very different experiences of themselves as sexual beings along the developmental pathway. Boys are confronted directly with the presence of their genitalia from birth onward. Their sexual apparatus is visible and accessible, more like a hand or foot than a kidney or liver. Thus there is ownership of something sexual from the very beginning. It may not be identified as sexual, it may be named pee-pee, but it's there in flesh and blood and is the ready source of pleasurable sensation from the very first days. Additionally, the way we have it arranged in this culture, if a boy accompanies his dad to a public bathroom, he sees that same organ in various permutations of size and age attached to all these other people he comes to know as male. As young boys move into puberty, they experience their sexual feelings in undeniably evident ways: they have erections; they have wet dreams; their sexual feelings have observable visual and tactile referents that boys quickly learn to associate with arousal. There is little guesswork. They get to know (if not to understand or accept fully) their sexual apparatus and appetite. They even (in most quarters) receive the latitude to explore their patterns of stimulation and arousal through masturbation.

Women, in contrast, pass from childhood into adulthood with their sexual apparatus hidden to them. As they move into puberty, their sexual feelings at low levels of arousal are diffuse, not focal. And there is no visual feedback. In the absence of direct sexual stimulation by self or a partner, they may only very gradually come to identify the nature of their sexual arousal, embedded, as it often is, in interpersonal longings. Having no real permission to be sexual experiencers, and no sharply identifiable markers of arousal, they may as adolescents talk with others only about "how far we went" while at some level remaining mystified about their full sexual capacities.

The result is a sexual gender gap. To counter parental silence and secrecy, boys and men have a sort of built-in permission to be sexual experiencers that girls and women do not have. Men can be and are sexual beings because in essence they get permission from their anatomy. It is never quite as free or clear as would be permission from the prior generation, but it's something. Women get no such compensatory permission.

Cultural Mythology

The result is that males in our culture become the de facto carriers of sexual drives, sexual knowledge, and sexual permission. As boys, they have slightly more freedom to acquire sexual information than do girls, although in general their "sources" are other adolescent youngsters. As men, they bear the burden of sexual performance and wizardry. They are supposed to know the territory and be able to navigate it flawlessly. Even in the 1990s, he comes as sexual virtuoso and teacher, she as driven snow. The sexual script is that he delights her and curries her undying admiration by gradually and sensitively unlocking her hidden sexual potential. Not knowing how to unlock her or— God forbid—himself is tantamount to abdication of his most important function as a male. Taking responsibility for her own sexual training qualifies her as an "over-experienced" woman at the very least. The sexual part of a relationship is, after all, the man's domain—we've set it up that way.

This was never so clear to me as in the case of Tom and Alicia, who, after nine years of marriage, decided to work in therapy on their sexual relationship. Although she was vastly more sexually experienced than he, Tom could talk about their sexual functioning; she could not. Tom was educated about a woman's anatomy and sexual response repertoire; she was not. When they decided to read together a simple primer on human sexual responses, she was fascinated that she could actually come to know things about her own sexual potential—the forbidden fruit.

Here again, we have, as a culture, subtly recast the truth. Truly, men and women are both sexual beings. Both have drives that ready them for sexual encounter. We learn to think of her as reluctant, him as eager; her as oriented toward relationship, him as oriented toward orgasm. We learn to think of ourselves in these ways as well. Apart from any intrinsic differences in sexual styles or levels of sexual desire that might indeed exist between the genders, we learn how we as men or women ought to orient toward these things.

The sexual pressure this creates for men and women is untoward. Like a family system where one member overfunctions and another underfunctions, this artificial division of sexual labor presses men to pursue sexual prowess rather than intimate expression and presses women to accept sexual naiveté and, ultimately, apathy. Neither becomes truly free or truly actualized. In the atmosphere of sexual warfare, peaceful coexistence is all anyone can hope for. There is no room for the concept of long-term development of sexual potential.

One of my roles as both therapist and educator is to help couples break away from the kinds of myths and assumptions people bring to the arena of gender differences. He needs sex to feel intimate; she needs intimacy to feel sexual. Really? Why? Why are intimacy and sexuality sequestered from one another in any of us? Is that really our nature? Or is it perhaps what our wounded culture has taught us to feel? Is sex the gateway to intimacy and vulnerability in men as a gender? Or is it more true that emotionally open states are "forbidden" to real men unless they're intoxicated—with sex or alcohol or adrenaline? If so, the work of therapy is not to endorse pop-psych stereotypes but to help people to transcend their constraints. Is emotional connection the prerequisite to sexual desire in a woman? Or does she have to "justify" sexual feelings and drives to herself, her partner, and the parents within her by confining them always to moments of intense emotional union? If so, the work of therapy is not to get her partner to exchange fifteen minutes of open communication for one sexual encounter. It is instead to search with her into the shame she may feel about being a sexual person at all.

Perhaps it is one of the most important functions of a therapist to challenge those personal, familial, and cultural myths that keep people from becoming most fully themselves—those myths that bind and constrict rather than free and potentiate. What is the real meaning of gender? The true essence of anima and animus? Why do we have it? Where might we go to find out? What do we really know about the meaning, the purpose, of sexuality? Rods and pistons, titillation, endless serial orgasms—is this our creative best, our highest human potentiality? Were we meant to join genitalia? Or perhaps to join souls? And if so, how do we achieve this? These are very difficult questions for any of us to raise (let alone answer), because they touch on premises. But in this realm of male and female, if we as therapists unquestioningly accept as true the premises of modern American culture, we merely teach our clients to cope more gracefully with the annihilation of meaning for both genders.

THE THERAPIST'S ROLE

In the Native American tradition, among some of the clans of the Cherokee, there is a group of men and women referred to as "firepersons." Firepersons are individuals within the tribe who have undergone years of special training in sexuality and spirituality. They themselves participate in rites of passage, in teachings on the healing powers of sexuality, in studies of genital anatomy and sexual preferences, in exercises identifying the various energy fields within and surrounding the human body, and in inducing types and levels of orgasm as means to spiritual transcendence. In what is called the Quodoushka tradition, the grandmothers of the tribe—women of "wisdom and knowledge"—get together in council to choose an individual fireperson for each of the tribe's adolescents. The role of the fireperson is to help educate and awaken the developing adolescent to the realm of his or her sexuality and spirituality. The fireperson's teachings focus on the experiencing of natural energy flows throughout one's whole being and of the harmonious exchange of energies between sexual partners. The council of grandmothers looks carefully to the sexual stewardship of each new generation.

In American culture, sadly, we have no council of grandmothers to be guardians of our sexual awakening. We have no firepersons to teach us our sexual and spiritual potentials. Instead, therapists are often put into the position of mediating the sexual struggles within individuals and between partners. For some clients, the therapist may be the first person in the client's life who is a nonjudgmental witness to her as a sexual being—a parent who gives her permission to talk, to learn, to ask questions, to experiment, to be sexual, to seek guidance, to cultivate potential, to understand the meaning of her sexual experience. As if by default, then, therapists function in the role of fireperson.

Fireperson by default—by the standards of the Cherokee culture, this would be roughly equivalent to our appointing neurosurgeons by default. In a culture that reveres the powers and potentialities of sexuality, the title of fireperson is earned through exacting training and soul-searching experience. But our culture does not revere sexuality. It may be afraid of it, fascinated with it, obsessed with it, impressed with its power. It may package and advertise it and buy it and sell it. It may even celebrate it. But it does not revere it.

Where does this leave us as therapists? Perhaps it leaves us exactly where it leaves most of our clients: with the unsettling feeling that we may not really know very well the water we have always swum in. Perhaps it leaves us with a certain knowing that our culture—our clan, our family—is deeply wounded around its sexuality, and that, perhaps, we cannot know the right answers if we've never really known the right questions. Perhaps it leaves us, as therapists, needing to know our own woundedness before

we attempt to heal that of another, needing to embrace a humility that resembles that of our clients.

∽

I close with a brief vignette, again from my human sexuality
class. Each quarter, a man named Corky Reilly comes to our
class to talk about sexuality and humanness. He speaks of his sexual experiences as a young man, and of his current experience of
his own sexuality at age forty. Corky suffered a C-5 spinal cord
injury in his late teens and has been paralyzed from mid-shoul-
ders down ever since. In simple and straightforward terms, with
authenticity, Corky and his partner explain to the class what it is
like to give and receive sexually from one another when the definitions of sexual interchange are radically altered. He talks about
being attentive to one another, about talking together and
dreaming together, about holding and caressing and searching
out the pains and pleasures buried deep inside both people. He
talks about orgasm, and about how he in his injured body can
experience profound physical orgasm that is not centered on his
penis but on his person. He speaks of a rich unlocking of sexual
potential in himself and in his partner.

Class by class, group by group, my students leave, and each
time I hear in response, "That man taught me more about what
it is to be alive to my sexuality than anyone else I've ever met."
I picture Corky as I close this chapter on talking and thinking
about human sexuality. Perhaps he, for one, has known enough
to raise the right questions.

NOTES

P. 5, *But such psychologists as Winnicott and Kohut:* Winnicott, D. W. (1975).
Through pediatrics to psychoanalysis. London: Hogarth; Kohut, H. (1997). *The
restoration of the self.* Madison, CT: International Universities Press;
Greenspan, S. I. (1989). *The development of the ego.* Madison, CT: International Universities Press.

P. 16, *the PLISSIT model:* Annon, J. S. (1974). *The behavioral treatment of sexual problems.* Honolulu, HI: Kapiolani Health Services.

CHAPTER

2

A THERAPIST'S GUIDE
TO THE PHYSIOLOGY
OF SEXUAL RESPONSE

Randolph S. Charlton and Teri Quatman

A basic understanding of human sexual physiology is prerequisite for any therapist who wants to treat sexual disorders. You don't need to have attended medical school to understand the rudiments of what the bodies of your patients are doing, or at least are trying to do, during a sexual experience. In fact, it's only been within the last twenty-five years that physicians themselves have garnered a very clear idea of how our bodies respond to sexual arousal and orgasm. In this chapter, we've put together the information any therapist, medically or nonmedically trained, should know in order to evaluate and treat sexual problems.

If you have an understanding of the *normal* human sexual response, you'll be able to compare it with what your patients tell you about their individual experiences. But remember: there is variation in what is "normal." For example, there are women who can reach orgasm with the stimulation of intercourse alone, and there are women without significant psychological problems who are unable to reach an orgasm without direct manual or oral clitoral stimulation. These are "normal variants" and are not an indication of a sexual disorder. There is variation in what is normal for any particular man or woman, teenager or octogenarian.

A BRIEF GUIDE TO THE WIRING AND PLUMBING OF SEXUAL RESPONSE

The human body is both elegantly simple and confoundingly complex. We'll stick with the elegantly simple in this review of the bodily systems necessary for human sexual response. A physician needs to know the details of each and every organ system in the body, but a therapist who treats sexual issues gets a break. You only need a rudimentary understanding of four organ systems—the nervous, genitourinary, circulatory, and endocrine—in order to grasp the basics of sexual physiology. Let's start at the top.

The Nervous System

The first requirement for an intact nervous system is a *brain* or *central nervous system*. There are multiple excitatory and inhibitory sites within the brain that interact to produce our complex sexual reactions. The brain is connected to the rest of the body by (1) *the cranial nerves*, which exit from the base of the brain and enervate vital functions connected to vision, hearing, breathing, heart rate, facial sensation, taste, and speaking; (2) *the spinal cord*, which encases *sensory nerves* carrying incoming messages about touch, temperature, vibration, and position from the body to the brain, and also *motor nerves* carrying signals from the brain to the muscles of the body; and (3) *the autonomic nervous system*, which extends throughout the body and regulates the involuntary muscles involved in circulation, digestion, elimination, and glandular secretion.

The human brain has been called the ultimate erotic organ. As you no doubt know, mental imagery can create sexual arousal all by itself. Because the control centers within the brain are connected through the spinal cord to the reflex centers that control sexual response, emotional experience can heighten or lessen sensitivity to erotic stimulation.

In addition to the brain and its primary connections, a functioning nervous system requires an intact *reflex arc* connecting the *sensory receptors* of the genitals to the *spinal cord* and thence to the *blood vessels* of the penis, clitoris, and adjacent areas.

The reflex process works like this: when the receptors in and around the genitals detect sensations of touch (the main sexual stimuli), an impulse is initiated in the *sensory nerves* that travel from the genitals to *reflex centers* in the spinal cord. The reflex centers, located in the sacrum or low back, process the sensory impulses and send a message back to the muscles that cover the walls of the small arteries of the penis, clitoris, and surrounding tissues. The outgoing messages from the reflex centers travel via fibers of the *parasympathetic* and *sympathetic* divisions of the *autonomic nervous system*. Stimulation of the parasympathetic fibers causes the tiny arterial muscles to relax, opening them to increased blood flow; stimulation of the sympathetic fibers causes the muscles to contract, closing off the arteries to blood flow.

When the genitals are touched, the spinal reflex stimulates parasympathetic impulses and inhibits sympathetic impulses to cause blood build-up: *engorgement* and *erection*. The process is reversed to empty blood from swollen genital tissues.

Ejaculation and *orgasm* also occur through a spinal reflex. The center controlling ejaculation and orgasm lies above that for erection—at about the level of the belly button. The outgoing signals that initiate the muscular contractions of orgasm travel over the sympathetic branch of the autonomic nervous system.

These kinds of reflex sexual responses happen regardless of consciousness and independent of input from the brain. This is what enables a man or woman with a severed spinal cord to get an erection or vulvar engorgement. A similar reflex arc controls blood flow to the nipples in both men and women.

The Genitourinary System

This system comprises the genital organs, which have a specialized blood supply and are sensitive to sexual stimulation.

The *penis* is composed of three cylindrical structures that run along its length. Constructed like dense sponges, they fill with blood in response to parasympathetic nervous system signals. A fibrous sheath surrounds each of the two *cavernous bodies* that run side by side along the top of the penis. A second sheath wraps around the two cavernous bodies, creating a single functional tube that creates the stiffness of a man's erection when the pressure of the blood pushes against the constricting sheaths. The *urethra*, the opening at the end of the penis, is contained within the *spongy body*. Much like the cavernous bodies, but without a surrounding sheath, the spongy body runs through the lower part of the penis and expands to form the sensitive tip, or *glans*.

The *clitoris* is composed of two cylindrical cavernous bodies, with no urethral tube or spongy body. The cavernous spaces fill with blood during sexual arousal, causing the clitoris to become engorged. The external female genitalia, the *vulva*, also fills with blood, as does the area surrounding the vagina. The increase in blood pressure is central in the creation of vaginal lubrication and the reshaping of the vagina to better accommodate penetration.

The clitoris and the penis contain many small sensory nerve endings that are very sensitive to touch. Sexual arousal is also generated by touching the *internal labia;* the *vaginal vestibule;* the area between the genitals and the anus; the anus; the skin of the inner thigh, buttocks, and testicles; and the breasts, especially the nipples.

The Circulatory System

The circulatory system functions to selectively supply blood to the genitals (as described previously) and to hold blood within the genitals during sexual excitement.

The mechanism by which this occurs is not completely understood, but we do know that the thin-walled veins that take blood away from the genitals are compressed and closed off when the cavernous tissues of the penis and clitoris fill with blood. It also appears that the outflow of blood is further slowed down by valves within the veins.

The Endocrine System

The glands of the endocrine system produce many hormones that are necessary for the healthy function of the body, but the ones we need to focus on are testosterone and thyroid hormone. Testosterone is the major male hormone and is made by the *testes*. It is also present in small amounts in the female and is a factor in sexual desire for both sexes. Thyroxin, the hormone produced by the thyroid gland, governs how quickly or slowly the body's metabolism functions. Too much or too little thyroxin can alter sexual function.

The Reproductive System

In nature, sex is inextricably bound up with the hormones that regulate reproductive physiology, but modern science has done much to separate sex and reproduction in the human being. Sexual pleasure is not necessarily diminished by birth control pills, a vasectomy, or a hysterectomy. In fact, sexual interest usually persists even with the removal of the testes or ovaries, and sexual function continues long after a woman is incapable of becoming pregnant. There are numerous religious prohibitions about sex for pleasure, but the body does not distinguish procreative sex from recreative sex.

Although we are not considering the specific function of the reproductive system, its problems can influence sexual function, either because the problems cause pain (ovarian cysts, endometriosis, pelvic infections, menstrual cramps, cancer), because they cause physiological irritability and decreased interest in sex (premenstrual syndrome), or because they lead to psychological conflict that diminishes sexual interest (birth control, infertility, miscarriage, menstruation, male sterility).

Other Organ Systems

In contrast to the four main bodily systems involved in sexual response, other organ systems do not play a central role in sexual function. They are obviously necessary for good health and can influence sexual activity. Skin disorders (psoriasis, fungal infection, herpes) may involve the genital area and make sex painful. Musculoskeletal diseases can make it difficult or impossible to move, impairing but usually not obliterating sexual function. Gastrointestinal problems rarely interfere directly with sexual function except as they lead to general physical debilitation or pain.

MEDICATIONS

Anything—trauma, disease, or medication—that interferes with the function of the neurological, circulatory, genitourinary, or endocrine systems can impair sexual response. We review the major diseases that alter sexual function in Chapter Four. At this point, we will concentrate on the effect drugs have on sexual physiology. There are only a few drugs used specifically to improve sexual function, but there are many that alter and interfere with sexual physiology. Let's look at the most commonly used drugs that alter sexual function.

Alcohol

In moderate amounts, alcohol can increase sexual interest through disinhibition of central nervous system sites. Further alcohol intake interferes with all levels of sexual response. Chronic alcoholism can damage both the brain and the sensory nerve fibers, interfering with sexual interest, arousal, and orgasm. The malnutrition and liver damage that are part of alcoholism lead to debilitation of all bodily systems. Because many drugs and hormones are metabolized in the liver, the alcoholic can be more sensitive to the effects of other medications. In addition, some men with liver disease are unable to remove the small amounts of estrogen produced in the male body; as estrogen is an antagonist of testosterone, these men may find their interest in sex diminished.

Selective Serotonin Reuptake Inhibitor (SSRI) Antidepressants

A common complaint of patients on the SSRI class of antidepressants—Prozac, Zoloft, Paxil, Effexor—is the diminishment of sexual interest or a difficulty reaching orgasm or both. In clinical reports, the frequency with which sexual difficulties are seen range from around 12 percent to as high as 69 percent. In our experience, one-fifth to one-half of patients on SSRI medications notice some change in their sexual response.

The most common side effect of these medicines is inhibition of orgasm. This phenomenon is somewhat dose-related, tending to diminish when the amount of the drug is decreased. Although there is variation in the frequency with which SSRIs affect sexual function, clinical research data suggests that they all can cause sexual side effects; the only way to know what a particular patient will experience is to give a trial of the medication.

Aside from lowering the dose or changing the medicine, there are several pharmacological ways to lessen the orgasmic inhibition caused by SSRIs. For instance, cyproheptiadine is an antihistamine drug usually used for hay fever and other allergies. When taken an hour or so before having sex, it can return the patient's ability to reach orgasm to the pre-drug status. A recent study has suggested that the sexual side effects of these drugs might be decreased without loss of their antidepressant function if the patient takes the medicine for five days and then skips the weekend.

Nefazodone (Serzone) is a newer antidepressant that blocks both serotonin and norepinephrine reuptake. Several recent reports suggest that nefazodone is significantly less likely to cause sexual side effects than other SSRIs and, yet, works as well to treat depression.

Antihypertensive Medication

Medicines that lower blood pressure can have side effects that influence sexual function. Blood pressure throughout the body is dependent on the muscles that surround the vascular system; these are the same muscles that cover the tiny arteries and veins of the genitals. Male erectile response is most sensitive to the side effects of these drugs, but decreased libido, diminution of arousal, and difficulty reaching orgasm can occur in both men and women. Medications likely to cause difficulty with sexual function include Alpha-methyl dopa (Aldomet), clonidine (Catapres), the thiazide diuretics, guanethidine (Ismelin) and guanadrel (Hylorel). Propranolol (Inderal), which is used for hypertension, angina, mitral valve prolapse, and performance anxiety, can lead to decreased sexual desire and impotence.

Sedatives: Tranquilizers and Sleeping Pills

Like alcohol, these drugs depress the function of the central nervous system directly. In low doses, they can increase sexual interest and excitement through a general decrease in inhibition. In high doses and chronic use, they decrease all phases of sexual response. When used in combination or with alcohol these drugs are additive in their effect. The most problematic medications are methaqualone (Qualude), chloral hydrate, and the barbiturates. The benzodiazepine class of tranquilizers (Librium, Valium, Ativan, Xanax, and others) do not usually alter sexual function in low doses. In high doses they can inhibit all stages of sexual response.

Many drugs have been reported to influence sexual function. In Table 2.1, we've listed these drugs alphabetically by their generic names. If a particular brand of the medicine is commonly

Table 2.1
Medications That Can Influence Sexual Function

Drug name	Potential effect
Acetazolamide (Diamox)	Decreased desire, potency
Alprazolam (Xanax)	Inhibition of orgasm; delayed or no ejaculation
Amiloride (Midamor)	Decreased desire; impotence
Amiodarone (Cordarone)	Decreased desire
Amitriptyline (Elavil)	Loss of desire; impotence; no ejaculation
Amoxapine (Asendin)	Loss of desire; impotence; retrograde, painful, or no ejaculation
Amphetamines	With chronic abuse: impotence; delayed or no ejaculation; no orgasm in women

Anticholinergics
    diethylpropion (Tenuate)
    phendimetrazine (Plegine)
    phenmetrazine (Preludin)
    phentermine (Fastin, Iodomin)
	Impotence

Barbiturates	Decreased desire; impotence
Carbamazepine (Tegretol)	Impotence
Chlorpromazine (Thorazine)	Decreased desire; impotence; no ejaculation; priapism
Chlorthalidone (Hygroton)	Decreased desire; impotence
Cimetidine (Tagamet)	Decreased desire; impotence; retarded or no ejaculation; no orgasm in women; spontaneous orgasm associated with yawning
Clofibrate (Atromid-S)	Decreased desire; impotence
Clomipramine (Anafranil)	Decreased desire; impotence; retarded or no ejaculation; no orgasm in women

Continued

Table 2.1
Medications That Can Influence Sexual Function *(continued)*

Drug name	*Potential effect*
Clonidine (Catapres)	Impotence; delayed or retrograde ejaculation; decreased desire
Clozapine (Clozaril)	Priapism
Cocaine	Priapism
Desipramine (Norpramin)	Decreased desire; impotence; painful orgasm
Dextroamphetamine (Dexedrine)	Impotence; alteration in desire
Diazepam (Valium)	Decreased desire; delayed ejaculation; retarded or no orgasm in women; erection difficulties
Digoxin	Decreased desire; impotence
Disulfiram (Antabuse)	Impotence
Doxepin (Sinequan)	Decreased desire; unspecified ejaculatory problems
Famotidine (Pepcid)	Impotence
Fenfluramine (Pondimin)	Loss of desire (in women on large doses); impotence; increased desire in some patients
Fluoxetine (Prozac)	Anorgasmia; delayed orgasm; decreased desire; ejaculation difficulties; penile anesthesia; spontaneous orgasm associated with yawning
Fluphenazine (Prolixin)	Alteration of desire; impotence; delayed ejaculation; priapism
Gemfibrozil (Lopid)	Impotence; loss of desire
Guanadrel (Hylorel)	Decreased desire; delayed or retrograde ejaculation; impotence
Guanethidine (Ismelin)	Decreased desire; impotence; delayed, retrograde, or no ejaculation

Table 2.1
Medications That Can Influence Sexual Function *(continued)*

Drug name	*Potential effect*
Haloperidol (Haldol)	Impotence; painful ejaculation
Hydralazine (Apresoline)	Impotence; priapism
Imipramine (Tofranil)	Decreased desire; impotence; painful, delayed ejaculation; delayed orgasm in women
Indomethacin (Indocin)	Impotence; decreased desire
Interferon (Roferon-A, Intron-A)	Decreased desire; impotence
Ketoconazole (Nizoral)	Impotence; decreased desire
Levodopa (Dopar)	Increased desire
Lithium (Eskalith & others)	Decreased desire; impotence
Lorazepam (Ativan)	Decreased desire
Maprotiline (Ludiomil)	Impotence; decreased desire
Mesoridazine (Serentil)	No ejaculation; impotence; priapism
Methadone (Dolophine)	Decreased desire; impotence; no orgasm; retarded ejaculation
Methantheline (Banthine)	Impotence
Methotrexate (Folex)	Impotence
Methyldopa (Aldomet)	Decreased desire; impotence; delayed or no ejaculation; no orgasm in women
Metoprolol (Lopressor)	Impotence
Naltrexone (Trexan)	Delayed ejaculation; decreased potency
Naproxen (Naprosyn)	Impotence; no ejaculation
Nortriptyline (Aventyl)	Impotence; decreased desire
Papaverine (Cerespan)	Priapism (especially in those with neurologic disorders)

Continued

Table 2.1
Medications That Can Influence Sexual Function *(continued)*

Drug name	*Potential effect*
Paroxietine (Paxil)	Decreased desire; delayed or no orgasm
Perphenazine (Trilafon)	Decreased or no ejaculation
Phenelzine (Nardil)	Impotence; retarded or no ejaculation; delayed or no orgasm; priapism
Phenytoin (Dilantin)	Decreased desire; impotence; priapism
Prazosin (Minipress)	Impotence; priapism
Propantheline (Pro-Banthine)	Impotence
Propranolol (Inderal)	Loss of desire; impotence
Protriptyline (Vivactil)	Loss of desire; impotence; painful ejaculation
Ranitidine (Zantac)	Impotence; loss of desire
Reserpine	Decreased desire; impotence; decreased or no ejaculation
Sertraline (Zoloft)	Decreased desire; retarded or no orgasm
Spironolactone (Aldactone)	Decrease desire; impotence
Sulfasalazine (Azulfidine)	Impotence
Tamoxifen (Nolvadex)	Priapism
Testosterone	Priapism
Thiazide diuretics	Impotence
Thioridazine (Mellaril)	Impotence; retrograde, painful, or no ejaculation; priapism; anorgasmia
Thiothixene (Navane)	Spontaneous ejaculations; impotence; priapism
Tranylcypromine (Parnate)	Impotence; painful ejaculation; retarded ejaculation

Table 2.1
Medications That Can Influence Sexual Function *(continued)*

Drug name	Potential effect
Trazodone (Desyrel)	Priapism; clitoral priapism; increased desire; retrograde or no ejaculation; anorgasmia
Trifluoperazine (Stelazine)	Painful ejaculation; spontaneous ejaculation

Source: Adapted from Drugs that cause sexual dysfunction: An update. (1992). *Medical Letter on Drugs and Therapeutics, 34*(876), 74–76. Reprinted by permission of The Medical Letter, Inc.

prescribed, it appears in parentheses. There may be other, less widely known brand names for some of the drugs. This chart does not consider drug interactions, and as always, a medical consultation is the best way to evaluate the effect of illness and medications on your patients.

MASTERS AND JOHNSON'S EXCITEMENT MODEL

Of all the human biological processes, sexual response was pretty much the last to be scientifically studied and observed. This attests both to the strength of our emotional bias about sex and sexuality, and to the courage and forbearance of Virginia Johnson and William Masters. Their work—mostly completed in the 1970s—focused on the physiological changes that accompany sexual experience. They identified that the basics of sexual response in both the male and female involved the alteration of genital circulatory dynamics leading to a redistribution of the pelvic blood volume and the contraction of the smooth muscles that surround the reproductive organs.

Masters and Johnson's Four Stages of Sexual Response

Based on their data, Masters and Johnson divided sexual response into four phases (see Figure 2.1). These phases are physiologically, not psychologically, based. It was assumed that in the normal individual, the subjective experience of excitement follows the physiological stages of arousal.

You might stop and think for a moment whether or not this is true in your own experience. Our guess is that you've had experiences where your subjective sense of interest, arousal, and enjoyment followed your body's physiological reactions, and you've had other experiences for which this was anything but true.

1. *Excitement.* Remember, this is a physiological concept, not a psychological one. It refers to the alteration in blood flow brought about by reflex vasodilatation of the genital blood vessels. In the male, this results in an erection, in the female, vaginal lubrication and the swelling of the genital tissues. The length of time it takes for this process to begin and to have demonstrable physical effects is widely variable. It varies both among individuals and from experience to experience in the same individual. It is generally true that men, especially young men, become aroused more quickly than their female counterparts.

2. *Plateau.* This is the phase of maximum physiological excitement. It occurs when the maximum amount of blood is contained in the genital organs. In the male this makes for the "hardest" erection. In the female, genital tissue is swollen to its maximum and lubrication is being generated at its maximum rate because of the difference in pressure within the intravaginal blood vessels and the tissues surrounding them.

3. *Orgasm.* Physiologically, orgasm refers to the rhythmic contraction of the smooth muscles in and around the genitals. The sense of physical pleasure that is associated with orgasm is

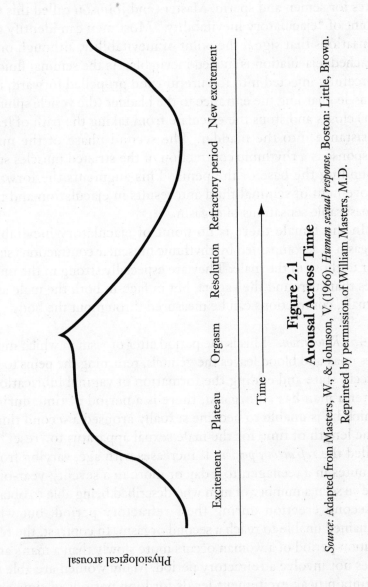

Figure 2.1
Arousal Across Time

Excitement Plateau Orgasm Resolution Refractory period New excitement

Time →

Physiological arousal

Source: Adapted from Masters, W., & Johnson, V. (1966). *Human sexual response.* Boston: Little, Brown.
Reprinted by permission of William Masters, M.D.

concurrent with these contractions. In the male this involves two phases. The first is the contraction of the walls of the storage sites for semen and sperm. Masters and Johnson called this the point of "ejaculatory inevitability." Most men can identify the sensations that signal the point of inevitability, although once reached, ejaculation is indeed inevitable. As the seminal fluid is forcefully injected into the urethra and propelled forward, the muscle guarding the entrance to the bladder (the vesicle sphincter) closes and stops the ejaculate from taking the path of least resistance into the bladder. The second phase of the male response is a rhythmic contraction of the striated muscles surrounding the base of the penis. This augments the forward movement of seminal fluid and results in ejaculation and the pleasurable sensations of orgasm.

In the female there is no point of ejaculatory inevitably; orgasm is accompanied by rhythmic muscular contractions similar to those in the male. They are especially strong in the muscles that surround the vagina, but in fact, in both the male and female, contractions can be measured throughout the body.

4. *Resolution.* This is the period after orgasm in which muscles relax and blood leaves the genitals, returning the penis to its flaccid state and ending the formation of vaginal lubrication. After a man has an orgasm, there is a period of time during which he is unable to become sexually aroused a second time. The length of time for the male sexual apparatus to "reset" is called the *refractory period.* It increases with age, varying from minutes in a teenager, to a day or more in a seventy-year-old. We've seen a number of men who described being able to obtain a second erection during their refractory period, but who remained unable to reach a second orgasm. In contrast, the resolution period of a woman occurs more slowly than a man's and does not involve a refractory period. Many women are able to maintain peak excitement levels for long periods of time and some are able to have multiple orgasms.

Clinical Insights

Masters and Johnson's physiological research clarified many aspects of sexual function and led to a new conceptualization of how sexual disorders could best be treated. Prior to their work, therapy for sexual problems was based almost entirely on a psychological perspective without understanding of the basic physical mechanisms that underlie sexual function. Some of Masters and Johnson's clinical insights can be summarized as follows:

• Sexual response is a multistage process, and problems can occur at any of the stages.

• The endocrine, neurological, vascular, and muscular systems govern sexual response by influencing the amount of blood delivered and contained in the genitals and the excitation of rhythmic muscular contractions. Anything that interferes with these systems can interfere with sexual function.

• Erection in the male and vaginal lubrication in the female are physiologically similar processes that depend on blood flow. Clinical experience suggests that the processes that create an erection in the man are more vulnerable to disruption than the analogous events that produce lubrication in the woman.

• A man who can't sense the "point of ejaculatory inevitability" will often be surprised to find himself ejaculating. He will have less control over the timing of his orgasm and is more vulnerable to premature ejaculation.

• Different individuals will have naturally different excitement curves. One aspect of sexual "fit" is the degree to which partners can manage the differences in the timing of their physical reactions.

• Short-term therapy directed at the reversal of specific sexual symptoms and based on an understanding of sexual physiology is effective.

Differences Between Men and Women

Common sense told us that men and women experience sexual arousal and orgasm in different ways, but it remained for Masters and Johnson to delineate the specifics of these differences.

• In general, the graph of a woman's excitement reveals a shallower excitement stage. This reflects what many women tell us in the consulting room: compared to men, they need and want more stimulation over a longer time to become fully aroused.

• In general, the plateau stage of maximum arousal is shorter for men than it is for women. Again, experimental results reflect clinical wisdom. A man is more likely to reach orgasm before a woman.

• Women who have multiple orgasms prolong the plateau stage of maximum arousal. The graph of their experience does not look like one humped camel of the "male-based" one orgasm per experience, but rather like a series of waves on the ocean.

• In general, the resolution phase occurs more quickly in men than women. The infamous scenario of a man reaching orgasm, sighing, saying how great it was, and rolling over to go to sleep is to some degree a function of this physical fact.

Clinical Problems

Although the paradigm that Masters and Johnson introduced was a significant step forward, it was not without problems for the psychotherapist. Each of the four issues listed here are related to the relationship between the mind and the body:

1.   Because the model is based on physiological criteria, the subjective nature of sexual arousal is more or less disregarded. As mentioned earlier, excitement is correlated with maximum physiological performance, and it is assumed that in the normal

individual, subjective arousal will correspond with physical arousal. However, many people, patient and nonpatient, have reported that subjective arousal is not always closely linked to physiological functions.

2. There is no specific consideration of sexual desire in this conceptualization. In this model, excitement begins when blood flow to the genitals alters. Certainly this can occur with the subjective sense of desire, but it does not have to.

3. From a physiological perspective, "successful" sex can be equated with biologically complete and functional sex. This paradoxically emphasizes the necessity to perform in order to be sexually functional. It also disregards highly passionate and sexual experiences that do not involve all four stages of sexual response.

4. The pleasure of arousal and orgasm is seen as the motivating force behind sexual interaction. Sexual therapy based on this model assumes that orgasmic sex is motivation enough to encourage patients to improve their sexual interactions. Although this is often true, it does not consider issues related to intimacy, which can be powerful motivators or fearful inhibitors of sexual experience.

Clinical Techniques

Masters and Johnson presented a specific form of evaluation and treatment for sexual disorders. Their focus was on information gathering, information giving, and a series of directive "homework" techniques created specifically to reduce anxiety around sexual performance.

• Much of the Masters and Johnson approach to sex therapy is based on the notion of reducing immediate anxiety, in the belief that the natural sexual function of the body will intervene and "push" toward successful, pleasurable sex. The specifics of their sensate focus exercise involving nondemand pleasuring will be discussed in Chapters Seven and Eight.

• It is sometimes helpful to draw Masters and Johnson's graph for a couple and to use it as a focus in a discussion of the differences between men and women in general (the "normal" response), and the differences between your patients (their actual response).

• Masters and Johnson separated the evaluation phase from the treatment phase of their work. They initiated what they called the "round table" discussion, in which the evaluators discussed the nature of a couple's sexual problems with them in the process of making the decision to proceed to therapy.

THE TRIPHASIC MODEL OF SEXUAL RESPONSE

From 1974 until her death in 1995, Helen Kaplan enlarged the scope of our understanding of human sexual response to include the desire phase of sexual experience and to clarify the physiological nature of the stages of sexual excitement.

Kaplan's clinical work with a large number of sexually dysfunctional patients led her to realize that a model based on Masters and Johnson's excitement and orgasm stages was limited. She understood something common sense tells us that was not included in the literature of human sexuality or sex therapy at that time: the first stage of human sexual response is not excitement but desire. Her focus on the psychology, neuroanatomy, and physiology of desire allowed therapists to understand and treat a new set of sexual problems—the disorders of desire.

The resulting model includes three stages: desire, arousal, and orgasm.

1. *Desire.* Desire is manifested by an interest in sexual experience. Desire can and often does exist without appreciable change in genital blood flow. Kaplan considered sexual desire a physical appetite, much like hunger. Just as the longer you are deprived of food the hungrier you get, the longer an individual

is deprived of a sexual outlet, the more that individual will experience sexual desire. Obviously there are a multitude of factors that can suppress or repress this natural process.

The hormone testosterone increases sexual desire in both the male and the female. In the male, testosterone is produced by the testes. The small but influential amount circulating in the female is made in the adrenal gland.

2. *Excitement.* This model follows Masters and Johnson in their understanding of the importance of genital blood flow for erection and vaginal lubrication. The important addition is an awareness that the parasympathetic branch of the autonomic nervous system is responsible for the change in blood flow. This means that medications which inhibit the parasympathetic nerves that activate the smooth muscles surrounding the genital blood vessels will alter sexual excitement and can cause impotence and female arousal disorder. These drugs are called *parasympatholytics* or *anticholinergics* and include some of the older drugs used in the treatment of high blood pressure; the antispasmodics used to treat gastric ulcer, spastic colon, and spastic bladder; and some of the drugs used to treat Parkinson's disease. There are also medications that work in the opposite manner; that is, they stimulate the parasympathetic nerves and inhibit sympathetic fibers. One such drug, Yohimbine, is used in the treatment of male impotence.

3. *Orgasm.* This model follows Masters and Johnson. As noted in the beginning of this chapter, the muscular contractions described by Masters and Johnson are primarily mediated by the sympathetic division of the autonomic nervous system.

Clinical Insights

Kaplan's background as a physician and an expert in psychodynamic psychotherapy helped her integrate the medical and the psychological models of sexual dysfunction. The following summarizes some of her conclusions.

- Sexual desire is the initial stage of human sexual response. If there is no interest, the rest of the sexual cycle never happens. The physical substrate of desire involves the presence of testosterone. A measurement of the level of circulating testosterone in the male is an important aspect in evaluating a sexual desire disorder. Neurological problems such as tumors, stroke, or serious Parkinson's disease can cause desire disorders, but most desire problems are the result of complex psychological and marital issues.

- Medications that inhibit the parasympathetic nervous system will primarily effect the arousal stage of sexual response.

- Medications that inhibit the sympathetic nervous system will effect the orgasm stage of sexual response.

- Masters and Johnson and the behavior therapists who followed in their footsteps focused on the immediate causes of anxiety, which they believed impaired normal sexual response. They accurately pointed out that psychoanalytic treatment for sexual disorders had for many years addressed the anxieties that originated in childhood experience, with little therapeutic success. In her model, Kaplan distinguished between immediate and distant causes of sexual disorders. She suggested that an integrated approach would be most helpful.

- Kaplan followed Masters and Johnson in using the sensate focus exercise to deal with immediate sexual anxiety. To this she added the notion of "bypassing" anxiety through the use of sexual fantasy. She suggested that when men were unable to obtain an erection or women unable to get aroused, they should move into their heads and create an exciting sexual fantasy. This often worked to improve sexual performance and to give permission for a patient to explore and enjoy sexual fantasies.

- Sex therapy prior to Kaplan's exposition pretty much disregarded the techniques of dynamic psychotherapy. Her training and expertise as a therapist helped her to incorporate interpretation and confrontation of unconscious dynamics into the sex therapy model.

Clinical Problems

Kaplan's model focuses mostly on the individual and has an underlying psychoanalytic assumption that sexual desire is instinctual. Although this can be very useful, it does not consider aspects of dyadic relationship, passion, intimacy, and the meaning of sexual fantasy. There are two principal difficulties with Kaplan's model.

1. If sexual desire is conceptualized as an instinct, much like hunger, then the longer one is deprived of sex, the more desire increases. Although this is partially true, there are a great many emotional and psychological factors that take precedence over the gradual "pressure" build-up to have sex. It is more accurate and complete to think of sexual desire as a multidetermined process. It is influenced by such physical factors as circulating hormones and the general state of health, by moods good and bad, by mania and depression, and most significantly, by the nature of the connection between two people.

2. The notion of bypassing anxiety through the use of sexual fantasy has the potential to create two people off in their own minds, using each other to masturbate. As far back as Freud's concept of genitality, the idea of being emotionally present during sex and orgasm was associated with psychological and relational health. The focus on lowering anxiety is helpful in sexual therapy, but it must be addressed with an understanding of relationship and intimacy.

Clinical Techniques

The most important aspect of Kaplan's model is the way in which it introduces the techniques and viewpoints of psychodynamic psychotherapy into the treatment of sexual disorders.

• Inclusion of desire disorders in the spectrum of sexual dysfunctions focused the therapist's attention on questions that had previously been the domain of psychoanalytic psychotherapy: what is exciting to a particular patient, and what is interfering with experiencing and enjoying that excitement?

• Kaplan's focus on bypassing anxiety led to the use of sexual fantasy as an adjunct to sexual arousal. Although this may have led to certain problems in the formation and maintenance of an intimate relationship, it also allowed some patients to experience erotic excitement on a scale new to them.

• The recognition of distant causes of sexual disorders validated the use of confrontation, interpretation, and clarification in a more flexible form of sex therapy.

• The recognition of the importance of interpersonal factors that interfere with safety and intimacy in a partnered relationship validated the use of the techniques of couple therapy in the context of treating sexual disorders.

THE QUANTUM MODEL OF SEXUAL RESPONSE

In his excellent book, *Constructing the Sexual Crucible*, published in 1991, marital/sexual therapist David Schnarch presents a new model of sexual function and relationship. He has endeavored to integrate the physiological and psychological aspects of sexual experience in a theory that stresses issues that have for the most part been left out of the field of sex therapy: intimacy, passion, and meaning.

In this theory, sexual function is dependent on the sum of all physical and psychological stimulation. As you might expect, physical stimulus is the amount of external, tactile stimulation received and processed by the body. Psychological stimulation is related to the amount of subjective sexual excitement experienced by an individual from cognitive and emotional sources.

The quality and quantity of physical and psychological stimulation are variable from person to person and encounter to encounter. In general, the psychological aspect of sexual arousal is more determinative of the total stimulus level than is physical stimulation.

The amount of physical and psychological stimulation required to trigger the vasocongestive responses involved in arousal and the muscular responses involved in orgasm must exceed a threshold in order to cause arousal and orgasm, respectively. When the total stimulus level, that is, the sum of physical and psychological stimulation, fails to reach an individual's threshold, arousal and orgasm do not occur.

By including the psychological dimension as an integral aspect of sexual function, this model spotlights the uniquely human, relational elements of sexuality. This adds a dimension to those theories that have focused more on the progressive phases of physiologic arousal than on relationship and psychological experience. Much like psychodynamic theory, this model recognizes the human capacity to assign complex meanings to any given sexual encounter, and acknowledges that sexual experience is contextualized in the larger setting of human relationship and personal history. Therapy guided by this model does not focus on sensate focus exercises, but rather on the process through which meaning is given to sexual experience in a relationship.

Passion and intimacy, the mainstays of meaningful sex, are seen to be interrelated experiences. Intimacy requires the capacity to be separate and yet related at the same time. Sexual passion requires the ability to recognize and present one's sexual self, one's sexual needs and desires, in the face of the potential for rejection and misunderstanding in a relationship. Sexual intimacy and passion are each a risky business. On the one hand, by the very nature of the risks involved, they cause anxiety. On the other hand, they lead toward intense, meaningful, and satisfying sexual experience.

The two sources of stimulation—physical and psychological—are additive and interactive. Thus, decreases in the stimulation from either source can be "counterbalanced" by increases in the stimulation provided by the other source.

Because the model focuses on the internal experience of the individuals participating in a sexual encounter, it moves toward the exploration of those processes that have been more traditionally the domain of psychoanalysis, psychodynamic psychotherapy, and marital therapy.

This brief summary of the emotional aspects of the quantum model is woefully inadequate. We encourage you to read Chapter Five, co-authored by Cynthia McReynolds and David Schnarch, which will give you a much better picture of the complexity and usefulness of the quantum model.

Clinical Insights

The quantum model of sexual function introduces the full range of sexual experience: the physical substrate, the psychological meaning, and the dyadic experience. David Schnarch has worked diligently to integrate insights from medical, psychiatric, psychological, and marital and family systems theories, and has done an excellent job.

• The inclusion of a simultaneous focus on the physical and psychological factors affecting sexual response allows for a more complete assessment of sexual function and dysfunction. It provides a space for sex therapy to be integrated with existing models of intrapsychic and dyadic processes from psychodynamic and marital therapy. It offers the clinician multiple avenues of understanding and intervention along both physical and psychological dimensions.

• A focus on the nature of a couple's relationship can correct one of the problematic aspects of sex therapy: the imposition of sensate focus and other sexual exercises onto a relationship that is "psychologically unready" to engage in intimate sexual expression.

• The concept of counterbalancing can help the clinician think in multiple ways about a given sexual disorder. In essence, any intervention that increases physical or psychological stimulation increases the likelihood that arousal and orgasmic thresholds will be reached.

• The theory supports inquiry and intervention based on a dyadic process model. This relieves individuals of the onerous "responsibility" for ownership of a sexual problem. Further, it encourages the clinician to think beyond stimulus-response factors into the complexities of history and process.

• The model provides a useful vision of intermittent dysfunctions in that difficulties can be caused by fluctuations in physical stimulation, stimulus transmission, the receiver's psychological processes, and changes in thresholds.

• Essentially, the quantum model asks the therapist to alter the basic assumptions underlying the therapy of sexual disorders from a focus on symptoms to a focus on relatedness, authenticity, and individuality.

Clinical Problems

David Schnarch's herculean effort to make sense of just about all that's been written about sexual function and sex therapy is quite remarkable, and we highly recommend his book to you. We think that the difficulties inherent in this model are a matter of degree and emphasis.

1. Because passion, intimacy, and differentiation are seen as the highest developmental level of sexual experience, there is the possibility of romanticizing individuality and creating a rather black-and-white approach. Differentiation is good, fusion is bad. Mature sexual pleasure can only be found in a differentiated relationship. Elements that bespeak fusion become signposts of psychopathology.

2.   Coming as it does from a marital or couple therapy approach, many of the concepts proposed in this model are presented as if they have been newly discovered and do not have a relationship to ideas presented in other related fields. Although the ideas and paradigms of the quantum model are new to the sex therapy literature, many of the concepts it espouses are represented in psychotherapy and psychoanalysis.

The danger is that a therapist may feel obligated to either adopt or reject the quantum model, rather than integrate it into a broader understanding of psychotherapy. For example, Freud's notion that genitality involves an individuated form of sexual expression that includes resolution of oedipal fixation and the discarding of anxiety-reducing sexual fantasy; Margaret Mahler's notion of separation-individuation as a process that involves growth from a primary fused state to a differentiated one; the self-psychological concept of transmuting internalization as a process in which a self-object relationship (a form of fused relationship) is a necessary and functional aspect of developmental growth—each of these ideas is expressed in other terms in the quantum model.

3.   Schnarch's approach is complex, as befits any theory that purports to explain human nature. Some therapists may not be willing to do the work necessary to understand the subtleties of Schnarch's emphasis on the assumptions underlying a therapeutic approach to sexual problems.

4.   Therapy based on the quantum model will most often be longer than that based on behavioral or Masters and Johnson models. Managed care evaluators may conclude that work focused on building intimacy and passion is not "medically necessary."

Clinical Techniques

This model adds techniques from marital and family therapy to general psychotherapeutic methods. The result is an approach that focuses primarily on relationship and authenticity.

- The assigning of homework by the therapist is contraindicated in this model because it removes the potential for differentiation and choice from the patients.

- The focus of the therapist's attention is on the dynamics of relationship. Sexual behavior is used as a metaphoric window into the nature of that relationship. Thus such techniques of couple therapy and individual therapy as observation, interpretation, clarification, and confrontation are useful.

- A major effort is made to expand a couple's tolerance for, and appreciation of differences in, desire, sexual preference, values, and emotion. The intent is to create room for each individual to enter the relational and sexual arena as an individual instead of as a symbiotic other. Thus the therapist pays attention to ways in which patients hide, suppress, and deny their own experience and desire.

∾

We hope this chapter has helped you to see that sexual behavior is the final result of multiple inputs. Sexual desire, excitement, and orgasm depend on the physiological processes of the human body and the psychological processes of the human personality. It is the combination of the physical substrate and the mental image that results in functional, meaningful sex.

With the basics of sexual physiology in mind, we'll move on to Chapter Three, which discusses the evaluation of sexual disorders.

NOTES

P. 35, *Nafazodone (Serzone) is a new antidepressant:* Feiger, A. (1996, May 4–9). Presentation on antidepressant therapy at the 149th annual meeting of the American Psychiatric Association, New York.

P. 42, *Masters and Johnson divided:* Masters, W., & Johnson, V. (1966). *Human sexual response.* Boston: Little, Brown; Masters, W., & Johnson, V. (1970). *Human sexual inadequacy.* Boston: Little, Brown.

P. 48, *Helen Kaplan enlarged the scope:* Kaplan, H. S. (1974). *The new sex therapy.* New York: Brunner/Mazel; Kaplan, H. S. (1995). *The sexual desire disorders.* New York: Brunner/Mazel.

P. 52, *marital/sexual therapist David Schnarch:* Schnarch, D. (1991). *Constructing the sexual crucible: An integration of sexual and marital therapy.* New York: Norton.

C H A P T E R

3

EVALUATION OF
SEXUAL DISORDERS

Randolph S. Charlton

The four basic attributes a therapist needs in order to evaluate
sexual disorders are

- A thorough knowledge of sexual anatomy and physiology
- An empathic understanding of emotional conflict
- The ability to talk directly, comfortably, and concretely
  about sex
- Common sense (the more the better)

In this chapter I will describe how to use these four attributes
to evaluate those patients who come to your office with problems and concerns relating to sexual function. This would
include *disorders of desire* (Hypoactive Desire Disorder and Sexual Aversion Disorder), *sexual arousal disorders* (Female Sexual
Arousal Disorder and Male Erectile Disorder), *orgasmic disorders*
(female and male orgasmic disorders and premature ejaculation),
sexual pain disorders (dyspareunia and vaginismus), *sexual disorders due to a generalized medical condition, substance-induced sexual
disorders*, and the *paraphilias* (exhibitionism, fetishism, frotteurism, pedophilia, masochism, sadism, transvestic fetishism,
and voyeurism).

The first step in the treatment of sexual disorders is a thorough evaluation. I will review the structure of the evaluation process, the questions you will need to ask, indications to make a referral for medical examination or psychological testing, and the creation of a diagnosis and dynamic formulation.

The model of evaluation I use combines psychodynamic understanding of conflict with a direct focus on sexual behavior and function. For many years, psychoanalysis was the treatment of choice for all forms of sexual conflict and dysfunction not directly caused by an obvious medical condition. Because psychoanalysis focuses on unconscious emotional conflict and relegates immediate precipitants and sexual symptoms to a secondary position, the evaluation of sexual function within an analytic framework is a protracted process. Understandably, an analytic format is not well suited to the prompt alleviation of a patient's troublesome and painful sexual symptoms, nor is it particularly workable in today's climate of managed health care.

A quarter of a century ago, Masters and Johnson observed, measured, and described the physiological elements of human sexual response. They went on to devise a form of brief evaluation and therapy that was aimed specifically at assessing and treating sexual dysfunction. Masters and Johnson used a two-therapist team and initially worked only with couples. Their six-session evaluation included clinical interviews with the couple, medical evaluation, and psychological testing. Nowadays, most individual practitioners who work with sexual disorders see patients without a co-therapist, and make referrals for medical and psychological examinations as needed rather than as an invariant part of the evaluation. Because of the expense and time involved, I rarely ask a co-therapist to join me in an evaluation, although, as will be discussed, there are a few circumstances when it is prudent to consider working as a co-therapy team.

Thanks to the work of Avodah Offit, Helen Kaplan, Bernard Apfelbaum, Joseph LoPiccolo, David Schnarch, and many others, we now have a way to combine the best of Masters and Johnson's brief format with insights gained from psychodynamic psychotherapy and behavior therapy. The type of evaluation you will learn in this chapter is

- Brief and efficient
- Focused on sexual function and feeling
- Especially useful in diagnosing the nature and causes of sexual difficulties
- In a format that allows you to determine if there is a medical problem that is influencing sexual function
- In a format that helps you decide what kind of therapy is indicated for patients presenting with sexual disorders

Individuals with sexual problems often come to the initial consultation with a great deal of anxiety and concern. A prompt evaluation often relieves their initial fears and sets the stage for treatment. It is especially important to complete the evaluation quickly and efficiently when time or financial constraints limit the number of sessions. Six to eight one-hour sessions are usually enough to accomplish this, depending of course on the complexity of the case.

STRUCTURE OF THE EVALUATION

Although some of the therapeutic techniques are different, the basic structure of the evaluation of sexual disorders is similar whether you are seeing an individual or a couple. A common format for a full evaluation usually looks something like this:

- If meeting with a couple
  Two sessions with the couple
  Two individual sessions (one with each member of the couple)
- If meeting with an individual
  Two to four sessions of individual interviews
- Psychological testing (when indicated)

- Medical examination (when indicated)
- Another meeting if needed (to obtain missing information)
- A final meeting in which feedback is given and a decision about how to proceed is made

The type of evaluation I am describing is similar to a medical examination in that the therapist takes charge of the questioning and makes sure that all relevant areas are covered. Issues of transference are usually bypassed during the evaluation, rather than interpreted.

For example, when Fred Wilms, a forty-two-year-old, successful venture capitalist, monopolized the conversation and answered questions addressed to his wife, I put up a hand, asked him to hold on, and directed her to tell me about her sexual experience in their marriage. Even though transference and emotional conflict are not interpreted in a situation like this, they must be recognized and taken into account. Your understanding of the nature of your patient's emotional experience influences the way in which questions are asked and discussions structured.

Tact and timing are always important for the psychotherapist, but when dealing with sex and sexuality, they are even more crucial than usual. Evaluations are particularly difficult because you don't yet know the patient, and they haven't developed a sense of alliance or trust. It is particularly important for you to keep track of the patient's level of anxiety, guilt, and shame, as these are the feelings most likely to disrupt the evaluation process.

In this example, Mr. Wilms grew red faced and impatient, while his wife, Jane, unaccustomed to taking the spotlight, began to stutter. I monitored their feelings, and as long as the anger and anxiety didn't totally disrupt the evaluation process, I did not address them directly. However, when Mrs. Wilms showed signs that she was unable to answer my questions fully even without her husband's interruptions, I pointed out the growing tension in the room and asked Mrs. Wilms about her apprehension. She said she was afraid that her husband was feeling left out. Mr. Wilms denied this, and though I didn't completely believe him,

I allowed his reassurance to calm Mrs. Wilms into continuing to tell me about her thoughts and feelings. It was necessary to focus on this dynamic in order to lessen her anxiety before continuing the information-gathering process.

Which Patients Require a Sexual Evaluation?

The answer to this question may seem obvious: patients with sexual complaints require an evaluation of their sexual feelings and function. Although this is generally true, we must be more specific in our understanding of when to focus directly on sex and when not to. There are patients whose chief complaint is of a sexual nature but who should not undergo an immediate evaluation and assessment of their sexual lives.

Psychosis, Mania, and Severe Borderline Conflicts. I once saw a young salesman who said that he was unable to have sex because his hair hurt. In all seriousness, he told me that the hair on his head was very, very sensitive, and whenever anyone touched it, he felt terrible pain. He'd been to several internists and a dermatologist, all of whom suggested he see a psychiatrist. His last sexual encounter was with a prostitute. He demanded that she not touch his hair. She agreed, but accidentally bumped against his head. He screamed at her and left in an angry huff. This paranoid patient had a somatic delusion that not only kept him from having sex but also kept him indoors and away from most other people. This is an obvious example of an alleged sexual problem that is in fact a sign of a serious mental disorder.

Some psychotic and borderline patients will present with sexual symptoms. You must evaluate the entire person when looking at sexual issues. When a major psychiatric illness is suspected, it's vital to address it before limiting your attention to sexual issues. I have supervised several therapists who missed a diagnosis of manic-depressive illness, manic stage, and incorrectly began the type of directed evaluation of sexual function we are discussing here without obtaining enough information about the patient's general psychological status. Manic and hypo-manic states are often characterized by an increase in goal-directed activity, which can include sexuality. In contrast to a patient with a more limited sexual dysfunction, manic patients exhibit an exaggerated sense of self-esteem, little need for sleep, rapid speech and flow of ideas, and a lack of consideration about the consequences of their actions.

I have seen manic patients complaining of premature ejaculation, but more often, their problems relate to the impulsive nature of their sexual actions. It is possible for a manic patient without a previous history of paraphiliac experience to be brought to your office after exposing himself, masturbating in public, or inappropriately approaching another person in a sexual manner. The suspicion of a manic or hypomanic episode is reason to obtain a complete psychiatric examination of your patient before proceeding with a focus on sexual issues.

Aside from the major mood and thought disorders, there are two other diagnostic categories that can present with sexual symptoms and that may require further evaluation and treatment *before* beginning a sexual evaluation. The first is depression; the second, substance abuse. In fact, depression and alcoholism are two of the most common causes of sexual dysfunction. Patients who would never seek therapy for either of these maladies will sometimes appear in your office with a sexual complaint. "I can't maintain an erection." "I'm too tired to have sex." "My wife says she's just not interested in sex anymore."

Depression. It is appropriate to conduct a brief evaluation of sexual issues with a patient suffering from a mild to moderate degree of depression. In fact, many patients with sexual dysfunctions will have some degree of depression. If they weren't depressed before their sexual function became impaired, they are likely to become so afterwards. Some of these patients will deny or minimize the degree of affect that accompanies depression. Instead, they may complain of a variety of somatic difficulties, including insomnia or hypersomnia, fatigue, weight gain or loss, agitation, and alteration in sexual function and interest. There are situations when depression is experienced in the body. A patient with a more serious, major depression will only rarely seek out help for a sexual problem. In my experience this is more likely to occur when a spouse or partner brings the patient in, with complaints such as "Our sex life has all but disappeared," or "My partner doesn't seem to care about sex anymore."

We must be alert for the signs of depression in all patients who come to us with sexual complaints. If a patient exhibits signs of a serious depression—psychomotor retardation, delusions of persecution, severe insomnia, tearfulness, hopelessness, or thoughts of suicide—it is not appropriate to focus your attention on the sexual problem. The depressive issues must be addressed first. With a seriously depressed patient, this requires a referral for psychiatric consultation in which medication and even hospitalization might be considered.

Alcohol and Drugs. An important early step in the evaluation of every sexual complaint is to take a thorough drug and alcohol history. Although alcohol is the most commonly abused substance that interferes with sexual performance, most of the "street drugs" (cocaine, heroin, amphetamines, sedatives, hypnotics, and anxiolytic tranquilizers) can have a deleterious effect on sexual performance. Further, there are a variety of legitimately prescribed medications (see Table 2.1) that influence sexual physiology. Drugs can influence all levels of sexual function (desire, arousal, orgasm, and sexual pain), so you can not rule out substance-related sexual disorders based only on the presenting symptoms of your patient. Although drug use can be a factor in the paraphilias, it is rare that the substance is the sole cause of the patient's sexual predilection. It is important to note, however, that acute intoxication can be related to loss of impulse control and to the acting out of previously inhibited fantasies.

The diagnosis of substance-induced sexual dysfunction is complex in that it requires that the dysfunction be *in excess* of that usually associated with the intoxication syndrome of the particular drug in question. Otherwise, we diagnose substance intoxication and include the sexual symptoms as part of the intoxication syndrome. This requires the expertise of a physician familiar with abuse syndromes and the side effects of a wide variety of psychotropic and commonly used medical agents.

Many patients cannot resolve their sexual problems unless they first resolve their substance abuse problems. If you have even the slightest suspicion that alcohol or other substances are involved in your patient's sexual problem, you must ensure that he undergoes a thorough physical examination, including appropriate laboratory tests. If the patient acknowledges a substance abuse problem, then you must evaluate its severity and its relationship to the presenting sexual problems. In most situations, it is advisable to deal with the drug dependency issues first. It is often impossible to know how well a patient will function sexually until she has stopped the substance abuse and her physical health is back to normal.

Conditions that suggest that a patient's sexual disorder is not substance related—even though the patient may be using a potentially problematic drug—include symptoms whose onset precedes the use of the drug, symptoms that persist over a month after completely stopping use of the drug, and a prior history of sexual dysfunction while not using the substance in question.

∾

To reiterate and underscore the important points: in each and every evaluation of sexual function, you should

- Look for signs of psychosis, mania, and severe borderline conflicts.

- Be alert for signs of depression.

- Ask your patients to list *all* the drugs they are taking.

- Ask specifically about alcohol and other "recreational" drugs.

Flexibility and Prioritization

There will be times when it is impossible to begin a brief evaluation of sexual function without first dealing with other, more pressing considerations. As previously discussed, you must alter the format of your evaluation when a major depression or drug abuse–related sexual problem is present. Additionally, there will be circumstances where a patient's anger, anxiety, guilt, or shame are at such a level that it is impossible to deal with sexual issues without first making other interventions.

Sometimes it will be obvious from the very first contact with the patient that you must do some preliminary work before initiating a sexual evaluation.

MR. AND MRS. KLOSTERMAN

Mrs. Klosterman, an anxious fifty-four-year-old housewife, called my office and asked if I would see her husband. With obvious bitterness, she said he was too busy to make the appointment and had asked her to do it. When I asked if she could tell me something about the nature of the difficulties, she said it had to do with sex, but it was her husband's problem—I should ask him about it.

When one adult calls to make an appointment for another it's like the beginning of a mystery story: something significant has just happened, but it's impossible to know what it means. In this case, it wasn't at all clear what was wrong or who was the patient. I ended up seeing Mr. Klosterman several times before Mrs. Klosterman was willing to come in to the office, and even then she wanted to be seen alone. When Mrs. Klosterman did appear, she angrily told me of what she saw as her husband's workaholism and outrageous sexual demands. She complained that her husband got home each night at about ten and expected her to be waiting for him, dressed in a sexy negligee and ready to seduce him into oral sex. As far as Mrs. Klosterman was concerned, if her husband was too busy to talk to her, she was too busy to use her mouth to satisfy him! It took two months of individual meetings before Mrs. Klosterman was willing to come into the office with her husband. Sex was still a central problem, but before we could address it directly, it was necessary to work through the effects of the Klostermans' underlying anger and resentment.

Common sense dictates that patients who have a history of traumatic sexual experience, such as physical or sexual abuse, rape, or sexual betrayal by a person in authority, will have strong feelings about discussing their sexual experience. In these cases, you must often deal with the aftermath of the traumatic experience before launching into sexual matters.

BILL AND MARGARET NESTOR

Several years ago I saw Bill and Margaret Nestor, a young couple who had recently arrived in California from the East Coast. Two years previously, Margaret had been forcibly abducted from her car, taken to a vacant house, and repeatedly raped. The awful experience left her unable to drive, unable to continue her job as a dental technician, and understandably terrified of sex. Individual therapy helped Margaret to resume most aspects of her life. However, she remained frightened and avoidant of sexual intimacy. I met with Margaret and Bill together for the first hour and obtained a history. It was clear in that initial consultation that Margaret was still suffering from aspects of posttraumatic stress. She was terrified to be talking about sex, especially to a man. I altered the usual pattern of the evaluation by introducing a woman co-therapist. When the four of us next met together, Margaret was still anxious, but far less so than before. The individual sessions were extended and split along gender lines: I saw Bill for four one-hour sessions and my co-therapist saw Margaret four times. We continued the evaluation more gently and slowly than in other circumstances, postponing the medical examination until it was clear that it would not evoke undue anxiety.

There are other situations in which you may begin an evaluation only to discover that the structure must be altered and the information gathering put aside in order to deal with pressing dynamic issues. For instance, a recently married young man was referred to me by his family doctor because of impotence. In our first meeting, he expressed a fear that his feelings would be disregarded, as they had been in his family of origin. His doctor had given him advice and medication to fix the impotence, but it had only gotten worse. He'd read several books on sex therapy and was worried I would want to bring his wife into the therapy and focus solely on his sexual performance. Because of this, I let him take charge and tell me about himself. Once he realized that I did take his feelings seriously, we were able to address sexual issues more directly and to consider the advantage of involving his wife in the therapy.

AREAS OF INQUIRY

The following lists of the main areas of inquiry in a sexual evaluation should help you to make sure you've covered all the bases. Remember that these are general guidelines about issues specifically relevant to sexual function and feeling; they are not a definitive compilation of everything you might need to know. I have tried to order the information in terms of how a "usual" interview goes; that is, the first items listed are the subjects I usually discuss first, and so on. Obviously, there is no such thing as a typical interview, so you will have to vary your questions depending on what is relevant in a specific situation.

Basic Information

- Nature and development of the sexual difficulty
  Emotional reactions to the problem
  Understanding of its genesis
  Attempts to resolve it
- Psychiatric history
  Previous illness, therapy, hospitalization
  Previous psychological testing
- Physical health
  Medical history, illnesses, disabilities
  Medicines taken
  Drug and alcohol use
- Motivation for treatment

History Specific to Couples

- How they met, what attracted them to each other
- Initial sexual experience together
- Changes in the nature of their sexual experience, wanted or unwanted, over the course of the relationship
- Method of and satisfaction with birth control
- What can't be talked about in the relationship

Sexual History (obtained in individual interviews)

- Family, cultural, religious background concerning sex
- Early sex play, education
- Discovery of arousal
- Initial shared experiences, same and opposite sex
- Abuse, sexual or physical
- Adolescence
  Dating
  Sexual experiences: petting, mutual orgasm, intercourse
  Body image, eating disorders

- Masturbation
  How often, how done
  Fantasies
- Other sexual partners
  Before present relationship (if any)
  During present relationship (if any)
- Feelings about sex not already discussed
  Likes and dislikes
  Wishes and fears
- What's important about sex
  Orgasm
  Closeness
  Verbal, nonverbal communication
- Feelings about partner(s) not already discussed

The Significance of Language

Remember as you discuss sexual issues with your patients that language can evoke emotion or bury it. Generalizations tend to flatten out feeling, especially where sex is concerned. Details can be used in an obsessive way to distance emotion, but for many people emotion is in the details. Evocative language is one way a patient allows the therapist to "be" in the presence of her genuine sexuality.

JIM FREDRICKSON

Jim, a sixty-two-year-old businessman, entered therapy to deal with a long-standing depression that included bouts of impotence. In response to my question about his sexual interest and energy, he told me that it was very difficult for him to talk about sex. We went over Jim's Midwestern upbringing, his embarrassment about bodies and bodily functions, and his unfamiliarity talking about sex with anyone, let alone another man. In the next session he spoke about his current sexual life in a general way. I was aware that his language was vague; he did not speak about "who did what to whom" and he avoided any direct references to his or his partner's body.

When I pointed this out, Jim commented that it was much more difficult to deal with the specifics. He could talk about the general issues without having to feel anything, but if he really told me what happened physically and inside his head, he would have to feel something. He was especially afraid he might feel aroused—that would be mortifying. There is a natural, culturally determined shame at revealing intimate details about one's most personal, sexual experiences. The inherent trust that this man had in me as a therapist and the trust he developed because of empathic, understanding responses allowed him to overcome low to moderate levels of shame and to begin to discuss his sexual life in a definitive and specific way.

Cultural and Religious Differences

I want to reinforce the notion that sexual norms vary greatly from culture to culture and generation to generation. Evaluation of clients' satisfaction with their sexual life involves understanding their experience in the context of their background and values. An example of this is the distribution of frequency of masturbation in American culture. Robert Michael and his colleagues discovered that college-educated Caucasians who are living with someone are the most likely to masturbate. Young women and older people generally masturbate less. People with conservative values, Catholics, and many people of color are statistically less likely to masturbate. Michael concluded that an individual's use of masturbation was more related to his or her social and religious background than to any other factor.

REFERRAL FOR FURTHER EVALUATION

Once the basic information has been gathered, it is time to consider medical examination and psychological testing. At the very beginning of your evaluation, you should ask about previous psychotherapy, including psychological testing, and obtain records of any therapy and tests that have been done. If the patient has a history of any medical problems, you should contact the physician and obtain the pertinent medical records and/or discuss with the doctor the possible effects of the patient's medical status on sexual function. The diagnosis of sexual dysfunction due to a general medical condition is one that requires a complete assessment and consideration of a variety of factors.

Medical Evaluation

A medical examination should be done in the vast majority of sexual dysfunction cases regardless of the general state of the patient's health. There are a variety of medical conditions, from diabetes to sickle-cell anemia, that can cause alteration of sexual function, and it is only through a thorough medical examination that some of them can be diagnosed. As with substance-induced sexual disorders, medical illness can influence each and every stage of sexual function. One of the most serious errors you can make is to overlook a medical condition that causes a sexual disorder. Not only would any psychological treatment the patient receives be limited in its effect, but there is also the possibility that an unrecognized illness would progress and cause irreversible harm to the patient in a situation where it could have been diagnosed and treated.

There are two important clues that would suggest that a medical condition might be causally related to a sexual dysfunction. First is a temporal association between the onset or exacerbation of an illness and the appearance or exacerbation of a sexual dysfunction. Second is an alteration in sexual function that goes against usual physiological function, as when a twenty-year-old man develops impotence without any stressors that might argue for a psychological etiology.

In my practice I have seen several men with impotence who were otherwise asymptomatic, who on medical examination were found to have diabetes. I have seen a young woman who presented with an arousal disorder and a thirty-three-year-old man with erectile dysfunction who were both diagnosed with multiple sclerosis.

Some sexual disorders are more likely to be caused by medical conditions than others. Pain with sexual interaction is a symptom that especially requires a complete physical examination. Pain with sexual intercourse is called *dyspareunia*. It can be related to insufficient vaginal lubrication as seen in post menopausal atrophic vaginitis, vaginal scar tissue, endometriosis, estrogen deprivation (as in lactation or breast cancer treatment), urinary tract irritation and infection, as well as some gastrointestinal conditions. *Vaginismus*, the involuntary spasm of circumvaginal muscles making penetration difficult or impossible, can also be related to a variety of physical abnormalities of the female genitourinary tract.

Withdrawal from alcohol or opioids is known to be related to the sudden appearance of premature ejaculation. Some men use drugs to diminish their sexual arousal and delay their orgasmic response; when the substance is no longer available, they will be unable to control the orgasmic response.

There are also a few maxims that offer clues to a psychological rather than a medical cause for a sexual problem. If a man complains of being impotent with his wife but is able to masturbate to orgasm, awakes with "morning erections," and is able to function in an extramarital relationship, it is a good bet that psychological factors are responsible for his problem. (See Chapter Four for more information about using a sleep lab to measure a patient's nocturnal penile tumescence.) The same is true for a woman who finds herself aroused and orgasmic in one relationship but not in another. Remember, however, that a physical illness can affect sexual function differentially. If an individual is more excited in an extramarital experience, he may be able to compensate for diminished physiological function. Thus, you should be very, very cautious about diagnosing a psychological etiology for your patient's sexual disorder without first referring him for a complete medical examination.

Finally, it is rare that a paraphilia is related to an organic condition. There are circumstances when a brain tumor or a hormonal abnormality might alter an individual's sexual function leading to unusual forms of sexual enactment, but paraphilias are most often long-standing, character-based sexual styles. If a perverse style of sexuality appears suddenly in an individual who previously exhibited no inclination toward it, either in fantasy or action, you should consider an unusual physical problem as one of the possibilities in your differential diagnosis.

When one or both members of a couple suffer from a sexual dysfunction, I most often refer each of them for a physical examination regardless of the identified patient. This examination is different from a routine visit to the gynecologist, internist, or urologist. I refer to an examining physician who is more than usually attentive to the patient's state of anxiety. I have found it helpful to work with one or two medical practitioners, a gynecologist, a urologist, and an internist who are interested and up-to-date on sexual matters. In the course of their physical examination, these physicians do more than silently assess the patient. They often discuss aspects of sexual physiology and answer any questions that emerge. In many ways, this type of physical examination is therapeutic. It serves to reassure patients that someone is paying special attention to the sexual aspects of their difficulty, and gives them a chance to discuss physical issues that are of concern to them. In Chapter Four, Harcharan Gill and Claire Appelmans review the medical evaluation of sexual disorders.

Psychological Testing

I've found psych testing very helpful in the evaluation of patients with sexual symptoms. This is particularly true for those individuals with dual diagnoses, personality disorders, potentially factitious disorders, and the gamut of paraphilias. The personality structure of such patients is often complicated, and it is consequently difficult to evaluate their capacity to engage in therapy.

Psychological testing can help sort out the degree of psychopathology, the motivation to get better, and the nature of hidden conflicts. Further, psych testing is useful with those individuals who have difficulty communicating verbally because of depression, shyness, or anxiety. In addition to patients with sexual symptoms who fall into the previously mentioned diagnostic categories, I often make a referral to a psychologist for testing when seeing a couple complaining of a sexual problem. The information obtained from such a consultation enhances and speeds the evaluation process.

MAKING A DIAGNOSIS AND CREATING A DYNAMIC FORMULATION

When making a diagnosis of a sexual problem, it is important to remember that notions of what is sexually "normal" vary from culture to culture and family to family. Socioeconomic, educational, and religious background strongly influence an individual's notions of sexual deviance, standards of performance, and gender role behavior. Sexual mores change from generation to generation. Activities commonly practiced by today's twenty-year-olds would leave our mothers' generation of friends embarrassed and confused.

Sexual symptoms can appear in a variety of situations. As we have already mentioned, sexual apathy and even anhedonia (lack of any pleasurable feelings) can accompany severe depression. Inappropriate sexual behavior can be seen in acute manic episodes. When making a diagnosis of a sexual disorder, you must first determine that the sexual symptoms are not better accounted for as an aspect of another psychiatric disorder. Furthermore, for a problem to classify as a diagnosable sexual dysfunction it must *cause marked distress or interpersonal difficulty*. Thus an individual who tells you that he is not at all interested in sex and is perfectly content with his celibate, abstinent state, does *not* have a diagnosable disorder of desire. On the other hand, suppose a man comes to you and says he is very upset because he is unable to delay his orgasm long enough to satisfy himself or his partner, and he does not have a medical condition or use any drugs or medications that could account for this symptom, and he is not diagnosable with an Axis I psychiatric disorder. By definition, he has premature ejaculation.

There are *three subtypes* that you can use to provide ancillary information about the nature of the sexual dysfunction.

1. The onset of the disorder can be defined as lifelong (since the onset of sexual functioning) or acquired (develops after a period of normal function).

2. The context in which the disorder appears is signified as generalized (disorder not limited to specific partner, situation, or method of stimulation) or situational (disorder limited to a specific partner, situation, or method of stimulation).

3. The causative factors of the sexual disorder can be either due to psychological factors or due to combined factors (both psychological and general medical condition or substance use are implicated in the etiology of the disorder).

The *Diagnostic and Statistical Manual of Mental Disorders* (4th ed.) divides sexual dysfunctions into six categories:

1. Sexual desire disorders
2. Sexual arousal disorders
3. Orgasmic disorders
4. Sexual pain disorders
5. Sexual dysfunction related to a general medical condition
6. Substance-induced sexual dysfunction

Sexual desire disorders are defined by decreased interest in sexual interaction. *Hypoactive Sexual Desire Disorder* (302.71) is manifested by persistently deficient or absent sexual fantasy and desire for sexual activity. *Sexual Aversion Disorder* (302.79) is a more extreme condition in which there is persistent aversion to and avoidance of all genital sexual contact with another person. Obviously, as with all sexual disorders, you must consider the age, personality, and background of the patient before making a diagnosis of a sexual desire disorder.

Sexual arousal disorders involve dysfunction of the lubrication-swelling stage of sexual response and are divided along gender lines. *Female Sexual Arousal Disorder* (302.72) is diagnosed when a woman manifests a persistent inability to maintain an adequate lubrication-swelling response in the presence of adequate stimulation. *Male Erectile Disorder* (302.72), commonly called *impotence*, is the persistent inability to maintain an adequate erection until completion of the sexual activity. Both of these disorders involve the blood flow response mediated by the parasympathetic nervous system and are thus vulnerable to medications that affect the autonomic nervous system.

Orgasmic disorders include *Female Orgasmic Disorder* (302.73), formerly called anorgasmia or inhibited female orgasm, is marked by a persistent delay in or absence of orgasm following an adequate excitement phase. Thus a woman suffering from this syndrome is able to become aroused, to lubricate and feel excited, but is unable to reach orgasm in spite of adequate stimulation. The judgment as to what is adequate stimulation must be made with care, and requires a knowledge of not only your patient's physiology but also her interests and "turn-ons." *Male Orgasmic Disorder* (302.74) was formerly called *retarded ejaculation*, a term I like, for it is descriptive of the problem. A persistent delay in or absence of orgasm following an adequate excitement phase is the signifier of this disorder. *Premature Ejaculation* (302.75) is the inability to have a reasonable amount of control over the ejaculatory reflex. A man suffering from prematurity often reaches orgasm with minimal stimulation, usually before he wants it or is ready.

Premature ejaculation has sometimes been diagnosed based on the length of time a man could delay orgasm, and sometimes by the degree of satisfaction the man's partner experiences through sexual interaction. Neither of these definitions is satisfactory, as they do not focus on the basis of the problem—control. Most men learn how to control the onset of orgasm by varying the amount of stimulation they are obtaining. In essence, most men learn how to regulate their excitement level, maintaining their arousal below the point of ejaculatory inevitability (that moment when the orgasmic reflex begins). An interesting aspect of this is that the premature ejaculator often is unable to register and measure the degree of his arousal. Some men will reach an orgasm almost before they know they are excited.

Sexual pain disorders include *Dyspareunia* (302.76), which refers to recurrent genital pain with sexual intercourse in a man or a woman. This is one diagnostic category that always requires a complete medical examination. *Vaginismus* (306.51) is the persistent involuntary spasm of the circumvaginal muscles when attempting penetration. It is most often noticed when intercourse is attempted, but sometimes is apparent during gynecological examinations.

Because some women are embarrassed to talk about their genital responses, and because some women do not even know that this disorder exists, it is important to ask any woman complaining of painful intercourse if she has noticed muscular spasm or difficulty when undergoing a pelvic exam. Sometimes a woman who is not aroused, and consequently is not lubricated, will complain of painful intercourse. A careful and complete sexual history will help differentiate cases of Female Arousal Disorder from dyspareunia and vaginismus. Physical examination will provide further information to confirm the diagnosis and pinpoint possible physical causes of the pain.

Sexual dysfunction due to a general medical condition is a particularly important category of sexual problems. As the name implies, this diagnosis is made when history, physical examination, or laboratory tests indicate that the sexual dysfunction is fully explained by the direct physiological effects of a general medical condition. All of the symptoms found in the specific sexual disorders can be caused by a general medical condition; thus you can not rule out the possibility of a physical cause of sexual dysfunction based only on the presenting sexual symptoms. Most sexual disorders caused by a general medical illness are generalized, and usually the sexual symptoms are concurrent with the onset or exacerbation of the illness.

Substance-induced sexual dysfunction is unfortunately all too common. To make the diagnosis, history, physical examination, or laboratory findings must indicate that the sexual dysfunction is fully explained by the substance use *and* either (1) the symptoms developed during, or within a month of, substance intoxication, or (2) medication use is etiologically related to the disturbance. Your history must include careful consideration of alcohol and drug use and a complete listing of all medications that your patient is taking.

Paraphilias, commonly referred to as *sexual perversions*, include eight forms of recurrent, intense, sexually arousing fantasies, urges, or actions involving either (1) nonhuman objects, (2) the suffering or humiliation of self or another person, or (3) sexual interaction with children or nonconsenting persons.

To make a diagnosis of a paraphilia, the sexually arousing fantasy or action must have been present for at least a period of six months and, like all sexual disorders, must cause personal or interpersonal difficulty. Many perverse sexual actions involve behaviors that are intrusive, destructive, and illegal, and thus patients with paraphilias are sometimes mandated to be evaluated by the court. The therapy of the paraphilias is often difficult, as it involves deep-seated anxieties and narcissistic conflicts. We will address these problems in Chapter Nine. The paraphilias include the following:

- *Exhibitionism* (302.4), exposure of one's genitals to an unsuspecting stranger
- *Fetishism* (302.81), use of nonliving objects for sexual gratification
- *Frotteurism* (302.89), touching or rubbing against a nonconsenting person

- *Pedophilia* (302.2), sexual activity with a prepubescent child or children
- *Sexual Masochism* (302.83), sexual arousal by being humiliated, beaten, bound, or otherwise made to suffer
- *Sexual Sadism* (302.84), sexual arousal by causing physical or psychological suffering
- *Transvestic Fetishism* (302.3), heterosexual male aroused by cross dressing
- *Voyeurism* (302.82), sexual arousal at watching an unsuspecting person who is naked, undressing, or having sex

Difficult Diagnoses

You will find there are times when you run into diagnostic difficulties. How would you diagnose a woman who is unable to have an orgasm with her husband but is orgasmic with a female lover only when she imagines she is with her husband? Or a man who is unable to have an orgasm with intercourse but is able to ejaculate while watching his wife pee in the toilet, an enactment he enjoys and she doesn't mind?

SAM AND DOROTHY ALLWORTH

During your history taking with the Allworths you discover that Sam, a fifty-four-year-old software engineer, is unable to control his ejaculatory reflex. He uniformly has an orgasm each time he penetrates Dorothy's vagina. However, this is not the problem the Allworths want to address. They have come to you because Sam is upset that Dorothy won't dress up in sexy lingerie and "talk dirty to him." Dorothy does not reach orgasm. In fact, she does not particularly desire sex, does not have sexual fantasies, and does not lubricate during sexual activity. Dorothy tells you that she was brought up to believe that a woman's duty is to please her husband, and though she'd like to oblige Sam, she is simply too embarrassed to say dirty words. Dorothy does not expect to have an orgasm, and says that she likes the closeness of sex and doesn't miss the excitement. Neither of the Allworths complain about Sam's "premature ejaculation" even when you ask directly about it. There is no history of drug or alcohol use, and neither Sam nor Dorothy is depressed.

What diagnoses do you make?

According to the schema presented in the *DSM-IV,* the disturbance must cause marked distress or interpersonal difficulty to be diagnosed as a sexual disorder. Sam is not experiencing any distress from his inability to control the timing of his ejaculation. According to Sam, his only problem is Dorothy's reluctance to be sexy. Dorothy doesn't complain of sexual or interpersonal problems because of Sam's "prematurity."

Must we ignore the obvious and conclude that Sam does not have premature ejaculation? Sam has premature ejaculation if the dysfunction is defined as a less than adequate amount of control of the ejaculatory reflex. However, if the prematurity must cause marked emotional distress or interpersonal difficulty, we are at a loss to make a diagnosis of premature ejaculation.

Sam's sexual problems are hidden behind Dorothy's disinterest in sex and sexual pleasure. How do we categorize Dorothy's lack of interest in her own sexual pleasure? Can we diagnose her problem as Hypoactive Sexual Desire, lifelong, generalized type, if she isn't complaining of distress in relation to her sexuality?

The Dynamic Formulation

In order to make sense of a sexual disorder you must remember that sex is an interpersonal experience. That is, sexual difficulties occur in the context of a relationship. Further, human beings are complex. We all engage in contradictory actions. We say one thing and do another. We deny our own problems by positing a difficulty in someone else. We repress and suppress those things that frighten us. We distance, displace, and distort those things we dislike about ourselves.

Formal *DSM* diagnoses are necessary to obtain treatment authorization from a managed care company, to obtain insurance reimbursement, and to begin to conceptualize the problem and its treatment. However, a *DSM* diagnosis is only the first step in understanding the nature of a psychological problem. The first step, not the only step.

An understanding of patients with sexual difficulties should include a formulation of the psychodynamics of each individual and a description of the nature of the relationship between the partners. You must be able to see how sex fits into the context of your patient's life. You must try to understand not only how the disorder got to be the way it is but also what function it serves in the psychic and interpersonal economy of the patient, what other conflicts and problems trouble the patient, and the ways in which the patient habitually solves or fails to solve problems both in the inner and the outer worlds.

What questions do you need to answer in order to make a dynamic formulation?

- What is the sexual dysfunction?
  How did it come to be?
  What functions does it serve, individually, in a couple?
- What do the patient's sexual fantasies tell you about the nature of the patient's excitement?
- What is the nature and degree of nonsexual psychopathology?
- What is the personality structure of the individual or the members of a couple?
- If seeing a couple, is there an identified patient?
  Who and why?
- What is the level of commitment to the couple relationship?
- What is the motivation for improving sexual experience?
  Individually and in the couple
  Do the partners' needs or desires function at cross purposes?
- How is conflict, hostility, and frustration handled?

- How does the patient define and experience intimacy?
  How much intimacy is wanted?
  How much intimacy can be tolerated?
  What is the capacity for problem solving (regarding childrearing, finances, relatives, and so on)?
  How much capacity exists for sharing pleasure (for example, sports, entertainment, hobbies)?

Let's return to the Allworths and create a diagnosis and a skeleton of a dynamic formulation of their problems.

According to criteria of the *DSM-IV,* we can't diagnose a desire, arousal, or orgasmic disorder. We could, and probably should, make a diagnosis of Sexual Disorder Not Otherwise Specified (302.9). A second diagnosis would be of a Partner Relational Problem (V61.1). "V codes" are used to indicate diagnostic uncertainty in situations that require clinical attention. Here we would be referring to a pattern of communication that involves negative communication (Sam's criticism) and distorted communication (Sam and Dorothy's unrealistic expectations about sexual life). As neither Sam nor Dorothy have a personality disorder, we can't list anything under Axis II. There are no general medical conditions present. Let's say Sam has recently been given a poor evaluation at his job and is experiencing some concern about getting promoted to vice president. Dorothy is having difficulty sleeping because their second child, thirty-two-year-old Mildred, is getting a divorce. Our *DSM* diagnosis would look like this:

Axis I: 302.9 Sexual Disorder Not Otherwise Specified

Axis II: V61.1 No diagnosis, Partner Relational Problem

Axis III: No diagnosis

Axis IV: Sam—job stress, mild; Dorothy—family stress, moderate

Axis V: GAF—Sam, 84; Dorothy, 81

A dynamic formulation is a bit like a biography of a patient's psyche. It must be consistent with the facts and explain the symptoms and interactional dynamics that you've observed. It should add a deeper understanding of the behavior, feeling, and motivation of each patient.

Between them the Allworths exhibit dysfunction in all three stages of sexual experience: desire, arousal, and orgasm. Dorothy, the identified patient, is functioning on a level where sex is not an exciting experience. For her, sex is something she must do in order to keep Sam's interest and affection. When sex works, that is, when Sam is satisfied, Dorothy feels closeness and safety. She does not complain of this situation because her aim is not to enjoy the sensual pleasure of orgasm but to maintain her relationship to Sam, something she believes she can do only if she can please him. Dorothy's present dilemma involves the conflict between her need to please Sam and her inner moral prohibition against speaking overtly sexual words—fear of loss versus fear of condemnation by her own conscience. A complete account of the case would delineate the origin of Dorothy's fear of sexuality, her anxiety about separation-individuation, and her submissive, masochistic solution to these problems.

Sam hides his anxiety by labeling Dorothy as the problem. He conceals his concern about performance, on the job and in bed, by focusing on Dorothy's inability to do exactly what he wants. Sam's personality style is obsessional, and he tries to control his own thoughts and actions as well as the behavior of those around him. He denies his inability to control his ejaculatory reflex because he would be mortified to admit (to himself, much less someone else) that he was defective. A complete account of Sam's psyche would include an understanding of the development and nature of his performance (castration) fears, his narcissistic inability to recognize the needs of those around him, and his domineering, sadistic solutions to these problems.

In terms of the couple, Sam and Dorothy are very committed to each other, and they are highly motivated to work out their difficulties. On the surface, Sam's motivation is to get Dorothy to help him become more sexually aroused; Dorothy's motivation is to be able to please Sam more effectively. Beneath the surface, Dorothy is trying to avoid separation anxiety; Sam, castration-performance anxiety. The system between them is breaking down because Sam's anxiety, and consequently his demands, have recently increased in relation to his job evaluation and his awareness of aging.

This very brief formulation makes it clear that the therapeutic task is to enlarge Sam and Dorothy's understanding of their problem in order to help each one of them deal more directly and more effectively with his or her fears. It acknowledges that both Sam and Dorothy have a sexual disorder and that the intimacy and pleasure of their sexual relationship could be greatly improved.

CASE EXAMPLE OF A BRIEF DIRECTED EVALUATION OF A SEXUAL DISORDER

I'm going to present an example of a complete evaluation, including history, diagnosis, and dynamic formulation. I've shortened the account somewhat, but you'll be able to use this example as an outline to help you conceptualize your own cases.

MR. AND MRS. BROWNELL

Mr. and Mrs. Brownell had been married for five years when they called for an evaluation of a sexual problem. They were each in their early thirties, had full-time jobs, and consciously wanted to have a family. The intimation of a sexual problem first appeared when they were unable to become pregnant. After a year of futile attempts, Mrs. Brownell underwent a complete medical-gynecological infertility evaluation. Mr. Brownell submitted a sperm sample, which was completely normal. When Mrs. Brownell's workup failed to reveal any medical abnormalities and she began to despair about ever having children, Mr. Brownell admitted that he had been pretending to have orgasms during intercourse. He told his wife that he was only able to reach climax with masturbation, and they decided together to seek sexual counseling. Mr. Brownell was seen by both as the identified patient. The stated motivation for therapy was to help Mr. Brownell have an orgasm with intercourse so they could have a child "naturally."

The diagnosis of Male Orgasmic Disorder (302.74), sometimes called retarded ejaculation, seemed obvious. As is often the case when seeing a couple, the Brownells' initial presentation raised questions about the nature of their relationship: Why did Mr. Brownell "pretend" to have an orgasm? How come Mrs. Brownell never realized there was no semen inside her after intercourse?

In the initial interview, Mr. Brownell said he couldn't understand why he was unable to have a climax with his wife. He reported that he had had orgasmic intercourse in the past and that the present difficulty had begun when he and his wife were first together. He felt attracted to her and didn't think that the problem was caused by anything she was doing. Mr. Brownell revealed that he had adult-onset diabetes, treated by diet alone. He drank alcohol "moderately," which meant two glasses of wine with dinner and a cocktail before bed. He did not take any prescribed medications and denied using any addictive drugs.

For her part, Mrs. Brownell had no awareness that her husband had been pretending to have a climax. She did not drink, use drugs, or take any medications. She was an intelligent, competent woman who had been raised as a Catholic. She'd learned as a child that sex was only acceptable as a form of procreation. She had never masturbated and had never had an orgasm.

Mr. Brownell's initial history revealed that he had an illness that could affect his sexual function. As I mentioned earlier, the suspicion or presence of any physical illness that might influence sexual function necessitates a comprehensive medical evaluation. Note that questions about medications, alcohol, and drugs were part of the first interview.

Mrs. Brownell's history is revealing as well. Her family and religious background both put a premium on being a good girl. Sex was not something to be discussed. Masturbation was shameful. Procreation was fine, pleasure was not. Mrs. Brownell said she was able to lubricate and become aroused, but she'd never had an orgasm. She wanted to become orgasmic, but she didn't know what to do to "make it happen." I had enough information to make a diagnosis of Female Orgasmic Disorder (302.73).

In his individual interview, Mr. Brownell admitted that he did, in fact, know something about his sexual problem. He'd been engaged before, to a woman he loved and enjoyed sexually. There had been no problem with orgasm. One day when he and his fiancee were ice skating, the ice broke and she fell in. She called for help, but he was too frightened to move. Paralyzed, he watched as she drowned. Since that moment, Mr. Brownell had been unable to have an orgasm except by himself, and then he was not enjoying the pleasure of the experience, but rather was berating himself for his cowardice and his desire to find pleasure in sexual release. Mr. Brownell said that his wife had no inkling of this situation and asked that his secret not be divulged. He feared that his wife would be hurt that he'd loved another woman and would be repelled (as he was) by his cowardice.

Mr. Brownell was imprisoned in guilt. I concluded that his sexual symptom was a reflection of deep-seated guilt and self-loathing. He'd all but given up on ever enjoying sexual pleasure himself, but he loved his wife and did want her to enjoy her experience. He said he would do whatever he could to help her reach orgasm and to have a child in a "natural" way.

Mrs. Brownell began her individual interview by stating that she'd known her husband wasn't really enjoying sex and that she felt it was her fault. His revelation that he wasn't reaching a climax during intercourse left her perplexed and insecure. In the year that they'd tried to conceive, she'd developed fairly consistent insomnia. During the time of her infertility evaluation, she often found herself tearful and blue. She saw herself as defective. She didn't know what was wrong with her, but she was sure something was.

Mrs. Brownell's interview reaffirmed the initial impression of an earnest, sexually suppressed and inexperienced woman who wanted desperately to change herself. Her propensity to blame herself was apparent. She'd come to experience herself as inadequate since childhood, and her physical symptoms and general mood made it clear that she was depressed.

Psychological testing supported my clinical observation that Mr. Brownell was struggling with an enormous amount of guilt. Further, he had a high need to control himself and to control those around him. There was indication of mild paranoia and significant underlying, hidden depression. Not surprisingly, sex and punishment were intimately connected in his mind.

Mrs. Brownell's tests corroborated that she was suffering from a clinical depression. In contrast to her husband, Mrs. Brownell did not want to control others; she expected and even looked for others to control her. The Minnesota Multiphasic Personality Inventory (MMPI) and the Thematic Apperception Test (TAT) underscored the clinical impression that both Mr. and Mrs. Brownell were depressed. Sexual inventory showed that Mr. Brownell's desire to be pleasured sexually was nil. He was not interested in what Mrs. Brownell did for him but only in what he could do for her. It is interesting to note that Mrs. Brownell's inventory was similar in that her main interest was in sexually pleasing her husband. However, she did show an interest in being pleasured and trying new things.

Physical examination revealed that Mr. Brownell's diabetes was more serious than had been realized. Visual inspection of his retina revealed early diabetic changes, and he was found to have a mild but measurable decrease in the perception of light touch in his extremities and genitals. The combination of Mr. Brownell's decreased sensitivity to touch and the degree of alcohol intoxication he was experiencing most evenings were clearly contributing to his sexual disorder.

Mrs. Brownell's physical and laboratory examinations were normal. The most important aspect of her medical evaluation was the way in which she engaged her physician. Mrs. Brownell told the doctor that she rarely looked at herself "down there." When the physician, a woman, asked if she'd like to see herself in a mirror, Mrs. Brownell accepted. Together they named all the anatomical parts and sent "down there" to the scrap heap of vagaries. The gynecologist answered questions about masturbation, intercourse, and orgasm.

The central problem in this evaluation was how to understand and treat the Brownell's complex intrapsychic and interpersonal problems. Individual therapy addressing Mr. Brownell's depression and self-punishment seemed indicated. Mrs. Brownell was conflicted about asserting herself, about her identity as a woman, and about openly enjoying sexual, physical pleasure. Her depression was situationally related to feelings of loneliness and alienation in her marriage, and I thought it likely that her depressive symptoms would abate if the marital relationship were to improve.

A great deal of emotional distance existed in the Brownell's relationship. They cared for each other, but something essential was missing. Mr. Brownell's "secret" was both a real and a symbolic representation of a wall between the two of them. In addition to a recommendation that Mr. Brownell begin individual counseling, conjoint therapy aimed at alleviating the sexual symptoms and lessening the withdrawal and defensive distancing in the Brownells' relationship seemed indicated. I was aware that as Mrs. Brownell became more assertive, Mr. Brownell might feel pressured, and for a time there might be an increase in the tension in the relationship. I decided not to reveal Mr. Brownell's "secret," trusting that the best way to handle the issue was to help him deal with his guilt and fear, in the hope that he would be more able to decide what to do about it himself.

The final meeting of the evaluation involved a discussion of my findings and conclusions. First, I went over the part played by Mr. Brownell's diabetes, his sensory deficit, and his alcohol intake. Mr. Brownell agreed to stop drinking and to see his internist to begin medication for his diabetes. I said that I thought Mr. and Mrs. Brownell were both conflicted about sexual pleasure, and that passion, intimacy, and excitement seemed to be missing from their lives. We went over their psychological tests, comparing their different personality and interactional styles. We looked at their sexual inventories and talked about what each of them wanted and didn't want.

Mrs. Brownell said that the process of talking about all of this had let her know that she very much wanted more closeness and aliveness with her husband. It was difficult to present the recommendation that Mr. Brownell see an individual therapist without going into his unrevealed traumatic experience, but somehow I managed. He didn't want individual therapy and said he'd only consider it if sex therapy didn't work. I pointed out that some of their goals overlapped but that Mrs. Brownell was the only one who wanted to increase the closeness and sexual pleasure of the relationship. Mr. Brownell agreed that he would like those things to happen, although he didn't quite see how they could. We decided to begin conjoint therapy with an aim toward improving the Brownells' sexual relationship. I explained that this meant helping Mr. Brownell to reach orgasm with intercourse, helping Mrs. Brownell to experience orgasm for the first time, and most important, helping them increase the communication and pleasure that was possible in their sexual interaction.

Evaluation of sexual disorders is a fascinating and complex topic. It involves all the skills a good therapist possesses and then some. It is often helpful to be able to discuss your cases with colleagues and supervisors, both to help with your understanding of the case and to help you deal with your emotional reactions to what your patients are telling you. I will end this chapter with a brief recounting of a recent supervisory experience.

DANNY AND BETH KLEIN

Dr. Mary Walker, a young psychiatric resident, recently asked me for help in evaluating a couple who'd come to her with a variety of sexual problems. Danny and Beth Klein were both twenty-seven, a year older than Mary. The Kleins had been high school sweethearts and now worked side by side at an auto manufacturing plant. Both were devout Christians who believed that sex before marriage was a

sin. They'd been married for four months and had yet to have intercourse. A majority of the first meeting was spent discussing issues
unrelated to sex. Finally, when time was almost up, Beth revealed
that she was scared intercourse would hurt. Danny chimed in that
he was scared he wouldn't do it right.

Dr. Walker felt pressured to give them some immediate advice.
However, she was scared she'd say the wrong thing and ruin the
marriage, so she didn't say anything.

I told Dr. Walker something Marcel Proust said: "Please, Dear
God, don't understand me too fast." I suggested that curiosity was
more important at this stage of her work than knowing the answers.

In the second session, Dr. Walker asked Danny and Beth about
their sexual experience. She discovered that they had tried once to
have intercourse. In that ill-fated experience, Beth felt herself
"tighten up" when Danny tried to penetrate her. Danny was unable
to stop himself from ejaculating on her leg. That's about all they
said. Both of them were ashamed and unable to talk about their fears
and feelings.

Dr. Walker thought Danny had premature ejaculation, but she
didn't have any idea what was wrong with Beth except that she was
obviously frightened of sex. I gave Dr. Walker Helen Kaplan's book,
The New Sex Therapy, and pointed out the chapter on sexual pain
disorders.

Danny began the next hour with a pressured confession that he'd
been masturbating most nights since the marriage. Dr. Walker was
able to ask him how he felt about this, but she was too embarrassed
to ask anything more. Her anxiety stopped her from being curious
about the content of Danny's fantasies. She didn't wonder what Beth
thought about Danny's practice. Without direction from Dr. Walker,
Danny went on to speak about his religious background and its prohibitions about sex. Finally, he asked Dr. Walker if she thought it
was all right to masturbate. Unsure what to say, Dr. Walker asked
him if he thought it was all right. Danny spoke at length about how
the Bible describes onanism as a sin.

Dr. Mary Walker brought her embarrassment about sexual practices into supervision. She wrestled with her own feelings and

decided it was time to begin her own individual therapy. I helped her get started with a colleague. In the ensuing months, Dr. Walker and I discussed sexual physiology, masturbation, sexual fantasies, and how to do a thorough evaluation of a sexual disorder. As she became more comfortable, Dr. Walker's questions to her patients became more clear and direct.

Dr. Walker made a diagnosis of a male orgasmic disorder (premature ejaculation) and a sexual pain disorder (vaginismus). She asked Beth and Danny to undergo complete physical evaluations. She had them take a battery of psychological tests. Her dynamic formulation included the place of shame, guilt, and anxiety in their sexual response. She understood the significance of religion and family life for Danny and Beth. When Dr. Walker discussed the nature of the sexual problems with Danny and Beth, she suggested that they would benefit from short-term sexual therapy aimed at helping Beth relax enough to enjoy intercourse. She also said that they could address Danny's feelings about masturbation and his fears about not performing adequately during intercourse.

It is not always easy to talk about what we do and how we do it. Sometimes it is even harder to discuss how we feel about what we do. Seeing patients with sexual concerns, doing evaluations, and discussing cases with colleagues will help you learn how to think about sexual function and dysfunction. Having therapy of your own is invaluable.

To do a complete evaluation of a sexual disorder requires tact and knowledge. You'll need insight and empathy, an understanding of the body and the psyche. Like Dr. Walker, you'll find that it is impossible to discuss another person's sexual experience without engendering feelings of your own. You'll find that it is impossible to learn about another person's sexual experience without wondering about your own. Each evaluation you do will be different. Each will teach you about human nature, about human sexuality, and about yourself.

NOTES

P. 60, *Masters and Johnson observed:* Masters, W., & Johnson, V. (1966). *Human sexual response.* Boston: Little, Brown; Masters, W., & Johnson, V. (1970). *Human sexual inadequacy.* Boston: Little, Brown.

P. 72, *Robert Michael and his colleagues discovered:* Michael, R. T., Gagnon, J. H., Laumann, E. D., Kolata, G. (1994). *Sex in America: A definitive survey.* Boston: Little, Brown.

P. 83, *However, a* DSM *diagnosis is only the first step:* Defense mechanisms may soon be included in the *DSM.* If this happens, a *DSM* diagnosis will include significant information that is now part of a dynamic formulation.

P. 92, *I gave Dr. Walker Helen Kaplan's book:* Kaplan, H. S. (1974). *The new sex therapy.* New York: Brunner/Mazel.

FOR FURTHER READING

Kaplan, H. S. (1974). *The new sex therapy.* New York: Brunner/Mazel.

Kaplan, H. S. (1975). *The illustrated manual of sex therapy.* New York: Quadrangle.

Kaplan, H. S. (1995). *The sexual desire disorders.* New York: Brunner/Mazel.

Masters, W., & Johnson, V. (1966). *Human sexual response.* Boston: Little, Brown.

Masters, W., & Johnson, V. (1970). *Human sexual inadequacy.* Boston: Little, Brown.

Masters, W., Johnson, V., & Kolodny, R. (1988). *Human sexuality.* Glenview, IL: Scott, Foresman/Little, Brown College Division.

Michael, R. T., Gagnon, J. H., Laumann, E. D., Kolata, G. (1994). *Sex in America: A definitive survey.* Boston: Little, Brown.

Schnarch, D. (1991). *Constructing the sexual crucible: An integration of sexual and marital therapy.* New York: Norton.

CHAPTER

4

MEDICAL EVALUATION OF
SEXUAL FUNCTION

It's all too easy for us to become isolated in our respective disciplines. Teaching psychologists and psychiatrists has shown me that it's unusual for most therapists to know what really goes on in the gynecologist's office, the urologist's examination room, and the sleep lab that monitors nocturnal erections. A therapist who understands what medical practitioners do and think about when they evaluate and treat the physical aspects of sexual dysfunction will be better able to make proper referrals and to interpret the conclusions of the examining physician.

When you've finished this chapter, you'll know more about what your patients will experience when you refer them for a medical evaluation. You'll know what the medical specialist will be looking for, and you'll understand the benefits and limits of the medical treatment of sexual dysfunction.

∾

GYNECOLOGICAL EVALUATION OF
SEXUAL DISORDERS
Claire Appelmans

As an Ob/Gyn nurse practitioner, I specialize in reproductive and sexual health matters for women of all ages. I work directly with a physician and provide many of the same kinds of services, with the obvious exception of surgery. In this chapter, I will discuss the ways in which gynecologists approach sexual concerns, when and how you might refer clients for medical evaluation, and some of the difficulties you may encounter in this process.

Almost all women have sexual concerns of one kind or another. These concerns lie somewhere on a continuum ranging from insecurities about their bodies, their roles as sexual partners, or their sporadic sexual difficulties, to significant sexual dysfunction. In talking to women about their sexual health, you should be able to elicit and identify these concerns and also determine when to make a referral to a medical practitioner. Because many women have difficulty using the health care system to meet their needs, I'd like to suggest that you take an interest in the way they choose and use their medical providers.

A WOMAN'S ROLE IN HER SEXUAL HEALTH CARE

Historically, women have been the objects rather than the subjects of their health care. That is to say that women have been kept from the information that would allow them to be active and assertive participants in their health care. Nowhere is this so true as in the areas of reproductive and sexual health. The prospect of "being taken care of" or of seeking "help" is for many women a prohibitive one. Women very often look to either abdicate responsibility for their health and their lives to a perceived authority (either a person or an institution), or are so invested in taking care of others that they can neither care for themselves nor allow others to take care of them. Ambivalent or contradictory feelings about asking for help often result in what is essentially self-neglect. I often see a client only after she has tolerated a sexual problem for a long period of time, during which she tried every conceivable self-treatment or over-the-counter remedy. As a therapist, you play a critical role in assessing and working through the dynamics that influence how your client cares for her body and her sexuality.

Issues of power and control are important in our relationships with those who engage our services. I think the words and labels we choose very much influence the way we think about things. So I prefer to talk about consumers of our services as "clients" rather than "patients."

Barriers to Sexual Health Care

There are a number of barriers that may make it difficult for a woman to use the medical system effectively.

• Many women have experienced physical and emotional harm in the guise of health care. It takes only one encounter with an insensitive gynecologist to create a lasting fear of pelvic exams. When I inquire why a woman has chosen not to have a Pap test in many years, the answer invariably relates to a profoundly humiliating or shaming experience.

• There is a glaring absence of an evolved systematic and conceptual approach to women's sexual concerns. The focus of medical science and research is predominantly on reproductive rather than sexual functioning. Do not make the assumption that because a clinician specializes in reproductive health, his or her expertise also extends into all areas of this vast field. Medical education programs have provided spotty education about human sexuality. Ask a medical student about the function of the vagina and you are likely to hear that it's the birth canal. Most women would rather see a professional who also appreciates that the vagina is an organ of sexual pleasure.

• Health care providers are often just as uncomfortable discussing sexual matters as anyone else in our society. As a teacher, I have found it next to impossible to get my students to elicit sexual health histories in a manner that doesn't make their clients very uncomfortable. Consequently, many a sexual history is inadequate.

For example, I saw Liz, a woman in her twenties, at a Planned Parenthood clinic. She came in for her annual exam and a renewal of her birth control pills. In the course of her medical history, Liz told me a lengthy story about a complex and invasive evaluation done to evaluate painful intercourse. Over a period of two years, she was treated unsuccessfully with antibiotics and underwent an elaborate diagnostic workup that included surgery. When I asked her to describe her pain and how it became manifest during sex, Liz stated that it hurt the minute her boyfriend touched her—before there was any penetration! This brought up the possibility that she might have once been touched in a way that caused her pain. I asked her about this, and she burst into tears as she acknowledged that she'd been sexually abused as a child. Liz would have fared far better with psychotherapy than with antibiotics and surgery. Unfortunately, Liz's story is by no means rare.

• Recently, the general concern over HIV has led more providers to screen clients' sexual behavior. The focus of this line of questioning is usually on the number of sexual contacts and on the orifices she and her partner(s) used in their sexual contacts. The result resembles an accounting ledger. Instead, the focus should be on the quality of a woman's sex life in the context of her overall health and vitality.

• There is a danger that in the interest of conserving time, money, and resources, managed health care may take us even further away from a complete evaluation of a woman's sexual concerns. Under managed health care, clinicians are expected to see greater numbers of clients in shorter periods of time—and I'm at a loss to think of a more time-consuming process than the evaluation of sexual problems! Another trend is toward the use of family practitioners and primary care providers, generalists who can provide a wide range of care. Unless they take a particular interest in sexual issues, they may not be able to give adequate attention to women's sexual problems.

What this means for you as a therapist is that you need not only to screen your clients for sexual concerns but also to give considerable attention to how they use the limited medical resources available to them.

Women's Sexual Health Care

An important aspect of how your client takes care of her body is how she deals with her medical provider. Although the majority of our clients are very competent and resourceful, some have difficulty discussing sexual matters. They may have difficulty understanding and participating in decisions affecting their care.

You first need to identify the nature of the problem and what kind of approach is appropriate for you to take. Sometimes a client may need help choosing a provider. Many women have a strong preference for seeing a female practitioner. Even though the sensitivity and caring of a clinician is less related to gender than to character, such a preference should be honored. Much will also depend on the kinds of referral sources available. Appropriate options include physicians, nurse practitioners, nurse midwives, and physician assistants. I would discourage you from basing a choice on a clinician's academic pedigree, as this is not necessarily predictive of the care he or she provides.

Your client may need to identify more clearly the questions she wants to ask about her sexual health. You may need to help her learn how to become assertive enough to have her questions answered so that she understands the working of her own body and her medical treatment. In some cases it is helpful to obtain a signed release of medical information, so that you can discuss the case with the medical practitioner. If you find yourself in the awkward position of suspecting that your client is not getting the care you believe necessary, you may need to suggest a "second opinion."

I encourage you to develop a referral system for women's health concerns. This is best done by word of mouth, so listen carefully to what your clients say about their gyn exams. I do this myself and have found this to be the most certain and expedient approach. Once you've identified a possible referral source, you might consider calling to ask how the provider handles sexual and other gynecological concerns. If you're considering referring an especially anxious client, you might ask whether the provider is willing to let the client have a support person with her. Is the provider willing to take extra time or schedule extra appointments to ensure your client has a safe and positive experience? Generally, providers will be direct with you about whether they have that kind of interest or time in their practice.

WHEN TO REFER FOR GYNECOLOGICAL EVALUATION

A gynecological exam is sometimes the only way you can rule out a pathologic process that might underlie your client's sexual disorder—and that could also compromise her physical health. Most of the time this isn't the case, yet the potential ramifications of such a diagnostic oversight could be awful for your client. Moreover, a gyn exam offers the possibility of reassuring her that there is nothing seriously wrong. Women need to hear this.

Keep in mind that gynecologists will not usually be using the same terminology or diagnostic criteria that you use. Most practitioners are not familiar with the *DSM-IV,* and there is no medical correlate to this manual. Whereas the *DSM-IV* refers to dyspareunia (painful intercourse) as a diagnosis, from a gynecologist's perspective, dyspareunia is only a symptom—when I discover the underlying cause of painful intercourse, then I have a diagnosis. Medical practitioners have an advantage over most therapists in that we can take what the client tells us and interpret her information on the basis of clinical examination and laboratory findings.

In my experience, women's sexual disorders are rarely purely physical or purely psychogenic. Often two or more problems exist concurrently. So I caution you against the tendency to set up a body-mind dichotomy, especially considering that many clients are likely to do this themselves. Whether the problem started out as a physical one or a psychological one, the fact is that once a condition has existed for a time, it becomes associated with a conditioned response, and the physical becomes blended with the psychological.

The simplest example of this is dyspareunia. Regardless of its cause, once a woman has experienced painful intercourse a couple of times, she learns to anticipate it. Her fear might turn her off to sex or make it impossible for her to become aroused. If a woman persists, attempting to have intercourse without lubrication, this adds another dimension to her pain syndrome. Thus, a woman might continue to experience sexual problems even after the physical cause underlying the initial problem has been successfully treated. It often takes time before a woman stops anticipating pain and can become adequately aroused and enjoy intercourse again.

Following are lists of symptoms related to complaints that strongly suggest a physical cause for a sexual disorder. If your client mentions any of these, you should consider a referral for a medical evaluation.

Genital and Pelvic Pain

- Any kind of genital or pelvic pain—before, during, or after intercourse
- Any coital or postcoital vaginal bleeding
- Painful intromission in the presence of adequate lubrication
- Bowel or bladder pain during or after intercourse
- Inability to accomplish penile penetration due to genital pain
- Changes in hormonal status (whether induced by surgery, medication, or aging)

Lack of Sexual Desire

- Recent or time-specific loss of otherwise normal desire (as opposed to a very long-term problem)

- Changes in hormonal status (whether induced by surgery, medication, or aging)
- Associated genital or pelvic symptoms
- Changes in other bodily processes: coordination problems, muscle weakness, sensitivity to heat or cold, fatigue, numbness or tremors in extremities, marked weight changes, body habitus, urinary or bowel incontinence

Lack of Arousal

- Associated genital or pelvic symptoms
- Changes in other bodily processes: coordination problems, muscle weakness, sensitivity to heat or cold, fatigue, numbness or tremors in extremities, marked weight changes, body habitus, urinary or bowel incontinence

Orgasmic Disorders

- Recent or time-specific loss of ability have orgasms
- Associated dyspareunia, lack of desire or arousal
- Chronic or recurrent urinary or vaginal infections
- Changes in other bodily processes: coordination problems, muscle weakness, sensitivity to heat or cold, fatigue, numbness or tremors in extremities, marked weight changes, body habitus, urinary or bowel incontinence

In addition to referring clients with an identifiable symptom, you should also attempt to identify women at risk. Women who have been in abusive relationships, whether physical or sexual, are at extremely high risk for many kinds of conditions that affect sexual health and lead to sexual dysfunctions. This also applies to women who describe sexual acting-out behaviors and women who are not actively attempting to protect their health. You should be concerned if contraception is not used when an unintended pregnancy could be disastrous, or if a client puts herself at risk for sexually transmitted diseases (STDs) or HIV infection. You might also deem it appropriate to intervene on behalf of women who aren't seeking routine gynecological care. Almost every time that I have identified a really serious gynecological problem, the client has been a woman who has avoided visits to a gynecologist.

EVALUATING SEXUAL CONCERNS

I discuss sexual concerns with all the women I see. Many are taken aback, especially when this has never before been a part of their medical care. A few women are embarrassed by my line of inquiry. I don't push them or pry. I only want them to understand that this is an arena in which their sexual concerns may be fielded. I feel my efforts have been rewarded when a woman returns to my office within a week to take me up on the offer to discuss her sexual life.

The most common presenting complaint in my practice is pain with intercourse. I also see many women with concerns about their inability to have orgasms. I explore ways in which women can learn to achieve orgasm and generally enhance their sexual relationships, but I refer those psychosexual concerns that are beyond my capabilities to a psychotherapist.

I generally approach sexual issues based on the stage of life of my client. For example, I have found that teenagers are often embarrassed to talk about their bodies, but they will sometimes be able to talk about sex in the context of fears about becoming pregnant or getting STDs. Or they might be able to begin a discussion by talking about their peers' sexual behavior, the pressure and expectations of their partners, or how sexual issues contribute to difficulties with their parents.

Young adults are starting to think about life goals and long-term relationships. Many young women in this age group are curious about their bodies and their sexuality.

Older, more mature women are keenly focused on the changes they observe as their bodies age. Or they may be in the process of questioning and reevaluating their sexual relationships. Often women enjoy a surge of sexual vitality in their forties and fifties. They have to cope with menopausal changes that may dramatically alter their sexual lives. Some women perceive these changes positively, others negatively.

During my screening, I try to learn about a woman's relationship with her partner and what role the partner plays in her sexual life. I try to learn about how the sexual concern has affected the dynamics of the relationship and vice versa. I also try to learn what her expectations of her partner are, as well as whether these expectations are satisfied. What she can describe to me about the nature of their communication around the subject of sex is information I find invaluable.

Health-related life events often influence women's sex lives in dramatic ways. This is very often the case in relation to pregnancy and childbearing. Medical illnesses and surgeries, both in terms of their impact on bodily self-image as well as in the logistical problems they engender, present significant sexual challenges for women. Problems with infertility, and the need for scheduled sex, often cause very major conflicts between couples. In fact, many relationships don't survive infertility problems.

I raise these subjects here because I believe there should be a place in our health care model for the "prevention" of sexual disorders. By addressing sexual problems before they become monolithic, we should at the very least be able to support our clients in enjoying richer and more vital sex lives—if not avert many sexual dysfunctions altogether.

Clinical Evaluation

I always begin a clinical examination by explaining to the woman what I need to do in order to adequately evaluate her complaint. As this may involve experiences that might be physically or emotionally uncomfortable, I ask her if there is any aspect of my exam that she'd like to defer to a later time. This gives women who have trouble defining how they want their bodies to be handled the opportunity to speak up, and gives us an opportunity to talk together about any problem areas.

The physical exam I do is fairly comprehensive. In addition to the pelvic exam, it includes a thyroid, lung, heart, and abdominal exam. If I need to rule out a possible neurological basis for a sexual problem, I include a neurologic and ophthalmoscopic eye exam. If I suspect an organic disease that is nongynecological, I refer the client to an internist or neurologist.

I try to keep laboratory tests to a minimum. In most cases, I do only routine urine and blood tests. Unless the woman has had a recent Pap test, I do this as a matter of routine. When her complaint is one of dyspareunia, I take a specimen of her vaginal discharge to examine under the microscope for signs of infection or inflammation. A complaint of painful intercourse also warrants testing for gonorrhea and chlamydia, which involves swabbing the cervix and sending the cultures to a lab. If the complaint relates to sexual desire, arousal, or orgasm, and the medical history suggests a possible endocrine disorder (involving the thyroid, adrenal, or pituitary glands, or diabetes), then I will order additional blood tests. This is only rarely the case.

As I prepare the woman for the pelvic exam, I observe her demeanor and body language. It is one of the most telling aspects of our encounter. A woman who is faced with the request to lie down on her back, place her feet in footrests that appear to be miles apart, and slide her hips to the end of the table so she feels like she's perched on the edge of a precipice, reveals a great deal in the way she manages these maneuvers. Even though I always elevate the head of the table so that we can maintain eye contact throughout the exam, the woman is nevertheless in a very vulnerable position. What happens in these brief moments often seems to reflect how a woman manages her sexual encounters. The majority of women display some degree of modesty.

I'm concerned about a woman who shows severe anxiety by recoiling, hyperextending her neck, and clenching her teeth, rolling her eyes back, or dissociating. I'm also concerned about women who are inappropriately passive—who just lie back, close their eyes, and wait for the exam to be over. Both of these extremes bring up the possibility of previous physical or sexual trauma. If I see that a woman is unable to be reasonably comfortable during the pelvic exam, I halt the process and work with her so that she can be more present and participatory. This can take a very long time, but the payoff is great. Observations such as these are invaluable in providing me with a sense of the psychological issues contributing to sexual problems.

As I begin to examine the external genitalia, I offer my client a mirror so that she can watch and ask questions. Many women are uncomfortable viewing themselves. If a client is embarrassed or anxious, I may later suggest that she practice exploring her body with a mirror at home. The use of the mirror also tells me how familiar a woman is with her anatomy and sexual functioning. Many women have to some degree disowned their genitalia. So I teach the names of various anatomical features, and encourage women to relinquish the proverbial "down there" that refers to a deep, dark void between the belly and the thighs. Using the mirror is for most women a novel experience. I marvel at the ever-expanding array of responses women have to this. A few exclaim, "That's disgusting," but most express curiosity and utter astonishment at being able to look into their vaginas and at their cervices.

Using the Clinical Evaluation to Make a Diagnosis

The pelvic exam is indispensable for the evaluation of painful intercourse. A woman should never be treated for a sexual dysfunction related to painful intercourse without a medical evaluation! I emphasize this because the majority of women are not able to describe their symptoms with the accuracy or certainty necessary for making a correct diagnosis without physical corroboration. It would be unconscionable to allow a woman to undergo unsuccessful and fruitless treatment (with attendant frustration and discouragement) for one kind of disorder if she in fact has a problem of a different nature.

Vaginismus, the involuntary spasm of the muscles surrounding the vagina, is a good illustration of this problem. From a client's description of what happens in this disorder, it is virtually impossible to distinguish it from the symptoms caused by an intact hymen, lack of lubrication, severe vulvar infections, or even vulvodynia (a severe vulvar pain disorder). But a woman with vaginismus will characteristically react to an examiner's touch with waves of spasms and pain just as she does when trying to have sex. When I observe involuntary muscle spasm like this, I can teach the woman how to relax her muscles using her fingers. It is often helpful if her partner is present and willing to become involved in the relaxation process. Because of the high correlation of sexual abuse and other psychological disorders with vaginismus, I invariably recommend the client support her digital dilatation measures with psychotherapy.

Vulvar and vaginal inflammations and infections are also common causes of dyspareunia, especially in younger women. Most of the time these are diagnostically simple problems with equally simple treatments. Here too, the clinical exam is indispensable for accurate diagnosis and treatment. With the increasing availability of over-the-counter vaginal medications, many women will attempt to treat themselves in the hope of avoiding an office visit. I have seen a great many women who have self-treated their vulvar burning with anti-yeast medications, when what they had was actually herpes.

Perimenopausal women are likely to experience dyspareunia related to thinning of the vulvar and vaginal tissues as their ovarian estrogen supply wanes. For some, the discomfort caused by this discourages sexual activity altogether. Though much consideration has been given to estrogen and its role in the prevention of osteoporosis, I find most women are much more interested in what estrogen can do for their vaginas than for their bones. Some women choose intravaginal estrogen creams; others prefer the oral medication. Recently, we've added a small amount of testosterone to the various schemes for hormone replacement therapy; this is most useful in women who have experienced menopause secondary to surgical removal of their ovaries. The testosterone helps to offset the diminished sexual desire often experienced with estrogen replacement.

The bimanual exam with two fingers in the vagina (introitus permitting) allows me to evaluate the vaginal muscle tone as well as the tone of the pelvic floor. This is especially relevant when a woman's complaints include difficulty controlling her bladder function as well as a diminished ability to enjoy orgasms. By learning to do Kegel's exercises, which involve voluntary, isometric contraction of the pelvic muscles several times daily, a woman can learn to improve the strength of the muscles around her vagina. This can make for stronger orgasms.

When the source of painful intercourse is significant pelvic pathology, a pelvic exam will usually point to the problem. During the course of the exam, I try to reproduce the pain and thereby discover the anatomical source of the pain. Common causes of deep pelvic dyspareunia include pelvic tumors, endometriosis, and pelvic infections caused by sexually transmitted infections. A woman whose uterus is tipped back may experience a "positional" dyspareunia; that is, she only experiences pain in certain positions and is otherwise pain free. This is a common source of painful intercourse. I recommend that these patients experiment with various positions until they find out what works best. The last resort is surgery, and the results are not always satisfactory.

The last part of the evaluation is a rectovaginal exam. I try to avoid subjecting women to this exam unless I find a compelling clinical reason to do so. The exam is done with the middle finger in the rectum at the same time as the index finger is inserted in the vagina. Sometimes tumors that are otherwise not detectable (especially in women with a "tipped" uterus), may be found in this manner. It is also one of the few ways in which a person can be clinically evaluated for rectal cancer.

Psychogenic Versus Organic Pain

As you can see, this kind of exam—as comprehensive as it is—yields information about only a very limited number of processes that may impair a healthy and enjoyable sex life. The exam is usually reliable, providing that the pain is truly gynecological in origin. I need to qualify this statement because much of the time I am unable to identify any source of pain at all. There is considerable controversy over the use of surgery in the evaluation of pelvic pain. Some physicians reserve exploratory surgery (usually by laparoscopy) for women who have dyspareunia in addition to an infertility problem. Others use surgery for diagnostic purposes quite freely. It's certainly indispensable when the suspected diagnosis is endometriosis, a cause of dyspareunia, chronic pelvic pain, and infertility commonly found in women of reproductive age.

As I've said, there is often no clinically apparent reason for a woman's complaint of painful intercourse. This doesn't mean that she isn't experiencing pain. From what we know about pain, and especially pelvic pain, a woman's experience of psychogenic pain is virtually indistinguishable from that of organic pain. Indeed, there's nothing clinically more perplexing in this area of gynecological practice than pelvic pain of unknown origin! Based on a woman's history and my observations of body language during the exam, I either refer her to a physician for possible surgical evaluation, or explore more substantially the possibility of a psychological source of her pain. Sadly, it's often the case that a woman who experiences psychogenic pain lives in denial and resists any suggestion to seek counseling.

Evaluating Sexual Function

It is next to impossible to clinically evaluate sexual performance in women through pelvic examination or laboratory tests. Whereas we have at our disposal very elaborate and sophisticated technologies to evaluate reproductive function, there are no generally available and accepted diagnostics for evaluation of sexual function. I suspect the disparity in the technological effort devoted to men and women has something to do with the fact that men's reproductive functioning is dependent on sexual functioning, whereas in women the two are independent of one another.

Unlike the evaluation of men, where elaborate contraptions measure penile tumescence and equally elaborate measures can enhance sexual performance, the art of working one's way through the complexities of sexual dysfunction in women depends largely on clinical perseverance as well as on sensitivity to a woman's psychosexual vulnerabilities. There is a very intricate interplay in the etiology of women's sexual dysfunctions, with just a few strictly organic causes at the one end of a mostly gray spectrum, and a great many others of purely psychogenic origin at the opposite end. As much harm can be done by overemphasizing the organic aspects of a woman's sexual disorder as can be done by attributing it to just being "in her head."

༄

Sexual disorders in women are clinically challenging to evaluate and treat. I've found that these efforts are most successful when the gynecological practitioner works in close contact with psychotherapists and counselors who are knowledgeable about the psychological aspects of women's sexuality. Together we can help many more women than either of us could on our own.

༄

UROLOGICAL EVALUATION OF SEXUAL DISORDERS

Harcharan Gill

As a urologist in a university medical center, I see a variety of male patients referred for evaluation of sexual dysfunction. In this chapter, I will review the nature of my assessment so that you'll know when to refer a patient to a urologist, what the urologist will be thinking and doing, what kinds of medical treatment a urologist might suggest, and what information the urologist will be able to give you.

WHEN TO MAKE A UROLOGICAL REFERRAL

A complete physical examination is advisable for men with sexual complaints in order to ascertain their general state of health and to review any medications they may be taking that could influence sexual function. This type of evaluation can be done by a urologist, family practitioner, or internist.

Sometimes patients will come to you having had a recent physical. In most cases it's best to contact their physician yourself to make sure there are no health-related concerns or medications—alcohol abuse being the most common—that your patient failed to tell you about.

The vast majority of the men I see who benefit from an in-depth urological evaluation are those diagnosed with symptomatic erectile dysfunction by their general physician, internist, or psychotherapist. Thus I would advise you to make sure that all of your patients with impotence are evaluated by a specialist.

I rarely see men with premature ejaculation, as it is extremely rare for this condition to be caused by physical illness. However, I often see patients with *retrograde ejaculation*. Retrograde ejaculation occurs when the muscle at the neck of the bladder fails to close, causing the ejaculate to be deposited into the bladder. This can be caused by surgery to the bladder neck and prostate, some medications used for hypertension, benign prostatic enlargement, and the psychotropic agent thioridazine (Mellaril).

The initial experience of retrograde ejaculation is strange, and can be upsetting. Normally, a man can feel his excitement mounting and will sense the point of ejaculatory inevitability. At this moment, he feels his genital muscles contract, and he expects to ejaculate. In retrograde ejaculation, nothing emerges from the end of the penis because the ejaculate follows the path of least resistance and ends up in the bladder.

Retrograde ejaculation is not a harmful condition in itself. It does not interfere with erection or the pleasurable sensation of orgasm. However, some men, especially those with anxiety disorders, or borderline and psychotic conditions, develop fears and even delusions that something awful is happening to them. The anxiety generated by the lack of visible ejaculate can lead to other sexual problems, including disorders of desire and arousal.

Once they understand what's happening, most patients are not too concerned about the symptom. An exception is the man who wishes to have a family. If the problem is caused by a medication, it can be reversed by discontinuing or changing the drug.

It is uncommon for me to see a man complaining of lack of sexual desire who is physically able to maintain an erection. The fact that he can obtain and keep an erection is evidence that the desire disorder is not likely to be caused by a physical problem.

To summarize, an up-to-date medical examination is advisable for your male patients with sexual disorders. Medical evaluation is unlikely to be productive for patients suffering from premature ejaculation, or for men who can maintain an erection either with masturbation or intercourse. A referral to a urological specialist is indicated for your patients with erectile problems.

ERECTILE DYSFUNCTION

The field of erectile dysfunction continues to undergo changes in terms of our knowledge of physical causes, diagnostic tests, and therapeutic options. Erectile dysfunction increases progressively with age but is not an inevitable consequence of aging: other age-related conditions increase the likelihood of its occurrence. Recent estimates in the United States suggest a prevalence of about 5 percent in forty-year-old men, increasing to 15 to 25 percent in sixty-five-year-old men. Prevalence rates vary across geographic, racial, ethnic, socioeconomic, and cultural groups.

The multifactorial nature of erectile dysfunction requires a multidisciplinary approach to its management. Most of the patients referred to a urologist turn out to have organic impotence, or at least the psychological component of the erectile dysfunction is not usually found to be the dominant etiologic factor. Despite this fact, I consider psychogenic causes for impotence as part of my evaluation. When a psychotherapist refers a patient, we can pool information, making my task considerably easier. In cases where I am unsure, I refer the patient for a psychological consultation. I believe it is important to eliminate psychological causes of impotence before proceeding to use any physically invasive diagnostic tests.

Categories of Erectile Dysfunction

Here is an outline of the issues I consider when evaluating a patient with erectile dysfunction:

I. Psychogenically caused erectile dysfunction
   A. Anxiety
      There are many presentations of anxiety, from performance issues to insecurity about a man's sense of masculinity.
   B. Depression
      Depression is one of the most common causes of impotence. Sometimes the sexual dysfunction is the presenting symptom of a man who denies his emotions and says he's not depressed.
   C. Unconscious sexual conflict
      This is your area of expertise, and if I suspect that there are sexual issues beneath the surface, I would refer the patient to you for evaluation.
II. Organically caused erectile dysfunction
   A. Disease of or injury to the *nervous system*
      1. The brain—strokes, tumor, trauma, Parkinson's disease, dementia, surgery
      2. Spinal cord—trauma, tumor, surgery, multiple sclerosis
      3. Prostate and rectal surgery, trauma
   B. Disease of or injury to the *circulatory system*
      1. Arteries—arteriosclerosis, diabetes, hypertension, trauma, aneurysm, surgery
      2. Veins—venous leaks, incompetent veins
      3. Blood—severe anemia, sickle-cell anemia

C. Disease of the *endocrine system*
1. Hyperprolactinemia
The hormone prolactin, which controls the production of milk in a nursing mother, is usually present only in minimal amounts in the male. One of its secondary effects is to diminish sexual interest and arousal. Tumors of the pituitary gland can cause an abnormal increase in the production of prolactin, leading to impotence in a man.
2. Hypergonadotropic hypogonadism: testicular
The testicles manufacture androgens, which are necessary for sexual desire and function. When the testes do not function properly, as sometimes happens after mumps, trauma, or abnormalities of fetal development, the pituitary sends out more gonadotropic hormone to try to "turn on" the under-functioning testes. Blood tests will diagnose this condition.
3. Hypogonadotropic hypogonadism: pituitary
Like the aforementioned condition, this disease is marked by insufficient androgens in the man's system. This time it's caused by a malfunctioning pituitary gland, so that the gonadotropic hormones that "turn on" the testes are low or absent. Again, blood tests are necessary to make this diagnosis.
4. Thyroid disease
Thyroxin, the major hormone produced by the thyroid gland, regulates the metabolic rate of the entire body. Both too little (hypothyroidism) and too much (hyperthyroidism) can lead to impotence. Physical examination and blood tests are the means to a diagnosis.
5. Adrenal disease
The hormones of the adrenal gland—steroids and adrenaline—regulate a wide variety of bodily functions. Again, too much or too little can cause erectile problems.
D. Drugs
There are a variety of medications and street drugs that can lead to erectile problems. The most common are antidepressants, antihypertensives, antiandrogens, estrogen, cimetidine, nicotine, alcohol, marijuana, and cocaine. See Table 2.1 on page 37 for a full list.

Most patients have more than one factor causing their erectile dysfunction. In a man with diabetes, for example, vascular, neural, and psychological factors may combine to cause erectile dysfunction.

Evaluation of Erectile Dysfunction

As I have said, I feel that despite the popularity of the new diagnostic tests, a detailed sexual and medical history is the most important part of the evaluation of a male with erectile dysfunction. The history helps define the actual sexual problem, the presence or absence of sexual desire, the degree of erectile dysfunction, and the interaction of physical and psychogenic factors. The sexual history is used to differentiate between true erectile dysfunction, changes in sexual desire, and orgasmic and ejaculatory disturbances.

As a psychotherapist, you will evaluate psychological factors related to erectile dysfunction. Obviously, this will include input from the patient and his partner. A complete medical history will complement your evaluation by defining the risk factors that may contribute to the patient's erectile dysfunction. The medical history should include the treatments for any chronic systemic disorders, such as diabetes, multiple sclerosis, chronic renal failure, chronic alcoholism, cirrhosis of the liver, or hyperlipidemia. A history of previous prostate, colon, or back surgery may be relevant. You should obtain a detailed history of the patient's use of medication, because various classes of drugs may cause sexual dysfunction. The physician's function would be to review your patient's medication and determine whether any drug or combination of drugs interferes with sexual function. The most commonly prescribed medications that have the potential for causing impotence are the drugs used to treat high blood pressure (antihypertensives). Drugs that have antiandrogen effects, such as estrogen, will also cause impotence.

I find the physical examination of a patient with erectile dysfunction most often does not reveal the cause of the erectile disorder. Regardless, my examination includes evaluation of the endocrine, vascular, and nervous systems. I carefully examine the patient's penis for local factors such as *fibrosis* (Peyronie's disease), which can cause the penis to bend to one side or the other, and *phimosis*, a condition in which the foreskin is contracted and can not be retracted.

There is no single series of laboratory tests that exclusively diagnoses impotence. The basic laboratory tests I always do include a complete blood count, urinalysis, blood urea nitrogen, creatinine, fasting glucose, cholesterol, prolactin, and testosterone. The patient's medical history determines whether I do any additional tests, which would include those for thyroid function, luteinizing hormone (LH), and follicular stimulating hormone (FSH).

Nocturnal penile tumescence (NPT) testing involves the monitoring of sleep-associated erections. If I suspect that there may be a major psychogenic component to the patient's erectile dysfunction, I get an NPT study. You'll learn how this is done in the next section of this chapter.

The aim of my neurologic evaluation is to identify the existence and extent of any sensory or motor deficit and to discern if there is a need for medical or surgical treatment. I routinely check the penis and genital area for sensitivity to touch, pain, and temperature. I also use a tuning fork to check for the vibratory sensation in the penis, fingers, and toes. I can check the integrity of the connections between the sensory nerves, the spinal cord, and the nerves returning to the genitals by testing the bulbocavernosus reflex. This involves squeezing the glans of the penis and noting the degree of reflex contraction in the anal sphincter.

Other more complex, invasive tests include biothesiometry, dorsal nerve conduction velocity tests, and tests of reflex latency time of the bulbocavernosus reflex. These are rarely necessary, and they are not available to most urologists.

Several tests are available for the evaluation of the vascular integrity of the cavernous body, the central cylinder within the penis. I do the basic and least invasive test first, leaving the more complex and invasive tests for the more complex cases. Pharmaco-penile duplex ultrasonography (PPDU) has essentially replaced the measurement of penile blood pressure that I did in the past. PPDU involves measuring the size and blood flow in the cavernous arteries of the penis using an ultrasound machine.

This is followed by pharmacologic stimulation of the body of the penis using an intracavernosal injection of a vasodilator (prostaglandin E2). After five minutes, the duplex ultrasound is again used to measure the peak flow rate, acceleration time, diastolic flow velocity, and dilatation of the cavernous artery. Reference values of the parameters of the PPDU test are well documented in the literature and are dependent on the dose of the pharmacological agent used. Although this test can be helpful, I strongly believe that its clinical effectiveness is limited.

I am usually able to make a diagnosis following these studies, but if the diagnosis is still in doubt, there are a few other tests available. Progress in medical technology now allows us to measure the flow into and out of the cavernous sinuses of the penis (cavernosometry) and to see the sponge-like interior of the penis (cavernosography and nuclear medicine imagining).

Therapy of Erectile Dysfunction

If there is no sign of a physical or medical problem, you would be informed of this; you could then treat the patient knowing that the problem is psychogenic.

If there are physical problems influencing the patient's sexual function, there are a variety of treatment options that can be used either in conjunction with your psychological treatment, or, if indicated, instead of your treatment. Therapeutic modalities for the treatment of organic erectile dysfunction include the following:

Oral Medication. There are several oral medications that operate to increase the likelihood of obtaining and maintaining an erection. They operate in slightly different ways, but basically they all function to increase the blood flow into the cavernous areas of the penis and to retard outflow. Success with these agents is variable. They include yohimbine, alpha 2 blockers, trazodone, vasodilan, and L-arginine.

Vacuum Erection Device. This mechanical device works to increase blood flow into the penis, creating a vacuum around the penis. Blood is "sucked" into the cavernous spaces, creating an erection. Many different vacuum erection devices are available, but they have three common components: a vacuum chamber, a vacuum pump, and a constrictor band. Patient acceptance and satisfaction with these devices range from 60 to 80 percent. The reasons for discontinuing include premature loss of penile tumescence, penile pain, pain during ejaculation, and inconvenience.

Intracavernous Injection Therapy. This is perhaps the most important advance in the treatment of impotence in the last few years. It involves a self-administered intracavernosal injection of a vasoactive agent prior to a sexual encounter. In plain English, this means that the patient learns how to use a syringe and a fine needle to inject a small amount of medication directly into the penis. Because the penis contains two cavernosal bodies running side by side along the top of the penis, injection is best accomplished at a forty-five-degree angle.

The agents currently available are phentolamine, papaverine, and prostaglandin E1. They work by opening up the arteriolar spaces, allowing blood to flow into the penis. These agents can be used alone or in combination.

I give the first test dose in the office and observe the response. On the second office visit, I teach the patient the injection technique. On the third visit, I observe the patient self-inject, and if the technique is satisfactory and an adequate erection of less than one-hour duration is obtained, I give the patient a prescription for the medication.

I warn the patient to call me or return to the hospital if the erection lasts longer than one hour. This condition, called *priapism*, can permanently damage the penis and requires immediate treatment.

I follow the patient at three- to six-month intervals to check dosage and to examine for any complications. The complications of this treatment include fibrosis at injection site, pain at injection site, bleeding at injection site, increasing dose required, and prolonged painful erection.

Although the process of self-injection is neither particularly difficult to learn nor particularly painful, a number of men are reluctant or unable to do it. For some men, the image of a needle, even a small one, going into their penis creates too much anxiety for them to feel comfortable doing the injection.

Penile Prosthesis. I offer penile prostheses to patients only as a last resort. Most of the men who undergo placement of the prostheses have tried other therapeutic avenues unsuccessfully. Some are uncomfortable with the artificiality of the vacuum erection device. Some are unable to inject themselves. Some also decide against such surgery, finding the idea of an implant unpalatable.

Penile prostheses are of two types. The malleable prosthesis is a long, smooth cylinder fabricated from plastic coils and silicone. Implanted under the skin of the penis, it is always semi-erect: hard enough that penetration is possible and yet soft enough that the man can walk around comfortably. The inflatable prostheses is likewise implanted under the skin of the penis, but it is soft when deflated and hard when inflated. A reservoir of biologically inert fluid is implanted beneath the muscles of the lower abdomen, and a pump is implanted in the scrotal sac.

Because surgical implantation destroys the natural circulatory dynamics of the penis, there is no possibility of a normal erection occurring once these devices are used. The main complications of the implants are infection (5 to 10 percent), malfunction (5 percent), and erosion through the skin (5 percent).

Vascular Surgery (Arterial or Venous). Penile arterial or venous surgery is limited to young men with focal arterial or venous disease. This is an extremely rare finding. A young patient diagnosed with vascular impotence should be referred to a medical center with experience in the evaluation and repair of such problems.

CASE EXAMPLES

The following four examples illustrate how I evaluate and treat
patients based on patient goal–directed principles.

MR. HORNER

Mr. Horner, a sixty-year-old married lawyer, was referred to me for
evaluation of his impotence. He told me that he had failed to obtain
any spontaneous erections following his recent pelvic surgery for
rectal cancer. Mr. Horner said he'd had normal sexual function prior
to the surgery. He had been cured of the rectal cancer and very
much wished to have normal sexual function again. His libido was
normal, and he was not taking any medications. Mr. Horner's impotence was neurogenic—secondary to unavoidable pelvic nerve injury
during surgery for his rectal cancer. After the history and physical
examination, Mr. Horner and I discussed the problem and possible
solutions, including vacuum erection devices, intracorporal self-
injection of a drug that would bring about an erection, and penile
implants. He elected to try the self-injection treatment. He learned
the technique easily and was able to get erection with 10 micrograms
of prostaglandin E1. At three-month follow-up, both Mr. Horner
and his wife were pleased with this treatment.

BILL McAVOY

Bill, a forty-four-year-old pharmacist, presented with reduced libido
and erections that were soft and inadequate for sexual intercourse.
The only significant finding in his history was a recent diagnosis of
duodenal ulcer. Bill was being treated with cimetidine. My physical
examination was unremarkable, and all the basic laboratory tests,
including serum testosterone, were normal. Knowing that cimetidine is a medication that can influence sexual function negatively,
I consulted with Bill's internist and recommended that the ulcer

medication be changed. No further evaluation was necessary. Six weeks later, Bill reported that his sexual function had returned to normal.

PHIL WESTIN

Phil, a twenty-one-year-old college student, was referred to me by his psychotherapist. They had been working intensively for some months for what was presumed to be psychogenic impotence. Unfortunately, the patient had not observed any improvement. In my detailed history I discovered that Phil was able to get an erection, but it lasted less than a minute and was inadequate for penetration. He did not remember ever getting an erection that was sustained. After a complete physical examination and blood work, I progressed one by one through all the tests I've outlined previously. I finally made the unusual diagnosis of a venous leak; like a balloon with a hole in it, blood was leaking out of his penis, causing his erection to disappear almost as soon as it was created. The test that confirmed this condition was an infusion cavernosogram, with which I was able to see the blood flowing into and out of his penis. Phil underwent surgical correction of the venous problem and has had normal erections since.

CARL LEVIN

Carl, a fifty-one-year-old executive, presented with decreased quality of erections. His erections were soft, not sustained, and therefore inadequate for sexual intercourse. However, Carl stated that he had had normal sexual intercourse on a number of occasions in the last few months. He worked six days a week, an average of sixteen hours a day. He smoked a pack of cigarettes a day and consumed a glass of wine daily. He was not on any medication. Physical examination was unremarkable, and all his basic laboratory studies were normal. I advised him to change his lifestyle, work fewer hours, and cut down on the smoking. I suggested that he could use a vacuum erection device in the interim in hopes that his confidence would return with some successful sexual experiences. Three months later, Carl called me to find out if he could get a refund on the vacuum device because he no longer needed it. The sexual problem of this hard-driving executive turned out to be easier to reverse than I had anticipated. I had planned to refer him to a psychotherapist for counseling if he couldn't alter his lifestyle, but in this case, the patient understood that the sexual symptom was a sign that he wasn't taking care of himself adequately. If only all our patients were so inclined.

The treatment results for men with physical or mixed physical and psychological erectile problems are generally encouraging. I've evaluated most patients with simple noninvasive tests, and when a physical problem is discovered, the therapeutic options I've described have been generally acceptable and successful.

I have found that reassurance is important for men with sexual problems, regardless of whether or not they have obvious organic reasons for their erectile dysfunction. I spend time explaining the causes for the sexual disorder and the way in which my treatment recommendations will work. Sometimes I provide the patient with relevant reading material.

As a psychotherapist, you should expect medical consultants to work with you; they should explain the physical problems, any physical treatment, and the patient's response to the diagnosis and suggested treatment. There are times when I send a patient referred to me by his internist or family practitioner to a psychotherapist for counseling. I have found that we can best help our patients with sexual disorders if the medical practitioner and the psychotherapist work together to understand and treat these fascinating and sometimes difficult disorders.

❧

SLEEP CLINIC ASSESSMENT OF ERECTILE DYSFUNCTION
Alex Clerk and Vincent Zarcone

Differentiating psychological from physiological impotence is a vital step in determining the proper treatment of your patients with erectile dysfunction. This is especially important in that the most invasive treatment for organic impotence—surgical implantation of a penile prosthesis—creates irreversible organic impotence.

You've already read about how to conduct an evaluation of sexually dysfunctional patients, and you know that a medical or urological examination is indicated for most men with an erectile disorder. There are times when the question of cause, psychological or organic, is still in doubt, even after a complete history, physical examination, and blood tests. Measurement of a patient's erection during sleep is the best way to eliminate the psychological factor and obtain an indication of the status of the organic "wiring and plumbing" of a man's erection.

We will briefly review the use of the sleep laboratory in the evaluation of men with an erectile disorder. You will thus be better able to refer patients for sleep lab evaluation, you will understand why your medical consultant makes such a referral, and you will be able to counsel intelligently and explain the procedure to those of your patients who use it.

NOCTURNAL PENILE TUMESCENCE (NPT)

Functionally, impotence is the inability to achieve and maintain an erection of sufficient rigidity for penetration during sexual intercourse. Nature's way of measuring the adequacy of an erection is simply to see if it is up to the job. Because anxiety is a frequent cause of Male Erectile Disorder, it's not possible to say for certain that a man who can't manage penetration does or does not have an organic problem.

One way around a patient's anxiety is to catch him sleeping—literally. While we dream, many aspects of our physiology are altered. Perhaps you've read about one of the more well known aspects of dream physiology, rapid eye movement (REM). In addition to this phenomenon, heart rate accelerates, blood pressure goes up, and blood flow to the penis increases. This happens regardless of whether a man is dreaming of Cindy Crawford, his great aunt Gertrude, or shoveling snow. A healthy man has an erection for about an hour and half each night. The purpose of nocturnal erections is unknown, but they are always closely associated with REM sleep.

Measuring and recording the functional aspects of an erection is a simple physics problem, much like measuring the factors that indicate if a building is strong enough to stand up in a stiff wind. We measure penile engorgement: *tumescence*, the amount of swelling of the penis; and *penile rigidity*, the strength of the erection, it's stiffness and resistance to bending.

Referral to a sleep clinic for NPT evaluation typically comes after an examination by an internist or urologist. To add to the material presented elsewhere in this book, we offer the following:

• The classic features suggesting psychogenic impotence include sudden onset preceded by a specific event, normal morning erections, and absence of chronic health problems and medications. A history of rigid erections under any circumstance is indicative of psychological impotence.

• Normal aging *does not* produce impotence. The impotence found in 55 percent of men over seventy-five is due to organic or psychogenic causes. Penile arterial insufficiency and the collateral effects of drugs for diseases that affect the elderly are the main organic factors. You should never dismiss impotence in your older patients.

• Although the exact relationship is not clear, sleep apnea is common in men with erectile dysfunction. As part of your history you might ask about sleep disruption and periodic leg movements in sleep.

• We check carefully for signs of Peyronie's disease, a fibrotic area in the penis that causes a bend during erection which can interfere with blood flow, maintenance of an erection, and penetration during intercourse.

In order to obtain accurate measurements, we ask the patient to spend the night in our sleep lab. Two gauges slightly smaller than the circumference of the flaccid penis are wrapped around the base and glans of the penis. This allows us to measure changes in penile rigidity and circumference throughout the night. In addition to these measurements, evaluation of erectile function should ideally include measurement of axial rigidity expressed as the force required to produce penile buckling. Unfortunately, this requires manipulating the penis until it buckles, which can be uncomfortable and often wakes the patient.

Simple methods for measuring nocturnal penile tumescence that can be used by a patient at home are the "stamp method" and the snap-gauge. The former, a very informal procedure, involves wrapping postage stamps around the penis before going to sleep. The patient cuts a strip of stamps, leaving a quarter-inch of overlap, which is licked and stuck to the beginning of the roll. This is at best a very inaccurate procedure, but it does give the patient who is totally unable to obtain an erection while awake some information about the presence or absence of nocturnal erections.

The snap-gauge is a more sophisticated measuring device based on the same principle as the homemade postage stamp method. The gauge consists of two pliable plastic bands that the patient wraps around his penis. When the penis enlarges, the bands break. The size of the erect penis is indicated by colored lengths of plastic. Studies have revealed that results obtained with the snap-gauge are not precise and do not reflect the functional integrity of the penis to a great degree. For this reason, we do not use the snap-gauge in our sleep lab.

~

As a psychotherapist who treats sexual disorders, you will undoubtedly come across patients who either have had or should have a nocturnal penile tumescence study. It is the best way to differentiate psychogenic and organic erectile dysfunction. If the report indicates that the patient has normal erections during REM sleep, you can be quite sure that some combination of anxiety, depression, and psychological conflict is behind the sexual difficulty. For those patients with organic impairment, the study will indicate the degree of physiological dysfunction. Knowing the degree of organic impairment will help the patient choose an appropriate treatment and help you work with the patient's reaction to his body's limitations.

NOTES

P. 124, *Penile arterial insufficiency:* Pentimone, F., & Del Corso, L. (1994). Male impotence in old age. *Minerva Medica, 85,* 261–264.

P. 125, *Although the exact relationship is not clear:* Hirskowitz, M., Karacan, I. , Arcasoy, M., Acik, G., Narter, E., & Williams, R. (1990). Prevalence of sleep apnea in men with erectile dysfunction. *Urology, 36,* 232–234.

P. 126, *For this reason, we do not use the snap-gauge:* Allen, R., & Brendler, C. B. (1990). Snap-gauge compared to a full nocturnal penile tumescence study for evaluation of patients with erectile impotence. *Journal of Urology, 143*(1), 51–54.

CHAPTER

5

PASSION AND INTIMACY
The Foundations of Sexuality

Cynthia McReynolds and David Schnarch

(Beloved), why this inconsistency?
That we live within love and yet we run away?

RUMI

Sexual relationships go awry in many ways, and therapists see all of them: dysfunction, alienation, boredom, conflict, affairs. In the multiplicity of sexual disorders and dissatisfactions, it is easy to lose track of what makes sex so compelling and challenging in the first place: erotic passion and the longing for intimate connection. What makes passion ebb and flow in relationship? Why do people sometimes pull back from the very things they most long for? What qualities of engagement and touch do a couple experience through their sexuality?

Given the elusive, subjective, and intangible nature of passion and intimacy, clinicians and clients may understandably focus more on the mechanics than the meanings and feelings that

---

Note: This chapter describes the fundamentals of sexuality and treatment using the Sexual Crucible model developed by co-author Schnarch. Case examples are from co-author McReynolds. Further applications and theoretical underpinnings may be found in Schnarch's 1991 publication *Constructing the Sexual Crucible: An Integration of Sexual and Marital Therapy.*

127

comprise sexuality. In this chapter, we are going to do just the opposite. We focus on passion and intimacy in sexuality, and find that these are the foundations on which the problems as well as the joys of sexuality arise.

We begin this chapter by discussing several issues that are fundamental in all interactions and particularly salient in erotic partnerships: self-definition, anxiety tolerance, and systemic tensions.

This framework of internal and interpersonal dynamics will help you treat individuals and couples with a broad spectrum of sexual difficulties. It will also give you a perspective from which to integrate the specific applications of sex therapy that are explained in other chapters.

Conflicts about passion and intimacy cannot simply be considered pathology. The dilemmas that arise are inevitable, and shape evolved relationships as well as dysfunctional ones. We encourage you to try these observations and frameworks on yourself. Your experiential understandings will help you recognize what is going on in your clients' lives, as well as what is happening within yourself as you work with your clients.

DIFFERENTIATION IN RELATIONSHIP

Let's look at two examples of couples' sexual interactions. You'll see significant differences in the emotional tone, the nature of the conversation, and the behavioral outcomes. We'll use these contrasts as jumping-off points for discussing the dynamics of passion, intimacy, and sexuality.

LEO AND SHELLEY DWYER

Leo and Shelley are in bed, and Leo wants to have sex. He says, "It's been forever since we've done it." Shelley feels pressured by his comment. She doesn't want to right now, and feels resentful that he so often pressures her and yet won't come right out and say what he wants. Disagreeing with Leo directly is even more stressful than feeling resentful, so, after a long moment of silence, Shelley says, "Oh, all right, if you really want to do it, I don't mind."

Leo becomes mildly anxious rather than aroused when he hears her comment: he perceives Shelley's half-hearted agreement and worries she will be resentful because he "pressured her." Feeling a vague concern that the situation may go awry and become a fight, he inquires, "Do you want to?"

She answers, "If you do."

Leo puts his hand on Shelley's shoulder and kisses her cheek, asking "What would you like me to do for you?"

Shelley thinks about this, draws a blank. She feels self-critical because she isn't as passionate as she thinks she ought to be, and mad at Leo for making her feel this way. Shelley pulls away from Leo slightly, saying, "I don't know. Here, do you want me to stroke you? Why don't you get out the lotion? Let's just do whatever you want." They continue in this way, until Leo ejaculates intravaginally about ten minutes later.

RAUL AND ALISON MARTINEZ

Raul and Alison live just down the street from the Dwyers. They too are in bed and Raul says, "I've felt sexy all day, and I really want to get it on with you tonight."

Alison strokes his chest and says, "I'm not really in the mood, but it's fine if you want to come."

Raul feels more aroused as Alison touches him, and he runs his hand down her thigh, saying, "Are you sure I can't persuade you?"

Alison laughs, "Pretty sure."

Raul puts his arm around her shoulder. "Well, how about if I get behind you and rub up against you?" Alison has a momentary qualm, wondering if something is wrong with her for not being interested when Raul is, but she lets go of that thought quickly by reminding herself that she often initiates sex. Alison tries something tonight that she hasn't done before. When Raul rubs his penis against her buttocks, she pushes back toward him, joining his rhythm with her body and murmuring, "Yeah, go for it."

Raul has a brief chuckle over how Alison has made getting turned down a turn-on, but he doesn't spend much time thinking about it now. Alison finds that she has unexpectedly aroused herself; she almost decides to get more actively involved, but doesn't. They continue on like this until Raul comes against Alison's butt.

So, who had sex? Who was passionate? For that matter, what is passionate sex? Who felt desire and who felt desired? In which house would *you* rather be? We don't know which couple logs more instances of intercourse per month, but we do know there are significant differences in the spirit of the two interactions and the possibilities each couple creates for good sex. What makes the difference?

The critical factor in maintaining sexual passion over the course of an important long-term relationship is the ability to remain fully and solidly oneself while emotionally engaged with the other person. Such self-development determines what happens in relationships in four key ways:

1. Self-definition
2. Contact with partner
3. Reflective choice
4. Anxiety tolerance

Self-Definition

Let's look at how Leo and Shelley, Raul and Alison disclose who they are in terms of their sexual desires and limits. Self-definition between Leo and Shelley is muted—their positions are shaped by trying to control the impact they perceive they will have on their partner. They speak in bland, indirect ways. They rely on inference and innuendo. In the second scenario, Raul discloses his *self* by being direct about what he wants. Alison does the same by giving an honest answer. Even when Raul and Alison discover they are not on the same sexual wavelength, neither one hides his or her own position or tries to obliterate the other's.

The tendency to lose the sense of self and define oneself through the responses of others is called *emotional fusion*. In fusion the boundaries of identity seem vague or brittle, unable to withstand much pressure or disagreement from others. Fusion means a high likelihood of being "infected" with the feelings, ideas, needs, and anxieties of others—in other words, influenced in ways you don't choose.

In emotionally fused relationships, partners try to meld both of their internal experiences into a single common reality. As a result, each person's well-being is inextricably linked to the other's experience and wishes. Both focus on each other in pseudo-mutual ways, trying to ensure consensus and avoid defining their own reality.

After Leo and Shelley negotiate in the way we have heard, neither wants sex any more even though one or both may have started with that desire. When holding a distinct, self-defined position frightens people, the very process of interacting creates a lack of clarity.

The opposite of fusion is *differentiation*—the ability to maintain a solid, self-sustained sense of identity while emotionally engaged with others. With higher levels of differentiation, the sense of self is more resilient. One has a greater capacity to handle the natural stresses of a relationship without losing a sense of self, and one's ability to choose a course of action is enhanced. Differentiation is what makes us able and willing to differ with others—to know and show our unique identity, expressed through thoughts, feelings, values, vulnerabilities, strengths, desires, fantasies, and eroticism. Well-differentiated people can tolerate multiple, distinct, co-equal realities: they can be themselves when they're with others, and can accept others being themselves.

Fusion and differentiation are two ends of a continuum; differentiation isn't an "all or nothing" thing. One's level of differentiation tends to stay relatively stable over time, although it may seem to fluctuate as a result of life circumstances. In terms of handling anxiety, differentiation can be compared to electrical wiring that conducts a certain amount of charge, but breaks down if the current exceeds the wire's capacities. People who have a low basic level of differentiation characteristically operate from fusion when they're anxious. However, even well-differentiated people operate from fusion when something raises their level of stress above what they can handle.

Contact with Partner

In emotionally fused relationships, we may pay a lot of attention to our partner in order to monitor the other's reactions, but this is not the kind of attention most of us crave in relationship or sex. At low levels of differentiation, relationships are a tyrannical harmony in which differences are threatening. We attempt to deny, minimize, or rapidly smooth differences out of existence. Contact with a partner is neither solid nor comfortable because closeness results in anxiety about losing our *self*, whereas separateness creates anxiety about losing the *other*. If the self is shaky, there is an inability to be separate and a natural resistance to really "letting in" another person—whether sexually, emotionally, or intellectually.

For example, as Leo became increasingly circumspect in expressing his desire for sex with Shelley, he also made less contact with her—he wasn't present, and he did not let himself be conscious of the full scope of her position. The spirit of his interactions was self-protective rather than curious: Leo didn't feel secure enough in himself to truly know or desire Shelley. This is one consequence of a fusion position. Undifferentiated people manage the pressures of sexual relationships with blustery and insistent demands, martyred suffering, or a withdrawn stance of not wanting sex.

When we are poorly differentiated, contact with our partner's differing reality is so difficult to manage that we create an illusion either of one reality or of no connection in the first place. There are three main ways to do this:

- Submission—trying to make oneself invisible
- Dominance—trying to make one's partner invisible
- Distance—trying to make one's connection with the other person invisible

The alternative to these distortions is allowing both oneself and one's partner to be visible. When separateness is maintained, the option to know another person exists. This is possible because one's self is solid enough to withstand the risks that accompany intense emotional involvement—the inevitability of misunderstanding, disappointment, disapproval, conflict, rejection, loss. We can only continue investing, loving, and risking passion if we can keep our own shape when we—or those important to us—are anxious. In this sense, we can only have as good a relationship as we can stand losing. This is one of the key dynamics that largely determines how much sexual intensity people are able to experience.

Would it surprise you to learn that a few years earlier many of Raul and Alison's sexual interactions went just like Leo and Shelley's? In some ways it was worse, because there were times sexual invitations ended in open disagreements and in long periods of no sex at all. The comfortable atmosphere between Raul and Alison that was evident in our first example arose from the ways they learned to handle these earlier situations that were filled with conflict. Let's take a look at what was going on between them then.

RAUL AND ALISON MARTINEZ
THREE YEARS EARLIER

Earlier in their relationship, Raul's anxiety about his desire for sex would get translated into criticisms of Alison for not wanting sex as often as he did. She'd criticize him in kind to "defend" herself, and the fight would be on. Through discussions in a women's group, Alison began to evaluate her sexuality by *her own* standards instead of Raul's. When she was able to hold on to her own values and needs in her relationship, she found that she was able to be erotic in ways that were more expressive of herself. She wasn't so much standing up *for herself against Raul*, but standing up *as herself for herself*.

One example was that she liked very light, teasing touches in the beginning of foreplay. She had been unhappy about the absence of this kind of exchange, and sometimes vented it by telling Raul he didn't know how to be sensual. One evening, she tried taking his hand and moving it on her body in the way she preferred. He got mad and said she was criticizing him. Alison was tempted to jump right back into the familiar routine of mutual attack, but instead she told him she wasn't criticizing him. All she wanted was to get more turned on with him. However, Raul stayed angry and withdrew. This was one of Alison's worst fears. She managed to calm herself down, resist getting back into the fighting loop, and tolerate the sadness and frustration she felt about not being able to control Raul's angry, distancing reaction.

Alison had managed to do something very, very important. If she had stood up for herself by denigrating Raul or by cutting off from him emotionally, her action would have been another version of a fusion response. Although these gestures often pass for individuality and strength, they are not.

If Alison and Raul recounted the details of this exchange in therapy with you, you could use the emotional and communicational events to help you clearly understand what happened. Meaning and differentiation are often contained in the details of interaction. How did Alison touch Raul? What did she say to him? Was she looking at him? What was she thinking? What did she do when he responded in a way she didn't like? What happened to her sexual desire throughout the interaction? Alison's ability to stay solid in her focus without cutting off from Raul was a very important step in their sexual relationship, but the positive results weren't immediate or guaranteed.

Reflective Choice

Thus far we've discussed two of the four important aspects of differentiation in relationships: self-definition and contact with a partner. The third aspect concerns emotional reactivity. We'll see the importance of this in Raul's experience.

Although Alison was unhappy about Raul's response, she also found that she had developed some immunity to Raul's judgments of her. His criticisms were no longer so provocative. When he complained again about their lack of sex, she told him that she too wanted more sex and wanted to show him more about what turned her on.

Raul refused her invitations, and after several weeks of increasing tension and alienation, they began therapy. In treatment, Raul realized he was anxious about moving into a new sexual style because he was afraid he might become impotent, as he had during two earlier relationships. Raul admitted that he was aroused by Alison's new sexual assertiveness—so much so that he felt vulnerable and out of control.

Now he faced a choice—to continue sidestepping his anxiety by fighting and withdrawing, or to walk into his anxiety and find out how much of his own arousal (and Alison's eroticism) he could handle. For several weeks Raul pulled back and protected himself from the humiliation he anticipated if he were to lose his erections again. All the while, Alison pressured him to be sexual with her. She reassured Raul that she would understand if the worst happened. I encouraged each of them to show themselves as much as possible, to say what they wanted, to say what they were afraid of—Raul in his choice to withdraw from sex and Alison in her desire to talk Raul into greater involvement. Then something happened that I'd been anticipating. Raul changed his mind. For his own sake—not for Alison's or anyone else's—Raul decided he wanted to know what would happen if he pushed his sexual and emotional limits.

Raul's initial decision to disengage from Alison sexually was reactive and self-protective. In therapy, I didn't try to dissuade him from his position. Actually I took his position (and him) more seriously than he did. I asked him questions that allowed both of us to recognize how this choice (1) made sense given the importance of his relationship with Alison; (2) accurately reflected his identity in terms of experiences and values he held about love, self-disclosure, and judgment; and (3) was costly in terms of vigilance, ongoing self-doubt about sexual performance, maintaining distance, and getting pressure from Alison. In other words, I took his reactive stance and offered it back to him respectfully, in a more complex and complete way than he was conscious of before. Raul began to recognize himself more clearly and experience his ability to make choices.

This set the stage for his next decision, which was to reengage Alison sexually. Making choices based on thinking rather than reacting further developed his sense of being in control of himself. In a subtle but significant way, Raul understood that he had taken charge of himself by facing sexual intimacy as an opportunity for self-discovery. As he deliberately decided to risk what he had thought of as failure, he actually judged himself successful and powerful for taking it on.

After a few months, during which his erections came and went, Raul found that the level of eroticism and arousal he could tolerate and enjoy increased significantly. Initially, he was more able to allow Alison to be in control. As he allowed her to show him what she liked, he also found that he enjoyed allowing her to take charge and teach him more about what she could do to make him aroused. Their sex increased in scope, playfulness, and the depth of connection. As he became more comfortable with a passive-receptive sexual role, Raul discovered that he gradually became more comfortable with his own sexual aggression. For instance, one time Raul held Alison's hands down and thrust into her forcefully while murmuring "I'm really going to do you, baby. You can't stop me now. I'm going to make you come whether you like it or not." Once this would have seemed like more than he could handle, but now Raul found that his level of sexual excitement had increased significantly, *and* he stayed erect. (Notice that tone, intent, and context are everything. Another couple—for example, one engaged in domestic violence—would deal very differently with a statement like Raul's.)

As we saw earlier, Leo and Shelley felt compelled to act in certain ways by their anxiety and their fear of what the other would do. Shelley felt pressured to have sex because Leo wanted it. She felt resentful because he didn't ask directly. Leo didn't want to arouse Shelley's resentment, so he tried to downplay his desire. This circular conundrum makes sense once we understand their emotional fusion. If Leo's feelings and reality are determined by Shelley's internal state, then he is going to shift and adapt his behavior to manage what is going on in her. She's going to be doing the same. Neither one feels free to be separate and advocate for themselves, or to be close and give to the other; both feel out of control. They are caught in the emotional reactivity that is a natural by-product of fusion. Feelings are enacted reflexively with little or no thoughtful processing.

We've described the opposite pattern—reflective choice—in Raul and Alison. They developed the ability to observe themselves, experience emotions without feeling compelled to act, and make choices that involve risk or anxiety. The reflective state of mind and the sense of choosing are more critical features of differentiation than the nature of behavior expressed.

Anxiety Tolerance

Differentiation is neither an antidote to relationship difficulties nor the cure for anxiety. Anxiety occurs at every level of development, but there is a distinction between anxiety generated by retreats into fusion and anxiety generated by differentiation.

We can see these different anxieties in how the women in the two couples, Shelley and Alison, handled their self-doubts. Shelley went blank when Leo asked her what she wanted. Her fear that she would be criticized, rejected, and abandoned if she voiced her desires left her unable to know what she wanted. She tried to get away from her anxiety by silently blaming her husband and then adapting to his agenda by offering to stroke him. Trying to avoid the natural anxiety of passionate and intimate relationship generates unproductive anxiety.

Alison's successful experience demonstrates the fourth characteristic of differentiation—being able to tolerate anxiety for the sake of growth. Alison felt uneasy for a moment, too, wondering if she should want sex because Raul did. But she didn't pull away from this concern—she felt it and thought about it. She did a reality check and calmed her internal criticism through reflection. Alison chose to step toward anxiety, whereas Shelley reactively stepped away. Choosing to tolerate the healthy anxiety of growth is both a hallmark of differentiation and also the way we develop. As a therapist who deals with sexual disorders, your job is to help your clients go through the anxiety generated in intimate sexual experience rather than reduce it or run away from it.

Alison also shows us how anxiety tolerance is linked with sexual arousal. When Alison challenged herself by being more active as Raul stimulated himself against her buttocks, she turned herself on. Her mastery of the fear of self-revelation gave her more flexibility and room to experience and reveal her eroticism.

Theorists often discuss the critical role that overcoming obstacles plays in generating sexual excitement, but what are usually described are external obstacles, such as partner unavailability or societal norms. However, the *internal* resistance to self-discovery and self-disclosure is one of the most significant obstacles to eroticism. When we extend ourselves beyond the levels of sexual self-definition already mastered, we tap into a potent source of sexual excitement. The same "wiring" that enables us to handle anxiety also enables us to handle excitement.

RELATIONSHIP DYNAMICS

How do you help a couple like Leo and Shelly become more like Raul and Alison? We suggest that you use the very dilemmas confronting your clients to help them develop candor, greater connection, genuine giving, and erotic zest. The same processes that generate the tensions in relationship also provide the leverage that a therapist can use to promote growth. These dynamics operate in all relationships. However, they become greatly intensified in monogamous, long-term, erotic relationships. You can use these dynamics to help your clients resolve dysfunction and become more capable of passionate, intimate relationships. The dynamics are created by (1) the natural drives toward togetherness/closeness and individuality/intimacy, and (2) the inherent tension between these two drives. The resulting emphasis in therapy is on self-validated intimacy.

Togetherness and Individuality

The drive for togetherness comes from a powerful, innate human tendency to belong, to be part of the herd, to be sensitive to others. In relationships, we fulfill our longing for togetherness by building closeness and creating a shared space of experiences, understanding, and connection. As we build more closeness, we take comfort—if we have the differentiation to tolerate it—in the

familiarity, stability, reliability, and trust that develop. We cultivate a sense of mutually knowing and caring for each other. It's
vital to realize that healthy togetherness is not the same thing as
fusion. In fact, as Leo and Shelley demonstrate, "togetherness"
in poorly differentiated couples involves channeling anxiety back
and forth, and limits the quality of interpersonal contact.

The drive for individuality comes from an equally natural
impulse to be independent, distinct, and separate from others.
We need to follow our own directives and fulfill our own purposes—feeling, thinking, and acting on our own behalf. When
we *express* our individuality in relationships, we generate intimacy—the candid recognition and revelation of one's inner self
in the presence of the other. The word *intimacy* is derived from
the Latin *intima*, meaning "innermost." Not only does intimacy
give our partner a deeper and more accurate sense of who we are,
but even more significant, we usually feel profoundly connected
with ourselves in intimate moments. Self-disclosure can be
enlivening and enlightening—if we have the differentiation to
tolerate it—and can strengthen a relationship by grounding it in
more reality. But there are no guarantees. Intimacy inherently
feels risky because we go out on an edge of individual expression
without knowing how the other person will respond. Whereas
closeness *affirms and sustains* relationship, intimacy reveals and
affirms individuality, and in the process, *changes* relationship.

The Tension

Quite naturally, we feel pulled to fulfill ourselves in terms of
both togetherness and individuality. Balancing these opposing
drives is the crux of differentiation—maintaining individuality
in the midst of togetherness. If we have enough differentiation,
we can reap the rewards of both closeness and intimacy. In fact,
it is possible to develop a positive synergy between these seem-
ing opposites.

It is when the demands of a situation exceed our ability to
handle them that anxiety drives us to seek emotional fusion.

Then the balance between togetherness and separateness goes awry. We swing between compulsive togetherness and reactive individuality in an either-or manner, unable to fulfill ourselves either way. Many things bring us to this out-of-balance point—external stresses, psychological disorders, immaturity, and the natural evolution of a successful relationship.

Most people don't realize that relationship success also creates systemic pressures that make balancing closeness and intimacy difficult. The more valued the relationship, the more there is to lose. We feel more anxiety in being intimate in the sense of being honestly and fully ourselves. Yet if we want passion, we need the spark and invigoration of intimacy. One of the central dilemmas of sexual partnerships is that the more important a relationship becomes, the more difficult it is to sustain passion. This is so because the tension between closeness and intimacy becomes increasingly profound. The paradox of closeness and intimacy is that the only way to really have either is to be willing at times to sacrifice closeness for the sake of intimacy. In other words, to be liked we have to be willing to risk not being liked, for the sake of being known accurately.

Look at what happens if we try to keep a relationship running smoothly by making sure our partner likes us and is comfortable with what we do. Consciously and subconsciously, we present ourselves in ways we think will be acceptable and lovable. But at some level we know that we are being loved for how we're showing ourselves rather than for who we really are. How reassuring is that? By succeeding in being liked for what we present, we imprison ourselves in the presentation we have created. What happens to our respect for ourselves? Or our respect and passion for a partner who is willing to settle for a facade? Usually both fizzle. If we choose closeness without risking self-revelation, we can have it, but only to a degree.

On the other hand, risking intimate self-disclosure without knowing the outcome creates the possibility that we might be liked for who we really are. At least we will have given our partner the chance. Choosing intimacy means we *may* be able to have both intimacy and closeness, but the price is the possibility of disrupting the closeness through criticism and rejection.

When we are in the comfortable balance between closeness and separateness already achieved in our relationships, we usually don't feel much tension or risk in being ourselves. However, when we push the erotic or emotional limits, uncertainty appears. By the time most couples come to therapy, the natural pressures of relationship are driving them to the limits of their development. Therefore, although they will feel that pushing themselves is terribly risky, continuing not to do so has very substantial costs as well.

Self-Validated and Other-Validated Intimacy

Consequently, the fundamental premise of sex therapy in a differentiation model is to strengthen each individual's ability to bring important aspects of self into the relationship, independent of the support or validation offered by the partner. Self-validation does not mean excluding awareness of the partner. To the contrary, it means mastering the anxiety aroused by engaging with the partner *and* by unilaterally disclosing self. The solidity of the relationship with self determines the resiliency of the relationship with the partner.

The more typical way to be self-revealing is to rely on a partner's support, reciprocity, understanding, or acceptance to soothe the natural anxiety associated with self-expression or new sexual behavior. There is nothing wrong with support from a partner. Problems appear when we *require* validation from each other as a substitute for increased differentiation as individuals.

People often fall in love with someone who provides validation. It's only later, as infatuation fades and projections are withdrawn, that the real battle begins. Pressure is used to coerce the other into delivering enough validation to diminish the anxiety that accompanies self-definition. This is how emotional fusion works. The more vigorously couples insist on other-validated intimacy, the more insecurity and anxiety they generate. This is so because a partner (or a therapist, for that matter) inevitably fails—whether from accidental misstep, reactivity in the face of anxiety, aggression, or the vagaries of illness and death—to protect an individual from facing his or her own limitations and lack of a strong, secure sense of self.

No matter how much validation we receive from our partner, it does not satisfy the inherent need for validation and esteem from ourselves. Other-validated intimacy is a widespread expectation and demand in relationship, but the actual foundation of long-term intimacy and eroticism is the capacity for self-validated intimacy.

Imagine that Leo and Shelley had been listening to what went on in Raul and Alison's bedroom. Both might say something like, "If you had only talked to me like that, it would have been a whole different evening." Perhaps that's true, but if Leo and Shelley or their therapist focus only on how Leo could have helped Shelley behave in a different way, or vice versa, they miss the point. Raul and Alison succeeded because neither one required the other to behave in a particular way. The distinction between trying to elicit other-validation and being able to validate yourself shows up in the tone or spirit of the interaction. The most sexually adept or psychologically correct interactions can still have the intention of controlling or shaping the partner, and no one is more (hyper)sensitive to this meta-agenda than a spouse.

Empathy, acceptance, and understanding are hallmarks of strong sexual relationships, but they are outcomes of individual development and not necessarily the means of achieving the relationship. Therapeutic approaches based on teaching couples behavioral techniques or communication skills can be based on the same cultural misperceptions that hamstring our relationships:

- There is a way to sustain passion and intimacy over the lifetime of a relationship without anxiety.

- The basis of a good relationship involves making sure partners don't push each other beyond their sexual comfort zones.
- Only when we feel secure can we really be our most honest, erotic, and good selves.
- If we really love someone, we'll feel passionate toward him or her.

Most clients who consult you for sexual issues will not say they want more passion in their relationship. Most desire a decrease in emotional pain and an increase in sexual performance. However, we think resolving sexual problems involves the same kinds of emotional development that increases the likelihood of greater passion. You can see this in a third couple, Eva and Jonathan.

EVA AND JONATHAN BERRY

Jonathan Berry storms into my office. Eva comes in behind him. Almost before they are seated, Jonathan tells me that things have gotten out of hand in their marriage. For the last five or six years Eva has been non-orgasmic and increasingly less interested in sex. During the year before marriage and for a few months afterward, their sex life was better and she was orgasmic. During their vacation last month, Eva had a friendly rapport with the waiter at their hotel, and this convinced Jonathan that she was having an affair.

Jonathan is forty-nine years old and used to getting his way. Now he finds himself in a no-win situation, feeling ripped off when they don't have sex and ripped off when they do. Eva is thirty-eight and initially has little to say, deferring to Jonathan but making it clear with body language that she does not share his vision of her. She's quiet, deferential, and uncommunicative about what she wants; he's demonstrative, angry, and demanding. I ask Eva if the conversation she's having with Jonathan is like the sexual intercourse she has with him. She says it is. It becomes clear that Eva maintains a sense of rebellious independence by not letting Jonathan have the pleasure of her sexuality. To prevent him from having the keys to her kingdom she has thrown them away.

They both agree he runs the show—manually stimulating her genitals, deciding when to penetrate her, and marking the end of the encounter when he climaxes in missionary position. Typically, Jonathan initiates sex by putting Eva's hand on his erect penis and then stroking her genitals. I ask how he touches Eva. Specifically, literally, how he touches her. Jonathan is uncomfortable and impatient with this discussion. I know he plays golf, so I ask him if he touches her genitals with the same focus he uses on a golf club. Jonathan says no. I suggest comparisons until he decides he uses about the same amount of concentration when stroking Eva as he does opening the car door—almost none. He teeters between intrigue and withdrawal as we talk about what it means that he doesn't pay much attention when he's having sex with Eva. Paying attention would mean realizing how remote and unmoved Eva seems, and feeling a level of his own frustration and urgency that Jonathan finds very disturbing.

As Jonathan discussed his feelings, Eva got uncomfortable. His more honest, open definition of self was generating more intimacy than she was accustomed to. Eva tried to reignite the fusion pattern of Jonathan's bluster and her submission by lamenting, "I don't know what to do. I can't just make myself like sex, can I? Or have an orgasm? What do you want me to do?"

At this moment, I felt a pull to step in and help Eva get her sexuality alive again. Would it work? No. Here's a point where my theoretical frame of reference is critical. What do I believe is more fundamental to resolution of Eva's dilemma—more sexual arousal through improvements in erotic behaviors, or more emotional differentiation? I hope we've been clear that sexual behavior without emotional differentiation is a sexual disorder waiting to happen. It's often easier for a therapist to offer information about sexual technique than to focus on the painful issues of individual differentiation, but this is exactly the point we want you to grasp. Growth is painful but not unbearable, and it is certainly not without enormous benefit.

Instead of offering Eva explicit information about self-stimulation
or techniques to make orgasm with intercourse more likely (things
I certainly might do at a different point), I used her questions as
points of inquiry, asking her about what kind of sex she likes, how
she knows if she's going to have an orgasm or not, and what's different for her when she does. Eva's answers began the process of
defining and communicating her sexual self.

When Eva said she particularly liked a kind of foreplay they had
during their courtship, in which they orally and manually stimulated
each other's genitals, Jonathan exploded. He took Eva's comments
as a personal attack and started attacking back. I was caught by surprise and felt frustrated. Then I made the error of trying to calm
him down so that he could hear that what Eva was saying was about
herself and realize it wasn't about him. My attempts to get Jonathan
to listen were my reactive efforts to control him.

The situation was unproductive until I remembered that what
was happening made sense and was something I should try to understand, rather than simply to fix or stop. When Eva talked about what
she liked sexually, this was beyond Jonathan's intimacy tolerance. It
was simply too much contact for him. Jonathan was trying to move
them back to the familiarity of fusion fights. When I saw this, I was
able to point it out; I asked Jonathan if he could tell this was too
much intimacy for him, and what might happen if he hadn't "protected" himself from it. Jonathan struggled with the questions, but
didn't run away. He saw the contradiction in claiming to want to
know what Eva liked and then interfering with the conversation once
she started to tell him. He finally realized that he was afraid that if
Eva was in charge of her own sexuality, she might really have an
affair. Her autonomy confronted him with his vulnerabilities.

I didn't presume that becoming orgasmic again was Eva's immediate goal. Instead I started by trying to understand how her current
behavior already expressed what she wanted and who she was. Eva
realized that she was so loath to validate her own sexual sensibilities
that she had set herself up to endure unpleasurable sex and not have
orgasms. This accurately reflected the self-protective measures she
had learned as a child and the kinds of suffering to which she had

become habituated. As she recognized her capacity to make choices and realized that no one but herself was going to make it different for her, she began to imagine and create other sexual alternatives for herself. Before she could take a new position, Eva had to intentionally claim the old one. Then she needed to be able to sustain the new position even if Jonathan did not support her. As we have seen, when Eva presented her erotic self more clearly, Jonathan reacted with anxiety and an attempt to return to a fused argumentative style.

Eva and Jonathan spent eleven months in weekly therapy. At the time they terminated, she still did not have orgasms, but she actively participated in shaping their sexual experiences. She could initiate and enjoy what she liked. For his part, Jonathan now noticed when Eva gave him what he called the "limp treatment." Instead of going into blustery eruptions or performance without presence, he would ask her what was going on and tell her how he didn't like having sex without her. They said sex was as good as when they were dating, but in a different way—not so "hot" but with more surprises and a greater sense of doing it together. Eva, Jonathan, and I all felt our work was successful. Eva said that if they continued as they were, her orgasms would reappear on their own.

PASSION AS INTIMATE SEXUALITY

What is passion? When people talk about sexual passion, they describe feelings of electric connection, vivid intensity, vitality, and turn-ons that permeate the atmosphere. The slightest touch, glance, or word can thrill. They speak of pouring out who they are and drinking in the partner, feeling desirous and desired, being deeply open to each other. Because passion manifests itself in highly meaningful interactions, we often confuse ourselves into thinking that the source of intensity lies outside ourselves—either in the physical behaviors themselves or in the other person.

When we believe passion resides in what we do with our bodies, we usually omit what makes sex most problematic and precious—the meanings we give to it. A defining characteristic of human sexuality is our unique neurological capacity for making and perceiving meaning. No other animal displays so many variations in sexual meaning nor so many difficulties in physiological function. These complexities create the uniquely human possibilities for ecstasy, despair, love, victimization, self-annihilation, and self-transcendence in sexual experience.

When we believe passion resides in our partner, we overlook the relationship dynamics discussed previously—the unconscious adaptations we make trying to satisfy both closeness and individuality. A change in partners can seem to provide the passion apparently unavailable with the current partner. This is because a new partner doesn't disrupt our fantasies of fulfillment by confronting us with too much reality about the partner or ourselves. A new partner can also provide a way around the differentiation necessary to continue being intimate in an increasingly important relationship. Remember that for a relationship to be important, the partner doesn't have to be thought of with affection; the relationship can revolve around other issues, such as emotional identification, economic dependency, and societal norms.

If passion is not in the strokes or the other person, where is it? The odds are excellent that the couple who complains of kissing (or anything else) without passion today can describe another time when the same behavior with the same partner was highly passionate. What makes the difference? It is the meanings and depth of self that we bring to the experience.

The first time doing any sexual behavior is a stretch into the unfamiliar and usually involves a mix of anxiety, excitement, thrill, and passion. Remember your first French kiss, or your first experience of oral sex? Sizzling? Disgusting? Disappointing? Whatever your response, it's likely that you still remember the moment, because first times have a particular intensity. But what happens after lots of French kisses, especially if they are with the same person? Once a new behavior is incorporated into your sexual repertoire, the thrill around the behavior gradually subsides. Mastery is gained, and eventually the behavior may even become uninteresting.

In sexual experience, there can be many firsts—with new behaviors or new partners. But eventually, over the course of a lifetime, there is a limit on how many new ways we can use our bodies and how many new partners we can engage. Now what do we do?

There is really only one area where we can keep stretching into new challenge—within ourselves. Passion occurs when there is the right mix of mastery (anxiety tolerance) and challenge (facing the unfamiliar). When what we desire is just beyond what we have already mastered, and we push ourselves to reach into the unknown toward it, we turn ourselves on. Thus, the newness we can explore over the long term with a single partner is interior. We generate passion within ourselves by increasing the depth of self we express and allow to be seen by our partner, and the depth to which we allow our partner to touch us.

What is intimate sexuality? Many people use the terms *intimacy* and *sexuality* interchangeably, but they are not the same. In fact, most people prefer to have one without the other. Experiencing them together is deeply challenging and precisely what passion requires: letting ourselves be deeply known in and through our sexuality. "Eyes-open orgasm" is a succinct expression of intimate sexuality—literally and metaphorically. This means letting our erotic selves fully see and be seen by our lover, opening a doorway into who we are.

If the top priority is to be liked by our partner and to minimize our anxiety in the relationship, we can't really bear seeing all of who our partner is, nor can we risk being seen exactly as we are. The natural pull toward being liked and protecting closeness in an important relationship makes it hard to really open our eyes and still be who we are sexually. How many of us keep our eyes and selves closed during sex? Sooner or later there is not going to be enough excitement or edge to feel truly passionate.

If this negotiation were put into words, it might sound like this: "It's so important to me that you are attracted to me, I can't stand to know if you aren't. I'm afraid that if you were to really know me you might not like me. So I don't mind hiding part of myself as long as you will love what I show you. We have a love that must never die—no matter what I have to do to you or me to preserve it."

Intimate sexuality means wanting to know and be known by our partner, in and through sexuality. Put into words, it might sound like this: "It's important to me that you are attracted to and like me. But even more, I want you to know me. I know there are no guarantees. But the one pain I don't want is knowing deep down that I never really showed you who I am. I'll do whatever it takes to be able to be who I truly am in your presence, and to hang in there as you do the same."

In the second scenario there is a sense of "going all the way" into ourselves and into our partner. We give our honest selves, and open ourselves to what our partner gives, without being sure what is going to happen. Our desire for real encounter motivates us to show our lover what we have never shown anyone, or possibly even seen in ourselves. We want our partner to want us in the same way, but there's no guarantee that will happen. When we do experience our partner wanting us deeply, we may feel ecstatic or terrified or both. When our partner doesn't appear to desire us as we hoped, we can feel profound levels of aloneness and grief.

Long-term relationships are the bane of sexual passion because few of us want to do what passion requires. The better the relationship, the more we must master ourselves to sustain passionate engagement with our partner. After all, how many of us want to subject what is deeply important to us to the kind of uncertainty we feel in the beginning of a relationship? How many of us want to stretch into the unknown in ourselves, not knowing what we'll discover, let alone how our partner will greet it? How often can we bear realizing that an important partner is not in our control and can be the source of great emotional pain? If we are to keep passion alive as part of a committed long-term relationship, we have to keep growing. We see that long-term relationships are also a perfect training ground for developing the selfhood that passion requires.

This perspective adds a critical and often-missed dimension to sex therapy. If the assumption is that sex is natural, normal, and positively reinforcing, therapists and clients can conclude that behavioral changes alone will be sufficiently rewarding to get couples back on track to a fulfilling and exciting sexual life. However, a focus on functional sex may mean missing intimate sex. A differentiation viewpoint helps us understand that what is natural about passionate and meaningful sex is its difficulty. Intimate sexuality is something we have to acquire a taste for and develop enough selfhood to be able to sustain. This is clear in the case of another couple, Art and Susan.

ART WONG AND SUSAN KETCHUM

Art and Susan come to therapy indignant and confused. They aren't married, but have a committed relationship of twelve years duration. Over the past several months, Susan has lost interest in sex, and Susan and Art are fighting a lot. This is particularly confounding because up until recently it would have been unthinkable. They tell me that for most of their relationship, Art would ejaculate too soon, often before vaginal penetration. Susan was solicitous and understanding, and Art was grateful for her loving support, but he felt inadequate and dissatisfied nevertheless.

They entered sex therapy eighteen months ago with another therapist, and successfully learned behavioral techniques for increasing Art's ejaculatory control. Susan learned to start and then stop giving him stimulation; Art developed more ways of calming his excitement by focusing on thoughts not associated with the sexual encounter. Eventually he could forestall orgasm for several minutes of intercourse without using these techniques, and then climax with a sense that he was pretty close to choosing it. For a few months, there was a noticeable upswing in his initiation of sex, and they glowed with a sense of accomplishment and excitement.

However, after a while Susan began feigning sleep and invoking her busy schedule in order to avoid having sex. Art was angry, and he challenged her to go to therapy because it seemed as though she was the one with a problem now.

Now that they can "have sex," Susan finds she doesn't particularly want the sex they are having. Art is agitated by her disclosure that she is dissatisfied. He bursts out, "How can you say that? We've never been more intimate. This is the best sex we've ever had—but you don't want to do it!"

I ask Art how he makes sense of the fact that he thinks they are closer than ever and yet doesn't know what Susan is feeling during sex. This opens up a discussion of their total involvement with each other. The focus in the prior therapy was on Art's ejaculatory problems and had not included issues of contact and intimacy.

Symptom reversal alone had exacerbated and surfaced the underlying issues of intimacy. Sometimes, symptom reversal can do the opposite—mask the other issues—but it rarely treats them. Therapy for sexual problems works best when it takes into account whole people and the complexity of identity, potentials, and relationship negotiation that is expressed through sexuality.

FIVE PRINCIPLES FOR TREATING SEXUAL DISORDERS AND RENEWING PASSION

Couples come to us believing something is "wrong." Most often, they've spent a great deal of time suffering, worrying, thinking, and trying to change. In the Sexual Crucible approach, our interventions support redefinition of each individual's concerns away from a partner-focused formulation of the problem to a more self-focused analysis. This heads right into the anxiety-laden conundrum they have created in their sexual relationship: a choice between suffering the consequences of fusion and reactivity, or suffering the anxiety of growing for the sake of self-definition and integrity. We don't try to help our clients get *around* this hot, pressurized crucible of development but rather try to help them move *through* it, because this is how they mature and resolve the issues that brought them to treatment.

Often the first step in treatment is to ask clients what the problem is, what their ideas or theories about it are, what they have done, and what the results have been. We try to understand individuals in the sense of seeing that what they do in their lives is a profound expression of who they are. We recognize that clients already are self-defining, albeit reactively and unconsciously. The best way to support the possibility of sexual and emotional intimacy for your clients is to focus primarily on the integrity of self and only secondarily on behavioral outcomes. When clients themselves can focus on their sense of self as expressed through their interactions, they'll have a much better chance of sustaining a passionate sexual relationship. As you work with sexually troubled couples who want relief, as well as sexually satisfied couples who want greater fulfillment, the following key principles can help you cultivate this focus.

• *It is normal for important relationships to push people to their limits and then require even more of them.* In long-term, committed relationships, the tensions between togetherness and individuality inevitably intensify and challenge the level of differentiation. This is not the storybook notion of "living happily ever after"; rather, it matches most people's real-life experience of "Oh my God, I didn't realize what I was getting into." The problems partners face arise out of their investment in the relationship. It is because the relationship is so important that they persist while suffering anger, self-doubt, withdrawal, even despair. This doesn't mean they need your comfort or sympathy, but they do need your recognition of the value of the relationship, the effort each partner has put into creating this dilemma, and the nature of the challenges facing them now.

For instance, if Leo and Shelly or Art and Susan came to your office, one of them might tell you that he or she doesn't feel important to the other anymore and that's why they don't have sex very well or very often. The opposite reality is probably more useful but often overlooked—that they have become too important to each other, and that is why they can't bear exposing themselves to real contact. This is why it's not just simply a matter of engaging, differing openly, making a direct request, or giving a forthright answer. If you as therapist agree that they need to become more important to each other, you may find yourself pushing in the wrong direction just as they are. However, if you recognize how important they already are to each other, and how risky it might feel to them to confront the inherent separateness between them, then you'll see a more comprehensive and realistic picture of the situation. This will allow you to work *with* the dynamics rather than *against* them.

• *Sexual and emotional interactions with intimate partners are as unique as fingerprints and show us who we are.* Each aspect of sexual and verbal intercourse exists in a context rich with meanings, assumptions, and choices. The details of sexual behavior reflect the meanings, beliefs, perceptions, and values that define identity. They show us how we approach the tensions between togetherness and individuality, how much contact we can manage with our partner, what sexually excites and frightens us, and where our anxiety tolerance is insufficient. It is important for you the therapist to ask about the specifics and listen to the answers. What is said, what is left out, what assumptions are made? Each detail is intimate—your client's self will be right there in his or her responses, even if it's not visible to either of you at first.

When does sex start? How do you tell? What do you do with your hands, eyes, legs, words? What goes on in your mind? How fast is your heart beating? Do you suddenly become disinterested? What happened just before that? Does your partner know what's going on for you? How do you tell? How do you decide to shift to the next action? What are you refraining from? And how do you manage that? When your partner is saying or doing X, what are you thinking about? If you wanted Y a few minutes ago, how did it come about that you don't want it now? How do you know when sex is done? Who decides?

In therapy, you work collaboratively with your clients—you bring general expertise in the meaningfulness of such details, and your clients bring specific expertise in their internal experience. Together you discover that whatever they are doing makes sense and, moreover, offers information about the choices they have made and who they are.

If you simply prescribe sexual "exercises" or techniques for your clients, the information potentially available from their spontaneous interaction can be obscured. You'll find that clients often pressure you for just this sort of intervention. In many cases clients are passively handing themselves over to you, the expert, for a fix. What can be lost in this process is their fear of and need for self-expression and emotional development.

This does not mean that you should discard your knowledge of sexual physiology, anatomy, and behavior. It is the timing and direction of your therapeutic efforts that we are asking you to observe. One of your major tasks in doing good sex therapy is to distinguish between using your comments and suggestions to help your clients sidestep the anxiety of greater self-definition, as opposed to using your therapeutic efforts to help them challenge themselves to be more honest and realistic. The therapeutic impact is completely different.

• *Paradoxes emerge at the developmental edge between the level of differentiation that has been mastered and the level required by the situation that has developed.* These paradoxes are not constructed or devised as therapeutic interventions but rather are inherent in life's dilemmas. As couples try to create the appearance of a good relationship through actions based in fusion rather than differentiation, their very efforts will undermine their goals. As you recognize the paradoxes your clients create for themselves, you can point out the dilemmas and acknowledge that there is difficulty involved in either way they choose.

For example, many couples talk about wanting more *safety* in their relationship. The safety that is desired usually means they want their spouse to stop doing things that make them insecure and trigger their reactive defenses. How safe is this kind of "safety"? Not very. It's a kind of brinkmanship. "If you make the wrong move, I'll lose control of myself. So I've got to control you—only I can't. So I'll try harder and then accuse you of controlling me!" This is the inherent paradox: partners who insist on controlling their spouses in the name of safety put themselves in a situation that is fundamentally unsafe.

Genuine erotic safety can only be created when partners deliberately take steps that feel unsafe: (1) challenge themselves to increase unilaterally the intimacy in the relationship, and (2) maintain a solid and whole sense of self even under the pressure of the anxiety felt in this process. Lovers like these have safety within themselves and therefore are free to keep discovering and exploring the erotic interplay between them.

Trust is another vital quality couples seek in order to restore or enliven their sex lives. In emotionally fused relationships, trust means requiring that your spouse feel or behave in predictable ways that reassure you and minimize your anxiety. Human nature is such that at some point all partners behave in ways that are disturbing, whether it's missing a cue for sexual engagement or having an affair. Issues of trust arise at the point where clients must decide between trusting themselves, including their perceptions of their partner's behavior, or distrusting themselves so that their partner can still "be trusted." When the latter happens, clients have little anchor in themselves or reality. Their perceptions are based less on what's happening and more on what they are afraid to see, know, or respond to.

So-called betrayals of trust—infidelity, financial deceit, intentionally caused pain—can create or intensify sexual problems. A critical factor in treatment is whether these issues are framed as betrayals of the partner or betrayals of one's own integrity. Often the situation is so inflammatory that the therapist feels pressured to join the couple (and the culture) in seeing that one partner has harmed or betrayed the other. The problem with this formulation is that it lands everyone right back in the fusion paradigm that gave rise to the problems that are being acted out.

Many couples don't resolve these kinds of issues—they distance from them with divorce or suppression, or they manage the unresolved emotions with a good guy–bad guy polarity. Resolution comes when one or both partners do the work of self-definition, which requires increasing the level of honesty with oneself and mending areas of self-betrayal, all of which results in more straightforward interaction with the partner. This might involve examining such issues as the original decision about who chose whom in the relationship, times of lying to oneself or stealing the partner's choice by lying to him or her, or relinquishing the fantasy of the partner as obligated to provide gratification. The paradox of trust in a relationship is that it must be based on trusting oneself, even if that includes distrusting the partner.

• *There is no anxiety-free option, only a choice between the anxiety of staying the same or the anxiety of differentiating.* The couple who comes for sex therapy is probably telling you that they want a way to improve or dissolve their erotic relationship without increasing their anxiety. An important step in therapy involves facing the reality that there is no anxiety-free choice. Any choice the couple makes engenders anxiety—either the anxiety that arises from not growing (and tolerating fusion) or the anxiety that accompanies maturing (and tolerating greater existential tensions). This is a critical awareness, and facing it makes therapy hot for both client and therapist.

When a person realizes there really is no "perfect solution," no anxiety-free path, the experience can be both dreadful and liberating. This awareness sets the stage for the development of adult self-containment and responsibility. It is here that we do our clients a disservice by implying that relating passionately is easy, natural, or the ultimate good. When we ignore the anxiety inherent in pushing a relationship into new ground, we subtly encourage our clients either to keep looking for a path with no anxiety or to pathologize themselves if they find such steps difficult, or both.

We want to emphasize that this difficult and stressful transition is part of a progressive developmental process for a couple or individual in or out of therapy. In the short run, emphasis on self-validation can give the appearance that the therapist favors individuality and sacrifices relatedness. But in fact, differentiation occurs *in* relationship; it means revealing ourselves while in emotional contact with important others. From a differentiation viewpoint, personal development and intimacy with a significant other are deeply intertwined, moving together like a DNA double helix.

Individuals may feel they've "been here before" when confronting problems of self-revelation, sexual experimentation, and emotional turmoil. In truth, they may have been "here" before, but usually on another, more limited level. As they work with their current version of the emotional and sexual challenges of relationship, they are likely to find themselves growing in many dimensions at once. Here is a summary of this cyclical process we see in our work with couples and individuals:

- When the pressures of the situation exceed the level of differentiation, emotional fusion generates reactivity, which shows up in unproductive fights, distance, lack of passion, and so on.

- Increased awareness heats up the crucible. Clients reflect on the choices already made and the options that lie before them. This is the first step of self-definition, but clients feel worse—stuck, despairing, frustrated.

- Facing these "worst fears" in an adult context of autonomy, responsibility, and no rescue is sobering. Now clients wrestle with a choice between continuing with unproductive fusion efforts to avoid anxiety or choosing to experience the useful anxiety of increased self-mastery and self-expression in relationship.

- As clients differentiate, they will experience a temporary and unfamiliar sense of separateness, disorientation, autonomy, difference.

- Healthy, realistic separateness makes possible greater and richer contact with the partner, which includes the potential for more free, spontaneous, and erotic interaction. This is the essence of an I-Thou relationship.

- Sustaining the tension between loving self and other in equal measure makes possible self-transcendence, authentic generosity, and maturation.

The process of differentiation is never complete. It cycles again and again, using each new synthesis as the stepping stone for further growth.

We'll demonstrate these steps in the individual treatment described in the following case example.

SUZANNE POMEROY

Suzanne, a thirty-four-year-old biochemist, came to therapy because she had recently discovered that her fiancee and fellow researcher, Josh Meeny, was fascinated by certain kinds of pornography. Even though they had known each other for several years and their sexual relationship was quite good, she feared that Josh might be a sex addict. When she saw that he was interested in pictures of bondage sex, she also became worried that he wanted to hurt her. Suzanne thought seriously about calling off the marriage.

She was caught in conflicted feelings at every turn. She loved Josh and wanted to know him on a deep level. But she didn't want to know about this. When he showed her blatantly sexual pictures, she hated them and wanted to get far away from them and him. She felt caught between losing Josh or giving up herself.

With her anxiety this high, Suzanne regressed into fusion, believing that getting to know Josh meant being the same as him or agreeing with him. Her reflexive reaction was to do what she had done in previous relationships when a sexual problem arose—

either withdraw, or engage in an unending battle until the man finally left her.

Fortunately for Suzanne, Josh was a solid enough partner that he didn't acquiesce, distance himself, or battle with her, so she had a good opportunity to work with herself. In therapy, she explored her responses to the pictures and thought out her position more carefully so that she could respect herself and express herself to Josh without losing control. Suzanne realized that (1) she could stand up for her own limits and (2) she knew very little about the meaning these images and fantasies actually had for Josh.

Suzanne told Josh what the pictures meant to her; she tried not to "protect" them from this intimate encounter by picking a fight. She asked him questions about his sexual interests and fantasies, and she tried to hear his responses as information about him rather than demands on her. He explained that he was excited by the idea of tying up a woman and being completely in control of her. He had no interest in actually hurting anyone. Suzanne began to ask herself why she felt closed off from such an experience.

There was a quiet poignancy in this process—Suzanne was dead set against capitulating and selling herself out, but she was also determined not to close herself off from caring about Josh or getting to know him as deeply as possible.

Suzanne lived with this tension for several months. After a lot of soul-searching, she decided to let Josh tie her up. They talked about what this would mean, how Suzanne might feel, what they would do if she got scared and wanted out. In the therapy hour before they went away for their "weekend experiment," Suzanne said she felt as though her nerves were vibrating. On the one hand she was scared, on the other she was sexually aroused. It was strange, she said, to be excited and curious and yet wish she was going to visit her grandmother instead.

When Suzanne returned for her next hour, a broad smile covered her face. She laughed as she related the details of her experience. She had been nervous and scared, and she felt embarrassed as Josh tied her hands and feet to the bedposts, but the overwhelming degradation she feared so much never materialized. Instead she found herself enjoying his ministrations and, to her surprise, also enjoying "resisting" him as the bonds allowed her to do. Suzanne was obviously feeling delighted with herself, and close to Josh. Because she had been woman enough to master reactive patterns and stay connected with herself *and* Josh, she was also strong enough to join her lover in an intense, meaningful, and generous sexual experience. Suzanne commented that this relationship was the best she had ever had but that this was, curiously, the first time in her life that she wasn't thinking that a relationship was the most important thing in life.

- *The therapist's level of differentiation is a critical component of the therapeutic process.*

Differentiation virtually defines the work of therapy. In clinical practice you must be able to (1) sustain a solid sense of self while emotionally engaged with your clients; (2) remain nonreactive in the face of your client's anxiety and reactivity; (3) express difference without blurring or rigidifying your own boundaries; and (4) remain present, caring, and neutral while clients struggle with themselves.

It's understandable, especially at the beginning of a therapist's career, to look toward clients for validation. It is natural to want your clients to "get well" according to your vision of wellness— to have good sex, stay together, talk to each other, become more differentiated. Or you may want their praise, attendance in therapy, or optimism at the end of a session to reassure you of your professional expertise or economic security. Your relationship with your clients can be important to you in many ways, and just as it does in personal relationships, this very importance can make it more challenging to stay neutral and clear.

As therapy progresses, clients struggle with intense, conflicted feelings. They blame, despair, collapse, regress, distance, and threaten. To the degree that your solidity as a therapist is dependent on the approval of your clients, you will be unable to understand these events.

Staying engaged but separate in the presence of clients' suffering can be heart-wrenching and stressful. Their pain can remind us of our own relationships and limitations—our intolerance for our partner's separateness, our avoidance of emotional and sexual intimacy, the limits of our own differentiation, and the inevitable poignancy and sorrow of life.

Witnessing clients' courage and triumphs can also be challenging. Sometimes they have more passionate sex, deeper relationships, and more success in work than we do. Being able to live with their success takes the same strength as living with their pain. When therapy is working well, everyone learns more about themselves, including the therapist.

WHY DO WE LIVE WITHIN LOVE AND YET RUN AWAY?

As a culture, we are terribly interested in and confused about sexual passion. On one hand, folklore implies that passion is totally out of our control. It fades with time, belongs to youth, depends on personal chemistry, happens in courting and affairs but not in marriage, and evaporates when children arrive. On the other hand, our culture treats sexual passion like a commodity that can be acquired through technique, appearance, social power, or a new partner. Sex has such a premier role in marketing and consumerism that everything from cars to cereal is sold on the possibility that it will create instant sexual passion.

There are seeds of truth in the folklore, but they are not complete. What happens to erotic passion in relationship is indeed something we cannot control. Sexual passion is larger than any single individual. It's part of the natural systems of human relationship. And yes, there are ways to rekindle passion, but they can't be purchased or fixed very well with external adjustments. Reviving and sustaining passion is an internal process that happens when individuals do the hard work of becoming more of who they can be.

Your clients come to therapy to do the work of resolving sexual problems, differentiating, and becoming more able to love as adults. When you focus your sexual therapy around the critical capacity of remaining true to self while deeply involved with a partner, you help your clients not only to have better erotic relationships but also to enjoy richer and more meaningful lives. In the process, you will have to challenge yourself as well. Perhaps as your clients become more able to live within love without running away, you will too.

NOTES

P. 127, *(Beloved), why this inconsistency?:* Moyne, J., & Barks, C. (1984). *Open secret: Versions of Rumi* (p. 67). Putney, VT: Threshold Books. Reprinted by permission of Threshold Books, 139 Main Street, Brattleboro, VT 05301.

P. 139, *Theorists often discuss:* See, for example, Morin, J. (1995). *The erotic mind.* New York: HarperCollins; Stoller, R. J. (1986). *Sexual excitement: Dynamics of erotic life.* Washington, DC: American Psychiatric Press.

P. 140, *from the Latin* intima: Malone, P., & Malone, T. (1987). *The art of intimacy.* Englewood Cliffs, NJ: Prentice Hall.

P. 159, *an I-Thou relationship:* Buber, M. (1970). *I and thou.* New York: Scribner.

FOR FURTHER READING

Kerr, M., & Bowen, M. (1988). *Family evaluation.* New York: Norton.

Schnarch, D. (1991). *Constructing the sexual crucible: An integration of sexual and marital therapy.* New York: Norton.

Schnarch, D. (1993, March–April). Inside the sexual crucible: The search for intimacy. *Family Therapy Networker,* pp. 40–48. Schnarch, D. (1994). A family systems approach to sex therapy and intimacy: Constructing sexual crucibles. In R. Mikesell, D. Lusterman, & S. McDaniel (Eds.), *Family psychology systems therapy: A handbook*. Washington, DC: American Psychological Association.

Schnarch, D. (1994, July–August). Joy with your underwear down. *Psychology Today*, pp. 38–78.

Schnarch, D. (forthcoming). *Passionate marriage: Sex, love and intimacy in emotionally committed relationships*. New York: Norton.

6

COUPLE THERAPY OF SEXUAL DISORDERS

Sandra Borrelli-Kerner and Bonnie Bernell

In this chapter, we will consider the treatment of sexual disorders in couple therapy. Our comments are addressed to those of you who are new to couple work, and to those experienced couple therapists who would like to increase their skill at handling sexual issues. The information we present should be added to everything else you have ever learned as a therapist. Couple therapy requires good clinical judgment and careful, responsible intervention. You'll need to call on your own creativity, because clients and their problems are unique. Therapeutic success depends on your values, attitudes, skill, training, style, and willingness to be present with sexual concerns as they become important in couple therapy.

Each of us has provided treatment for couples for more than twenty years. A quarter to a half of our day is spent working with couples. We think you'll find that our approach to psychotherapy balances compassion for each person with interventions that challenge growth. Our work is informed by psychodynamic, ego psychology, object relations, cognitive behavioral, behavioral, and systems theories, integrated with creativity and grounded in common sense. We seek to create a therapeutic atmosphere where open expression results in a constructive exchange and the eventual resolution of problems.

COUPLE THERAPY VERSUS
FOCUSED SEX THERAPY

What's the difference between focused sex therapy and a couple therapy approach to sexual disorders? Sex therapy is short-term, ten- to twenty-session, goal-directed treatment specifically designed to ameliorate sexual symptoms. For the most part, other dynamics are considered only when they affect the sexual arena. The techniques of sex therapy involve education and support about sexual interaction, discussion of sexual anxieties, and homework assignments specifically designed to alter destructive and unsuccessful behaviors.

In contrast, couple therapy is usually not time limited. The couple therapist has the curse and luxury of being able to address the broad range of sexual and nonsexual symptoms in a relationship. Thus, even when treating a couple with a distinct sexual disorder, the focus of couple therapy is not necessarily centered on sexual issues. Specific sexual homework assignments are not routinely used in couple therapy.

Can you integrate couple therapy and sex therapy? Definitely. We believe that a good couple therapist can work with sexual problems and a good sex therapist can work with the range of emotional issues that appear in the course of sex therapy. In our experience, the difference between sex and couple therapies is one of timing and focus, rather than of philosophy.

When you find that a sexual disorder emerges in the course of your work with a couple, you should use the criteria we discuss later in this chapter to determine if it is best to shift your focus from a general couple stance to one that concentrates on the sexual symptoms. We don't find that this needs to be a black-and-white decision. Sometimes it is necessary to blend couple and sex therapy. This means that you continue to work on the general issues the couple has presented and introduce, perhaps gradually, techniques focused on specific sexual problems.

Because sexual disorders involve a physical component, it is also important for the couple therapist to consider the necessity of obtaining medical and psychiatric consultation. The determination of physical as opposed to psychological causes of sexual disorders is covered elsewhere in this book, and we refer you to that information.

We want to encourage you to be pro-couple. This means believing that each person in a relationship has a valid point of view and has deep psychological reasons for being with this particular person in this relationship. Such an attitude allows you to assist each member of the couple in hearing the other's point of view.

We do not believe that every couple should stay together no matter what. If one person in the couple is not willing or not wanting to do the work necessary to be in a partnership, separation or divorce may be the necessary choice.

Being pro-couple means supporting the principle that people want to be with another person to meet a variety of needs and for a variety of functions or purposes. Not everyone must be in a relationship to be happy. If your clients choose to be in a relationship with each other, we expect that you will do your best to help them with that choice. If your clients' work leads them to consider separation, you would do your best to help them understand and manage that choice.

DECIDING HOW TO CONDUCT TREATMENT

As a therapist who sees couples, you will have to address some basic questions when treating sexual disorders.

When Sexual Issues Emerge in the Course of Couple Work

Should I continue to treat the couple as before?

Should I shift my focus and mode of working to a short-term sex therapy format?

Should I refer the couple to someone else for a medical examination, sex therapy, or individual therapy?

When a Couple with a Sexual Disorder Is Referred to Me

Should I see them in couple therapy?
Should I see them in focused sex therapy?
Should I do neither?

All diagnostic categories of sexual disorders—desire, arousal, and orgasmic—are potentially treatable in couple therapy. The decision to use a couple format, to alter the organization of your therapy to a brief, focused sex therapy approach, or to refer patients to another therapist is not made based on the sexual symptoms but on a comprehensive evaluation of your capabilities and the nature of dynamics within the couple. The evaluation of sexual disorders in couple therapy conforms to the presentation in Chapter Three, and we encourage you to review that material as it pertains to specific disorders and the need for medical evaluation.

We suggest the following guidelines to help you make decisions on how best to treat a couple with a sexual disorder.

When to Use a Sex Therapy Format

Couples who in the course of your therapy reveal a well-defined sexual disorder are usually best treated in *brief, focused sex therapy* when they have

- A committed relationship
- Motivation to work specifically on the sexual problems
- A willingness to interact sexually
- A lack of significant individual psychopathology
- A level of nonsexual conflict that is not disruptive to sexual interaction

When to Use a Couple Therapy Format

Couples with sexual disorders are best treated in a *couple format* when they require medium- to long-term therapy that deals with a range of nonsexual issues. This includes situations in which

- One or both members have significant individual psychopathology but are still able to work on their relationship
- The commitment to the relationship is a significant and immediate issue
- Resentment, distance, mistrust, and inability to communicate indicate that brief sexual therapy would be impossible or unsuccessful
- The sexual issues or disorders are mild or peripheral to the immediate conflicts facing the couple
- The couple has tried and failed a course of focused sex therapy

When to Consider Referral for Psychiatric Evaluation

Couples in which one or both members exhibit paranoid, borderline, or severe narcissistic personality disorders are notoriously difficult to treat in any format. These patients, as well as those who are severely depressed, alcoholic, or suffering with sexual problems secondary to medical illness or substance abuse, are best evaluated by a psychiatrist prior to attempting any form of treatment for their sexual problems. These patients may require *individual therapy or medication or both.*

When to Refer Patients for Individual Therapy or Couple Therapy with Another Therapist

Couples in which one or both members have a paraphilia are best evaluated for *individual psychotherapy.* Often the conflicts and defenses that these patients exhibit make couple therapy difficult if not impossible until they are able to manage their anxiety and join empathetically into a relationship.

The decision of when to see, or continue to see, a couple and when to refer them to another therapist needs to be made on a case-by-case basis.

We've found that it is possible to shift from an open-ended couple approach to a more directed sex therapy approach. In general this works best with couples who

- Are working well in our couple format
- Show a high degree of motivation to contend directly with their sexual problems
- Have the stability and flexibility to move into sexual issues and back to more general couple issues

We'd recommend that in your consideration of changing from a couple therapy to a sex therapy format, you talk it over with the couple and make the decision together as part of your therapy. You can use the way the clients confront and discuss the problem as both an indicator of how they're doing and an indicator of whether or not making the change of focus is a good idea.

There are several reasons why you might decide not to switch to a sex therapy format yourself but rather to refer a couple you've been seeing to a different therapist.

• They need the support of your continued couple therapy to tolerate and manage the stresses inherent in sex therapy.

• Your understanding of the way one or both members of the couple relate to you precludes a direct focus on sex and the use of sexual homework assignments. For instance, this might happen in a couple seeing a male therapist in which the woman feels overwhelmed by and frightened of men and male sexuality. In that case a referral to a woman sex therapist might be indicated. You could either interrupt your couple therapy until the sex therapy is completed, or continue concurrently.

• There are situations when the time-limited nature of sex therapy has therapeutic advantages. For clients who procrastinate or avoid sexual issues by diffusing them into a morass of emotional confusion, it may be helpful for them to know that they will be seeing a sex therapist for fifteen sessions. No more, no less. We would not recommend that you shift out of your open-ended couple therapy with a decision that you will change focus and see the couple for fifteen sessions of sexual therapy and then stop. It makes much more sense to refer them to a colleague and remain available as the couple therapist.

THE EMERGENCE OF SEXUAL PROBLEMS IN COUPLE THERAPY

Let's start at the beginning. We find that about half the time, clients who come for couple therapy bring up a sexual issue in the first session. Usually it is the man who will say that he wants to have more or better sex, or have more affection. He might go on, often with a great deal of pain and frustration, "Sex used to be so great, but now she's always too tired." Woman are more likely to say something like, "He's never romantic," or "I have so much to do after coming home from work. He doesn't help me, so how the heck am I supposed to be interested in sex?"

When sexual issues are not voiced early in the course of couple therapy, we find that they may make their appearance at any time: after a month, six months, a year, or not at all. When a sexual disorder appears in the course of couple therapy, it may have been present all along but had been denied, suppressed, or simply ignored. Sometimes new sexual symptoms will emerge in the course of couple therapy. This often happens because the therapy is working to alter defenses and break up a stalemate between the partners in the couple. The new symptoms can serve as a defense against previously unknown levels of intimacy and pleasure. They can be an expression of new levels of anxiety that are being encountered for the first time in the relationship.

We've supervised a few therapists who say sex rarely comes up in the course of their couple work. If that is true in your practice, something is wrong. The first person who must be willing and able to talk about sex is you. Some therapists unconsciously avoid sexual issues. By not asking about them, the therapist can give the impression that sex is not important to talk about. It's possible to become infected with your patient's fears and doubts about sex. It's difficult to reveal the personal details of intimate sexuality, but you'll never know what your clients believe about sex or what they are experiencing if you don't talk directly and specifically about it.

Many couple conflicts have a sexual component, and there are typical ways sexual problems arise in the course of couple therapy. Let's look at them one by one.

Disappointment

We hear a lot about disappointment during couple therapy. One of the most common ways that disappointment appears is in relation to romance and sex. For instance, Ron Funi, a twenty-six-year-old mail carrier, expressed his frustration this way: "When we first got married we were crazy about each other. Sex was a visit to paradise. Now I don't know what to think. Maybe I just don't turn her on any more. Or maybe she just faked liking sex to get me to marry her. I feel betrayed. I'm a very physical person. I don't want to live out the rest of my life not feeling loved. If it wasn't for the children, I'd get a divorce."

A thirty-one-year-old airline stewardess, Amy McWilliams, talked about her pain: "I thought that if we really loved each other things would work out. Maybe we just don't love each other enough. Our relationship went downhill after we started having children. Sex is boring; I sometimes wonder why we bother. My friends are more interested in what I have to say than my husband is. Maybe we've just grown apart. We're so different; it just seems like we don't understand each other. Is there any hope?"

The unavoidable disillusionment of a waning romance can be tolerated. We've found that disappointment is uniformly present and usually quite strong in couples struggling with sexual disorders.

But we try to help couples put disappointment into a context. Almost everyone arrives in a marriage not knowing how to make an exciting sex life that will continue beyond the "in love" stage. Helping a couple feel that they are not alone in this dilemma is a good starting point.

Many couples don't realize that marriages will feel quite different once they mature past the romantic phase. They are confused and upset that whereas they had no trouble enjoying sex at the beginning of their relationship, with time their sexual ardor disappeared. They may even fear that because time has brought more distance instead of more intimacy, their relationship must be doomed. It's a real challenge to make a relationship work after the Cloud Nine phase ends. Reality and the pressures of everyday life catch up to all of us.

It is important to instill hope and to give a couple a way to understand what has happened to them. We often find ourselves explaining that paradoxically the sensation of intimacy is often stronger at the beginning of a relationship. Being in love is a pretty strong motivator. It gets us to make time to be together. In love means showing interest and learning about each other. We say, "I love you," and hear it in return. Enveloped in the glow of physical and emotional attraction, we put our best forward. We are most aware of each other's positive attributes and believe we are the best of ourselves in this relationship. This stage of enchantment with each other always ends. Gradually, we see the differences and the negative aspects of ourselves and our partner.

Thankfully, there is also good news in this difficult process. When a relationship is more seasoned, the opportunity for a deeper, more knowing love occurs.

ELIZABETH AND DAVID

For example, Elizabeth brought her boyfriend of two years, David, into counseling because she had lost interest in sex and no longer felt "in love" with him. She did feel that she cared deeply about him, but on a recent romantic vacation, Elizabeth was uninterested in sex. She wondered if they should break up because the thrill was gone.

The therapist suggested that they explore their feelings and wait before taking further action. She reassured Elizabeth and David that the romantic "in love" phase of a relationship normally ends, and worked to help them understand their disappointment and frustration about this aspect of their relationship.

Asked when her interest in sex began to change, Elizabeth replied that just before they went on their trip she found out that a friend had become engaged. Encouraged to talk more about these feelings, she said tearfully that she couldn't understand why she and David weren't engaged.

David didn't know what he felt about Elizabeth's reactions. He said he loved Elizabeth but didn't want to jump into marriage. He thought Elizabeth needed more time to recover from a difficult divorce, and he didn't want to rush her. With some help from the therapist, David came to understand that he'd been very hurt by Elizabeth's slow disengagement from her former husband.

Elizabeth heard David's pain and added that she knew he'd also been terribly hurt when his previous girlfriend left him. She began to understand that David's hesitance about engagement was not because he didn't care about her but because he feared rejection. Her smoldering resentment cooled, and she felt a rush of love for David.

Elizabeth and David thus managed the first step in their reconciliation and reconnection, but in order to prevent such a misunderstanding in the future, they needed to learn to communicate more effectively with each other.

The loss of infatuation is not the only source of disappointment in a couple's relationship. There's a variety of hopes and expectations about intimacy: of how nice or warm or smart the partner is, of material and social success, of having children and raising a family. All of these experiences can lead to disappointment. The manifestations of disappointment often appear in a couple's sexual relationship.

Unresolved Conflict

Probably the number one killer of sexual intimacy, unresolved conflict results in feelings of resentment and distance.

Without conflict, we are less motivated to find out what another person is thinking and feeling. When feelings, thoughts, and conflicts are kept bottled up inside, it's easy for partners to make assumptions about what's going on based on their own projections.

Elena, a thirty-six-year-old housewife with a sexual desire disorder, complained, "I don't feel close, so how am I supposed to feel interested in sex?" Her husband, Albert, responded angrily, "How can you not feel close when we've been married for ten years and have two kids?" Like many couples, Albert and Elena were so busy handling their everyday lives that they didn't take the time to focus on each other. When they had a rare time away together, they avoided dealing with problems, partly because they were so desperate for enjoyment and partly because they had no confidence that they could resolve anything.

There is rarely a natural time to talk about conflict, especially sexual conflict. Who would want to talk about difficult subjects during a nice dinner, or first thing on a Saturday morning, or last thing at night when you're tired? We advise many of our couples that it's important to set aside a time to talk. It doesn't matter when, as long as there is relative privacy and freedom from interruption. It could be Wednesday nights after the kids go to bed, or Friday lunches at McDonald's.

Sally and Jeff avoided talking about sex because they were afraid it would upset the precarious balance of their relationship. Under the surface, Jeff was bothered that Sally was passive in their lovemaking. She never approached him, and when he came to her, he felt it took hours to get her aroused. Sex wasn't much fun for either of them. Sally was harboring feelings that she wasn't attracted to Jeff because he didn't shave and only took a shower twice a week.

Diagnostically, Sally had a sexual desire problem that she was concealing. Jeff had a growing depression that he was barely able to hide.

Jeff and Sally needed a safe way to talk to each other and a time to do it. Initially they used their couple therapy to do this, but as they progressed they agreed to a weekly dinner out where they would address difficult as well as pleasant feelings.

Blame

Masters and Johnson realized that spouses must take responsibility for themselves, whether they are communicating verbally or sexually. They taught couples to use "I" language. This means speaking of your own experience, rather than blaming the other person.

Couples in therapy will often reveal the ways in which they blame each other for the sexual problems that have cropped up in their relationship. We hear "You always ignore me when I want to have sex," rather than, "I feel hurt when I think you are ignoring my sexual overtures."

The Littletons came into couple therapy in hopes of finding a way to forestall a divorce. In the first five or six sessions they were anxious and reserved, but as they began to talk more about their experience it became clear how much each one blamed the other for their problems. Maryanne said that Paul was an insensitive lover who always came before she was even beginning to get excited. Paul retaliated that Maryanne was about as exciting as an avocado in bed. Maryanne turned red with rage, threw a box of Kleenex at Paul, and ran from the consulting room.

In this case the sexual problem appeared with an explosion of anger and accusation. It took many months before Maryanne and Paul could talk reasonably with each other again.

Transitions

The stress of transitional periods frequently results in sexual problems.

Rosa Anders lost her interest in sex after the birth of her first child. This continued the entire time she nursed her baby girl.

Her husband, a disk jockey at a local radio station, resented her withdrawal and unavailability, and started an affair. They arrived in couple therapy totally unable to talk to each other.

When a couple does not expect or understand the normally occurring fluctuations in sexual desire, these kinds of painful misunderstandings can result. Even those who try to prepare themselves may not have the psychological strength to deal well with the changes associated with putting one's own needs aside after a baby is born.

Tracy and Cal came into couple therapy because they were arguing all the time. They felt that having a child had ruined their relationship, and now they were stuck with each other in a lousy marriage because they didn't want to break up and hurt the child. Over time it emerged that the root of their predicament was the fact that Tracy had sworn off intercourse after a very difficult labor and delivery two years previously. She remained afraid long after the reason for her pain had gone. Her continuing fear prevented her from becoming sexually aroused. On the rare occasion when they tried intercourse, she did not lubricate but went ahead anyway. This made sex truly painful, validating her fear and making her stop all over again.

The normal transitions of life—leaving home, getting married, having children, midlife issues, menopause and old age—are all stressful. Unexpected and untoward situations, such as medical or psychiatric illness, financial reversals, the illness and death of parents, friends, or a child, can wreak havoc on a couple's ability to relax and be sexually intimate.

Infidelity

Affairs are more likely to occur during the stressful periods we've just mentioned. Although a new sexual relationship offers the allure of an escape from pain, turmoil, and uncertainty, infidelity more often creates new sexual problems instead of fixing the original ones.

ANNA AND GEORGE

Anna, an attractive social worker, was diagnosed with breast cancer when she was fifty-one. She was treated with a radical mastectomy and a course of chemotherapy. Her husband, George, a brawny sixty-two-year-old electrical contractor, found it difficult to deal with Anna's anxiety and depression. He withdrew emotionally and stopped initiating sex soon after Anna's surgery. A year of growing conflict led them to enter couple therapy. They seemed to be getting off to a good start when Anna called the therapist and announced that she had begun an affair with one of her colleagues at work. She said that she was sick and tired of George's sexual and emotional distance and was considering divorce. She asked that the therapist keep the affair secret.

Secrets pose special problems in couple or sex therapy. If you agree to keep a secret, what happens if you accidentally slip and divulge it? If you keep a secret are you allying yourself with one partner against the other? If it ever comes out that you have kept a secret from one member of the couple, it's very likely that any trust you've won will be destroyed. On the other hand, what happens if you divulge the secret? Will it motivate a couple to work on their problems, or destroy the relationship?

One way to deal with sexual secrets is to announce in your first interview that anything either member of the couple reveals to you will be open for discussion. This lets both of them know that information will not be kept from the other. If one of them later divulges something the other does not know, it almost always means that they are looking for a way to reveal his or her secret. The disadvantage of this technique is that it will force some patients to keep information to themselves that might be helpful to know in the course of the therapy. This may not be a significant problem, however, because the dynamics behind a secret are usually observable. Often, it is of secondary import to know the *content* of the secret; the reasons for its very existence are most important.

A second, and more difficult path to take is to tell the couple that they must trust your judgment on whether or not to reveal something that is told to you privately. This puts the therapist in the difficult position of being the one to decide whether or not revelation will be to the couple's benefit. Therapists who use this latter method will often meet with the individual with the secret to discuss the reasons for keeping information from the spouse and the reasons that the patient decided to tell the therapist.

The therapist had not mentioned the issue of secrets to Anna and George. Not knowing quite what to do, she asked Anna to come in for an individual session. In the course of their discussion, Anna decided to tell George about her infidelity, knowing that it would bring up the seriousness of their lack of sexual and emotional intimacy.

When George heard about the affair, he was hurt and then angry. He revealed that he had stopped being sexual because he thought Anna was uncomfortable about her disfigurement. He felt betrayed, and couldn't understand why she'd go to someone else just when things seemed to be getting better.

Anna and George voiced many previously unspoken thoughts and feelings over the next few weeks. Most of them involved disappointments and hidden resentments. They were gradually able to reconnect, but when they again tried to be sexual together, George was impotent.

This situation, of a new sexual symptom emerging after the revelation of an affair, is not particularly unusual. In this case, the therapist elected to continue in a couple format. She helped George understand the effect of his unilateral decision to stop having sex.

The techniques she used to work with George's impotence and Anna's anger are described in the next section on treatment.

THE TREATMENT OF SEXUAL PROBLEMS IN A COUPLE CONTEXT

We use a number of techniques in our couple work to deal with the spectrum of sexual disorders: discussing our clients' sexual experiences in a way that is specific and includes who did what to whom and how it felt, recommending books, focusing on sexual communication, helping couples to arrange a specific time to be alone, and assigning homework. Most of these same techniques are used in brief sex therapy as well. The difference between sex therapy and a couple therapy mode of treatment is not in the techniques used, but rather in the fact that couple therapy involves significant exploration of nonsexual areas of couple conflict and is thus useful with patients who are unable or unwilling to remain focused on their sexual interaction.

The PLISSIT Model

PLISSIT is an acronymic reminder of the basic issues involved in couple therapy for sexual problems. The letter *P* stands for *permission*. The most common and often most important way to help a sexually dysfunctional couple is to offer them permission to be sexual. This can come from your use of the language of sex, from direct and honest questions about physical connections, or from your knowledge of and comfort with sexual issues. Many of us have learned that being sexual is not OK and that being fully sexual is even less OK. Therefore, conveying an attitude of acceptance and approval of healthy sexuality helps to offset guilt, fear, and anxiety.

The *LI* stands for *limited information*. For example, it may be that a couple has gotten into a pattern of avoiding intercourse during menstruation because of misinformation. Basic information and education may free one or both partners from a tremendous group of prohibitions and inhibitions.

The *SS* stands for *specific suggestions*. For example, recommending the use of sexual aids, such as Astroglide, a sexual lubricant, can improve a couple's sexual experience. This small suggestion can mean that intercourse which had been avoided because of pain becomes worth having again. Providing such help in a neutral way often erases blame, distrust, anguish, and frustration within the partnership.

IT stands for *intensive therapy*. We've found that intensive therapy is required less often for sexual issues that come up in the course of couple therapy than are permission, suggestions, and information. When the sexual problem is straightforward and the couple relationship is basically sound, brief sex therapy is appropriate. In cases where sexual or relationship problems or both are complicated and intractable, integrated couple and sex therapy would work better.

First, we'll go through the most common ways we help our patients to work through their sexual difficulties.

Books

We have found that reading about sex can be a helpful adjunct to couple therapy. We discuss a couple's feeling about sexual material prior to suggesting specific books, and we try to use the couple's curiosity and interest to guide our recommendations. We've also found that if you suggest books to only one member of a couple, that person can become the identified patient. We suggest that you have both members of the couple read the same book or each of them read a different book.

There are a number of excellent books on sex and sexuality available. *The New Male Sexuality*, by Bernie Zilbergeld, helps to identify and confront myths about being a sexual man and can be helpful for both a man or a woman to read. *For Yourself*, by Lonnie Barbach, is a good resource for women who don't know how to masturbate or who are uncomfortable with their own bodies. *Night Thoughts: Reflections of a Sex Therapist,* by Avodah Offit, is a sensitive, well-written account of sexual feelings and behaviors. Clients will find valuable discussions of a variety of issues, from oral sex, sex and nursing, to midlife sexuality. *Mars and Venus in the Bedroom,* by John Gray, is an explicit sex manual for couples. It builds on the communication skills presented in *Men Are from Mars, Women Are from Venus.* Pat Love has written *Hot Monogamy,* which combines directions for good communication with innovative and well-grounded suggestions for better sex. This is a book for the mainstream client. It is encouraging and respectful. Our favorite books on general issues in couple relationships are by Harville Hendrix: *Getting the Love You Want* and *Keeping the Love You Find.*

Catalogs

Good Vibrations in San Francisco puts out two catalogs, one for their erotic books and another for lotions, potions, and vibrators. They're available free by a simple telephone request. If you are concerned about how a squeamish couple would respond to pictures, descriptions, or book titles, you might make copies of a few pages of the catalog and show them to the couple in a therapy hour.

RICHARD AND NANCY

Richard and Nancy Iliff came to therapy to work out their distance and anger. During the course of their work, Nancy acknowledged that she wasn't able to get sexually aroused with Richard and was using a lubricant to make intercourse possible. When the possibility of obtaining the Good Vibrations catalog was brought up, both Richard and Nancy thought it would be a great idea. However, Richard had a surprising amount of difficulty making the necessary telephone call. The first time he tried, a woman answered, and he became embarrassed and hung up. Gathering his courage, a day later he called again from work. This time, a man answered. Richard started to ask about the catalogs just as someone came by his desk to ask a question. Richard put down the telephone. Later, he called Nancy at home and asked her to make the call. She didn't want to do it either. Three tries later, Richard managed to finish his request. In the next therapy session, Richard said that if he had not made a definite commitment to call, he would not have been able to overcome his hesitancy.

When the materials arrived, both Richard and Nancy were a bit afraid to open the package. Slowly, one step at a time, with support and gentle prodding, they explored the material. Like many sexual situations in couple therapy, gentle encouragement is an absolute necessity.

The Date

So many of our couples do not even think to make a planned time to be alone together, without other adults or children, that we've come to use the concept of a date to help them get together. Our idea of a date is that two people who are attracted and interested in each other spend time together with the possibility of sexual contact. A date with a specific time, planned in advance by one or both people, can set the tone for romance, sensuality, and sexuality. When we find that a couple can have an enjoyable date, we may suggest an overnight romantic getaway.

For example, Mike and Robert, a gay couple who were in graduate school together, had good incomes and the means to do all sorts of activities and go on trips together. Mike planned gala dinner parties, fascinating trips for groups of their friends, events for the children, all kinds of celebrations. Robert appeared to enjoy these occasions, but resented that the only thing they did alone together was have sex. He became depressed and asked Mike to join him in therapy. One of the suggestions that helped Robert feel better was to set up a regular date night just for the two of them. Mike had a hard time relaxing into quiet, intimate times, and brought up a therapeutic discussion of his fear of intimacy. The two gradually felt closer to each other.

Sex Talk

There are many opportunities to talk about sex in the course of couple therapy. How you the therapist talk about it, the words you use and your comfort with them, is an integral aspect of creating a safe and therapeutic space in which to deal with sex. There are many taboos about sensuality and sexuality. Clients are frequently uncomfortable discussing this private area of their lives. Using sexual phrases descriptively and comfortably can make sex seem as natural as scratching an itch. Listen carefully to your clients' words for describing sexual anatomy. Use their words when appropriate. If they don't have a sexual vocabulary, then comment on that fact and begin to create one.

Sometimes it is easier to introduce the idea of a sexually explicit description using a nonsexual physical experience. For instance, "When you are asking someone to scratch your back, you might easily say, 'A little higher . . . no not quite . . . a little to the right . . . yes, just right, ooooooooooh . . .' If you could give directions like that about how you like your penis [or breasts, or vagina] to be touched, your partner might find it easier to please you."

For some people, dirty talk is bad talk. For others, dirty talk is good talk, even great fun. What about the word *fuck?* Is it the only way, the best way, or the worst way to refer to having sex? How does a couple decide what is OK to talk about? Does one person do the deciding? Both of them? There are the clinical words—vulva, penis, vagina, intercourse, and so on—words used by a scientist or a physician in a medical setting. There are the slang or street words—fuck, cunt, dick—that can also be used as curses. There are sexually explicit anatomical words such as tits, ass, and pussy, which are comfortable for some and derogatory for others. What language is acceptable in what settings is inevitably determined by the couple, but it is growth enhancing for people to learn to be clear in their sexual communication. We encourage people to explore the ways they use sexual words. This often paves the way to begin dealing with the shame, anxiety, or guilt.

Constructive Dialogue

We teach our clients a constructive and responsible way to handle a discussion using "I" messages. We sometimes instruct couples to take turns speaking and listening. The goal is for them to learn about themselves and each other rather than to blame or defend. Though it's understandable to blame and get defensive in an argument, not much will be accomplished in that state of mind. We advise our couples to save tough conflicts for couple therapy at first, where we can walk them through the process. In general, it's better to start with the easier issues, then move into more difficult concerns later.

The first step in attempting to constructively resolve a sexual conflict is for each individual to take a turn expressing his or her position, as simply and as clearly as possible, avoiding blame and emphasizing his or her own feelings. When he's verbalized his position, then she responds with acknowledgment that she has heard by reflecting back a paraphrased version. For example, she might begin with "If I heard you correctly . . ." and end with, "Is that right?" He might then respond, "You almost got it. Let me repeat it in a different way." Both are adopting an attitude of wanting to understand.

What may seem like a simplistic process is often totally new for couples with sexual conflicts. This basic communication process can achieve miraculous results; anger frequently disappears, and more vulnerable feelings emerge. Couples typically describe feeling very grateful to be heard.

As therapists, we have used this technique of paraphrasing what we have heard our clients say to establish a feeling of trust that we understand them. We also model reflective listening to demonstrate how a couple can talk to each other in ways that will help them grow in trust and understanding.

There are many benefits to practicing some form of constructive dialogue. It helps couples make their relationships conscious, in that they become aware of what motivates their feelings and behavior. It is safer to talk about loaded issues when there is a commitment to engage in a process based on acknowledgment and respect. Partners are better able to respond to each other in a nondefensive manner. Few couples, if any, continue the formal structure we've taught them, but they often incorporate the principles into the way they talk with each other. They can always return to the structure when things get rough.

Homework

There are several reasons that homework is especially helpful in the treatment of sexual disorders:

- Sex is a contact sport and can best be learned by doing.

- Having a couple actually come up against their inhibitions, anxieties, and symptoms is the best way to understand and alter the sexual disorder.

- Trying out new sexual interactions or returning to ones that were difficult in the past is always an anxiety-provoking experience. Couples need a safe space in which to be sexual together; for most this will be in their home, but for some it might mean someplace away from memories, children, and telephones, such as a hotel.

- Sex is an intimate experience meant for the couple to share; this excludes the therapist from all sexual encounters.

In this era of managed care, it is especially important that people multiply the therapeutic impact of office visits by learning about themselves and practicing new behaviors at home. Specific assignments are tailored with each couple's dynamics in mind. The first few times homework is used, we will usually create the assignment ourselves. As the couple comes to understand what the process involves, we include them in brainstorming about what might work best. This creates a give-and-take process in which we share our ideas with the clients and listen to their ideas. The resulting homework assignment then becomes a therapeutic product of our joint endeavor.

Clients are instructed that any result of their homework experience will be helpful to their progress. If it goes well, wonderful; if there are difficulties, they will help us understand where problems lie. The assignments we use involve physical behaviors, but we include an emotional component as well. Homework will often trigger anxiety, and this too is to be expected. Anxiety accompanies the effort to change. When clients experience so much anxiety that the tasks cannot be accomplished, it is wise either to back up a step or include relaxation suggestions as part of the homework, or both. These experiences are not likely to be completely comfortable, but we aim for a tolerable level of anxiety.

Nonsexual Touching

An example of the positive use of homework assignments involves a couple we introduced earlier.

DAVID AND ELIZABETH

Elizabeth, disappointed in the loss of her infatuated excitement over her sex life with David, was considering separation. Once they'd made an emotional bridge, the therapist didn't wait patiently to see whether they'd become physical again. Elizabeth had avoided sex for the entire six years of her first marriage, and the possibility of history repeating itself was too great. The therapist asked them to exchange nonsexual back rubs as an initial homework exercise. There are three reasons why the therapist did not specify what David and Elizabeth might do after their back rubs: (1) the couple had already been able to recreate a sense of emotional closeness; (2) the problem was one of re-finding sexual desire and was not a performance-related issue; and (3) the therapist wanted to see what the couple would do when given free rein.

The back rub progressed naturally to a spontaneous and enjoyable lovemaking. Elizabeth said she was surprised at how effective the nonsexual contact was in helping her want to be close sexually.

___

Masturbation

Most people have difficulty talking directly about their experience of masturbation. We're taught from an early age that touching yourself is bad, or wrong, or at least must be done in private and never discussed publicly. For those of us who find the idea of talking about masturbation difficult, letting a partner know you masturbate is impossible.

Learning about sexual response through self-exploration is a common homework assignment in couple therapy of sexual problems. Often the support of the therapist is enough to give the patient permission to learn about self-pleasure and to talk about it in a therapeutic session. For someone raised in a climate of sexual repression, the next step, pleasuring oneself in the presence of the partner, can be a real stretch. It's important to keep a client's values—moral, religious, and sexual—in mind when discussing such issues as masturbation and sexual interaction.

___

GEORGE AND BETTY

George and Betty came into couple counseling to get help with their newly blended family. Sex came up as an issue because they both wanted to preserve their sex life while being good parents. When the therapist asked them about masturbation, they both looked a bit sheepish and waited for the other to begin. Betty laughed nervously and said that she worried that if George knew that she "took care of herself" he might feel inadequate. She knew George pretty well, for he answered that he did wonder what her masturbation meant about her satisfaction with him as a lover. Betty gulped and said that he was a fine lover. The problem was really hers. When she masturbated, she didn't have to ask him to do certain things that would increase her pleasure. George asked her what those certain things were, and Betty was about to tell him, when the therapist interrupted. The therapist had noticed that Betty was stretched pretty thin. She'd revealed herself a couple of times, and George had yet to say anything about his own masturbatory experience. The therapist asked George if he had noticed Betty's anxiety and embarrassment. When George said no, they talked for a time about his awareness of Betty's feelings and then returned to the issue of his own masturbation and his embarrassment in talking about it. George said he wasn't used to talking about such things, but he did masturbate, mostly because he didn't want to burden Betty with his sexual needs. The ensuing discussion involved needs, feelings, and behaviors that they had never talked about before. George and Betty moved from embarrassment to relief as they talked. The result was an increase in their ability to be open and to trust each other.

Sexual Touching

Homework was critical for another couple we introduced earlier.

TRACY AND CAL

Tracy had been avoiding sex ever since a difficult delivery had resulted in chronic painful intercourse. Because fear was the cause of her present difficulties, the couple therapist taught Tracy a series of relaxation exercises that involved breathing and letting go of the tension in her muscles from her head to her feet. Cal was asked to give her a back rub to start. Tracy's job was to do her best to relax and enjoy it. If she noticed any tension returning, she was to ask Cal to stop for a moment while she repeated her relaxation exercises. In this way, they progressed from back rubs to front rubs to front rubs with genital touching included. Then Cal gently inserted one finger, then two, then moved them in a careful simulation of intercourse while Tracy worked to relax and enjoy. Actual vaginal penetration was done next, again gently, and in the beginning without any thrusting. The therapist suggested the female-on-top position for this, but Tracy was uncomfortable about this because she felt too vulnerable sitting up there. She said that "doggie" style might feel better.

While Tracy was working to relax, Cal was working to contain his sexual arousal. The therapist encouraged him to talk about his interest and frustration, and between the three of them they came up with a homework assignment in which Tracy stimulated Cal manually to orgasm. As long as she knew that vaginal penetration would only happen when she was ready for it, her fear did not return.

The homework worked well. Tracy was able to experience penetration and quiet containment without pain. The therapist had them repeat the exercise until Tracy said that she was excited about trying more movement. Both the feeling of security from having Cal hold her in the "spoon" position and the increased stimulation helped her go a long way toward neutralizing her fears.

When clients come back to therapy after homework has been assigned, it's essential to follow up and ask how it went. After a brief "how are you" establishes how they have been doing, bringing up the subject of the homework (if they haven't already) gives the message that homework is very important. Even in the case where major issues must be dealt with before dealing with the assignment, it is critical that the homework be addressed during each hour. Otherwise the sequence and follow-through of the therapy will be affected. It's best to review the homework in detail. We ask questions that help reticent clients describe what went on. We want to know about what they were each doing, thinking, and feeling during every aspect of the experience.

FOUR CASES

The most common sexual complaints we hear in couple therapy involve some form of avoidance of sex. Sometimes nonsexual couple therapy interventions are sufficient to bring sex back into the relationship, but most often, sexual problems have to be addressed directly.

In a case like that of Tracy and Cal, brief structured sex therapy might have resolved Tracy's avoidance of sex if they'd sought help when the problem first became apparent. By the time they eventually did appear for therapy, however, Tracy's fear had become deep seated and generalized, and they were better treated in couple therapy where the therapist could address a wide variety of emotional issues.

At this point we would like to tell you the stories of four couples with complicated sexual problems that were treated in a couple format either because sex therapy alone failed or would most likely have failed if it had been tried.

Sexual Aversion Disorder

MARIAH AND EVAN

Mariah and Evan were referred for couple therapy because they hadn't been sexual for years. They stopped having sex early in the relationship because intercourse was painful for Mariah. Mariah had developed diabetes as an adolescent, but consultation with her medical doctor suggested that her disease was mild, in control, and unlikely to be the cause of a sexual problem. Mariah and Evan continued a caring friendship but didn't want to consider marriage, knowing their relationship was incomplete without sex. Mariah's psychologist sent them to a couple therapist rather than a sex therapist because of the severity of Mariah's aversion to sex. She believed the case would require more than a short-term, structured program could offer.

Evan had an aversion to kissing. This was a big problem for Mariah because she loved kissing and needed it to become turned on. Evan said he learned to avoid kissing Mariah because it only led to frustration. He couldn't remember it being a problem in previous relationships, but he acknowledged that his earlier sexual experiences had mostly taken place in an alcoholic haze. We eventually discovered that Evan's lack of enthusiasm about kissing was related to his having been an asthmatic child who feared being unable to breathe.

Over a period of three months, Mariah and Evan progressed in their homework from doing back rubs to front rubs. When Evan even approached the genital area, Mariah felt anxious and needed to stop. This left Evan rejected and anxious. It had been so long since they had dared to be sexual that any sexual experience seemed alien to both of them. Mariah said she didn't know how she could go on. Evan was also nervous about trying again. Together we decided that they could try front rubs with just soft touching of Mariah's breasts. When this was successful, Mariah let Evan caress the area close to her genitals without any direct touching. She learned to relax by preceding the homework with a hot bath. She learned relaxation exercises and used them whenever she got tense.

Many sessions went by where they did nothing or just the first phase of the assignment, namely back rubs and occasional nongenital front rubs. We used the sessions to deal with financial issues, family problems, illness, and school and work pressures. Only when these issues were relatively quiet were they able to return to the sexual problem. One hallmark of a couple format is the freedom to move in and out of the sexual arena depending on the level of anxiety.

Even when we were not directly dealing with sexual issues, Evan and Mariah were encouraged to be as physically intimate as they could. The therapist regularly reminded them that fear and avoidance were major causes of their lack of a good sexual relationship. Even when they seemed to be regressing or merely marking time, part of each session was devoted to checking on the status of their physical intimacy and addressing their fears. Suggestions for improvement in their sexual exercises were made regardless of what else was going on. They were told that fear wasn't just going to go away but that they could progress in spite of it.

Working in both individual and couple therapy, Mariah was able to see that Evan was not like the brutish lovers of her past. Evan realized that if he didn't take the initiative to be sexual, it might not happen at all. His fear of hurting Mariah lessened, and he was able to be sexually freer with her. Mariah reminded him to keep on kissing. They found that once Evan was turned on, he enjoyed kissing. Mariah found that when she was turned on, she could move past her fear and enjoy the sensations of intercourse. It took more than two years for this couple to reach a point where they could enjoy sexual intimacy.

Premature Ejaculation and Secondary Orgasmic Problem

In this case, the sexual problems themselves were not particularly complex; it was the individual conflicts and the relationship problems that were deep seated and problematic. The overall picture made couple therapy preferable.

ALICIA AND BOB

Alicia and Bob, a couple in their fifties, had so much else to deal with that sexual concerns did not come up at first. Alicia's individual therapist made the referral, noting that Alicia was an extremely fragile person who frequently contemplated suicide. The couple presented as a classically polarized man and woman: Alicia carried all the feelings, and Bob was a rock of rational stability. Alicia frequently spent part of each session hysterically crying that Bob didn't care or didn't understand. Bob either verbalized his idea of a logical interpretation or glazed over and tuned out. Sitting between them was like being an interpreter for two people speaking different languages.

The first order of business was to consult with Alicia's individual therapist about the possibility of referring her to a psychiatrist for a medication evaluation. We agreed and took the necessary steps. It turned out that antidepressant medication was very helpful for managing Alicia's depression.

For some time the couple work involved putting out one emotional fire after another. One day Alicia called and said she was having a flirtation with another man. She was spending a lot of time with him but hadn't quite become sexual with him yet. This experience made her realize that Bob was too cold and that she desperately craved affection. She was scared to talk about her interest in another man, but agreed to do it as long as it was in the safety of the therapy office.

When Alicia revealed her affection for her male friend, it was interesting that Bob didn't seem to care very much. The therapist suggested that Bob's indifference was partly a result of his being cut off from his feelings and partly that he felt relieved that someone else was going to take care of Alicia's intense emotions. In fact, Bob never asked that she stop seeing the other man, but eventually she did on her own.

It took a long time for Bob and Alicia to recognize and talk reasonably about their feelings. The antidepressants and the therapy helped Alicia to calm down and not be so overwhelming. Therapy gradually helped Bob to identify his feelings. Eventually, Bob realized that he was frightened by Alicia's threats of suicide and as a result had become more distant than ever. Alicia needed a lot of support when Bob finally got angry. Bob's resentment had to be expressed and acknowledged without Alicia's falling apart. Their courage led to the return of closeness.

When Alicia and Bob finally tried to be sexual again, problems inevitably appeared. First off, intercourse was painful for Alicia, and they had to stop. Questioning revealed that in addition to the fact that they hadn't had sex for several months, Alicia was going through menopause and noticed that her skin had become drier. Even when she was aroused, she wasn't lubricating very much. A sexual lubricant was recommended, and sexual intercourse became possible again.

Next are the stories of two couples who experienced a failed course of sex therapy but went on to have success with couple or individual therapy that included attention to the sexual issues. We are not going to go into all the details of treatment, as they would resemble interventions that have been reviewed elsewhere.

Vaginismus

PRISCILLA AND NED

Priscilla, a twenty-eight-year-old tennis instructor, and her husband, Ned, twenty-nine and a graduate student, were referred to couple therapy after a behavioral sex therapy approach had failed to cure her vaginismus. Their eight-year marriage was unconsummated, yet they asserted that they had a wonderful relationship in every other respect.

Given the diagnosis and previous treatment failure, we sent Priscilla for a gynecological evaluation by a doctor who was well versed in sexual problems. The diagnosis of involuntary contraction of the vaginal muscles was confirmed. The physician was able to help Priscilla relax by talking to her and was able to complete the exam using a smaller speculum. Priscilla's ability to relax in this way brought into question her previous treatment failure; usually, women who can relax with a doctor will be successfully treated by short-term sex therapy for vaginismus.

We began with a homework exercise that required Priscilla to insert a lubricated finger gently into her vagina and then relax her body. She did it a couple of times and then said she just didn't have time to stop everything else and do it. Priscilla denied that she was anxious about the homework and said that she could put her own finger inside her vagina without tensing up. When it was suggested that the next step would be to involve Ned in the process, she said she wasn't ready for that.

After several months of therapy, it gradually became clear that Priscilla had all sorts of feelings about Ned, sexuality, and her body. She recalled that he made her feel bad when she told him about her only other intimate sexual experience. She'd petted with a boyfriend when she was away at college, and Ned was very judgmental and shaming about it. She also said that it bothered her when Ned masturbated looking at pornographic magazines. Finally, she confessed that she was ashamed of her body. She thought she wasn't sexually attractive, and this made her feel squeamish about sex.

The couple therapist referred Priscilla for individual therapy to work on her shame and inability to voice her needs and feelings. As Priscilla began to feel better about herself, she became more angry at Ned. The relationship became rocky. Couple therapy helped them to communicate better and they began to work on a series of old resentments. In spite of this, Priscilla was not interested in being sexual with Ned. Quite the opposite: she began thinking about divorce. She realized that she was outraged at the way Ned had treated her throughout their relationship. In a tearful session, she revealed that she was terribly frightened of Ned and that he occasionally hurt her physically.

Ned acknowledged his bouts of rage and physical abuse, and he began individual therapy. Priscilla decided she wanted to end the relationship; couple therapy continued until they were able to separate. Priscilla continued in individual treatment. She worked through her guilt and ambivalence about the divorce, and a year later she met a man who turned her on, body and soul. She was able to enjoy sex with him and to have intercourse without a problem. Priscilla's vaginismus was an unconscious attempt to keep out a man who frightened and hurt her. In that sense, the vaginismus was less of a problem and more of a communication about the real problem.

Impotence

DEMETRIUS AND IRENE

Demetrius, a sixty-seven-year-old retired history professor, had been successfully treated for depression with antidepressant medication.

Feeling better, he put his energies into writing poetry and traveling. About a year-and-a-half later, he called and asked to start couple therapy with his girlfriend of about a year, Irene, a forty-four-year-old teacher. They had been good friends, but a few months earlier their relationship had become something more. They were upset because their lovely friendship had become a roller coaster ride of highs and lows ever since sexual passion had appeared on the scene.

Demetrius knew that he'd had trouble with his sexual and loving relationships and openly asked for help. Irene acknowledged that she was an incest victim who had never married, avoided sex, and wasn't at all confident she knew how to have a good relationship either. They hoped for guidance about their relationship in general and specifically wanted help figuring out how to have a satisfactory sex life.

Demetrius had been impotent on and off for many years. He'd tried sex therapy several years previously, before his marriage broke up, with no improvement. Consultation with a physician revealed that his chronic diabetes and high blood pressure could be responsible for his impotence. They tried changing his medications a number of times with no improvement in his sexual function. Injection of a vasoactive medication into the cavernous body of Demetrius's penis resulted in only a weak erection. The option of a penile implant was discussed and summarily dismissed by both Demetrius and Irene.

Demetrius and Irene had more than their fair share of disadvantages, but they had one indestructible advantage. They really loved each other and were willing to do whatever it took to make their relationship work. Couple therapy focused on ways they could extend their affection into a passionate expression of pleasuring each other. Demetrius was more interested in pleasing Irene and being close to her than in having an orgasm. When he realized that she felt the same way, they were able to cuddle, hug, kiss, and use their hands and mouths to pleasure each other. Having known isolation and loneliness, they were both so grateful to each other that they were able to accept their limitations and appreciate what they did have.

We are couple therapists because we truly enjoy working with two people in their efforts to realize a relationship. It takes courage and creativity to become and remain intimately open to another human being. Couple therapists spend their time in the vortex of emotion that makes relationship. We see the best and the worst of people. We see their pain, their struggle, and their triumph.

Intimate connections involve our minds, our feelings, and our bodies. In many ways sex is the meeting place of all three. It is one way of connecting more deeply with a partner and with oneself. If we've helped you think about working with sexual problems in couple therapy, if we've piqued your curiosity about the many ways couple therapy can help resolve sexual problems, if we've given you the feeling that we find this a rewarding and valuable way to spend our professional days, then we've succeeded in what we set out to do.

NOTES

P. 176, *Masters and Johnson realized:* Masters, W., Johnson, V., & Kolodny, R. (1986). *Masters and Johnson on sex and human loving.* Boston: Little, Brown.

P. 180, *The PLISSIT Model:* Annon, J. S. (1974). *The behavioral treatment of sexual problems.* Honolulu, HI: Kapiolani Health Services.

P. 182, *Good Vibrations:* Catalogs can be obtained by calling 1–800–289–8423.

FOR FURTHER READING

Bader, E., & Pearson, P. (1988). *In quest of the mythical mate.* New York: Brunner/Mazel.

Barbach, L. G. (1975). *For yourself.* New York: Doubleday.

Fromm, E. (1956). *The art of loving.* New York: HarperCollins.

Gray, J. (1992). *Men are from Mars, women are from Venus.* New York: HarperCollins.

Gray, J. (1995). *Mars and Venus in the bedroom.* New York: HarperCollins.

Hendrix, H. (1988). *Getting the love you want*. New York: HarperCollins.

Hendrix, H. (1992). *Keeping the love you find*. New York: Simon & Schuster.

Kaplan, H. (1995). *The sexual desire disorders*. New York: Brunner/Mazel.

Love, P. (1995). *Hot monogamy*. New York: Penguin (Plume).

Moultrip, D. J. (1990). *Husbands, wives, and lovers*. New York: Guilford.

Offit, A. (1995). *Night thoughts: Reflections of a sex therapist* (Rev. ed.). Northvale, NJ: Aronson.

Paul, J., & Paul, M. (1983). *Do I have to give up me to be loved by you?* Minneapolis, MN: CompCare.

Tannen, D. (1990). *You just don't understand*. New York: Ballantine.

Westfall, A. (1995). Working through the extramarital dilemma. In G. R. Weeks & L. Hof (Eds.), *Integrative solutions* (pp. 148–194). New York: Brunner/Mazel.

Zilbergeld, B. (1992). *The new male sexuality*. New York: Bantam.

7

DISORDERS OF DESIRE

Marty Klein

*Some people leave marriages because of sex lives that
other people would kill for.*

DAVID SCHNARCH

This chapter focuses on some of the most common, mystifying, and aggravating problems in sexual counseling—sexual desire disorders. Sexual desire disorders are identified by a diminished or absent interest in sexual fantasy and sexual behavior that causes marked distress or interpersonal difficulty. Working with these issues demands a great deal of patience, medical knowledge, and self-awareness from a therapist.

WHAT ARE THE COMMON DESIRE PROBLEMS?

The *DSM-IV* describes the common desire problems as (1) Hypoactive Sexual Desire Disorder (302.71), deficiency or absence of sexual fantasies and desire for sexual activity that causes marked distress or interpersonal difficulty, not caused by a general medical condition; and (2) Sexual Aversion Disorder (302.79), aversion to and active avoidance of genital sexual contact with a sexual partner that causes marked distress or interpersonal difficulty, not caused by a general medical condition.

These groupings, however, do not sufficiently describe the situations and complaints about sexual desire that you are likely to see in your clinical practice. Let's begin our discussion with a consideration of the desire problems a psychotherapist is most likely to treat.

Desire Discrepancies

The most common and troublesome problem is not lack of desire but rather what happens in a relationship in which Partner A's desire for sex with Partner B is markedly different from Partner B's desire for sex with Partner A. The conflict usually starts out small and gets bigger as increasingly anxious partners adjust their sexual strategies to exaggerated projections of each other's actual desire. Thus, A may start out wanting sex once a week whereas B wants it two or three times a week; after a while, A is making preemptive strikes and accepting sex only once or twice a month, whereas B initiates or comments about sex every day.

Here are common statements patients make (or would make, if they could) to their partners about their relationship's desire discrepancy:

- You value certain activities (for example, cunnilingus) that I dislike, which makes me back away from sex altogether
- I like to be wooed into a romantic mood; you approach me so matter-of-factly ("wanna do it tonight?") that I can't get turned on
- Our conditions for good sex seem mutually exclusive (for example, I need us to shower first, you don't; you need the house to be clean, I don't)
- We relate to local relationship events differently (for example, I need us to be feeling close with each other to get turned on, you don't)
- We each want different things from sex (for example, closeness, escape, giving, making up).

Inhibited or Hypoactive Desire

The typical clinical versions of this problem are the self-diagnosed patient, the patient identified by a partner, and the couple in which both partners wish they had stronger mutual desire.

In each of these presenting complaints, there is a recognition that sexual desire is not what it might be, what it should be, what it used to be, or what it is with a different partner. The identified patient is often considered (by self or partner) inhibited specifically in *contrast* with the partner or with his or her own past functioning. Thus, there is a relativity to this evaluation.

Put another way, there is the unstated assumption that the person with inhibited desire *could* have more desire if something were "fixed." Indeed, that is how these patients usually present: "fix me" or "fix him (or her)." This assumes that the low desire is not constitutional but rather is a local pathology—analogous to saying a person ran a race slowly because of a pebble in her shoe, rather than because she is slow. Inhibited desire cases are marked by issues of blame and comparison.

Sexual Aversion or Panic

The severity of this problem makes it unusual in most clinical settings. It is hard to gauge how common it is in the general population; people with this problem are often either single (removing the motivation to seek help), or in relationships that are sexless, either by design or by default. Sexual aversion is marked by a powerful, unpleasant, physical response to sexual activity, which can include nausea, migraine headache, dizziness, or outright panic. Some patients deal with their anxiety by phobic avoidance of erotic situations.

Hyperactive Desire

Like the majority of people living in America's sexually conflicted culture, therapists make judgments about sex. High sexual desire is sometimes categorized as a form of psychopathology. Many therapists are quick to pathologize those who enjoy casual sex as "promiscuous," "compulsive," or "out of control" without understanding the dynamics underlying the particular individual's sexual desires. This is also true of individuals who pay for sexual services or those who take calculated risks with their marriage, health, or job in order to pursue their interests (in the same way that athletes and businesspeople do in other areas). Most psychotherapists assume that such behavior reflects primitive functioning rather than rational choice.

What exactly is hyperactive desire? There is an old joke about nymphomania—"That's a woman who wants sex one more time than her partner." This is one way hyperactive desire is evaluated: as something that disrupts relationships. Indeed, it is useful to ask these patients questions such as, Why do you initiate sex when you know the answer will be no? Why do you think you keep choosing partners with much less interest in sex than you have? What do you suppose you're wanting from sex—and why is it so hard to get it?

A person's choosing to take a risk in the pursuit of sex does not, per se, reflect psychopathology, though it certainly raises the question as to why the person would make such a choice. It makes more sense to think of hyperactive desire existing when patients have no choice about their sexual actions. "I didn't want to, but I couldn't help it," or "I knew the risk of AIDS was real, but I wanted it so bad that I just didn't care if it killed me." As with these two examples, if sexual desire and its attempted fulfillment disrupt a patient's nonsexual life, then we can think about a clinical syndrome. If patients' pursuit of sex fills up their time, leaving them unable to manage their work or relate to their family successfully; if it endangers their health, leads to arrest, or destroys significant relationships; then there is cause for concern.

The term *hyperactive desire* is a layperson's way of defining those situations where sexual desire is a singular, fixed, unconscious way of reducing anxiety. Whereas most people do this to some small extent—an appropriate strategy when it is one among many—sexual behavior that is a major and compulsive means of anxiety reduction represents a developmental problem that can drastically limit life satisfaction. When you closely examine syndromes of so-called hyperactive desire, you will often find that the patient manifests a generalized anxiety disorder, an agitated depression, or a narcissistic or borderline personality disorder.

Since the late 1980s, authors such as Patrick Carnes—addiction counselors who applied their concepts of drug and alcohol problems to sexual behavior—have considered hyperactive desire to be a form of "sex addiction." I do not find this idea particularly helpful. It is based on the assumption that the patient is suffering from a biological illness. Although this is perhaps true for a patient with an extra male chromosome, such people rarely present for treatment. Most so-called sex addicts are either (1) people whose sexual interests are nonnormative, which disturbs either them or others; or (2) people whose anxiety-driven choices, though gratifying in the short run, are eventually self-destructive. Neither state is an "addiction."

HOW DO COMMON DESIRE PROBLEMS APPEAR IN PRACTICE?

Desire issues come into our offices in three ways: as the presenting problem; embedded in some other sexual problem; or arising in the context of something else entirely (marital conflict, depression, relationship loss, and so on). Thus we must be sensitive to the possibility of a desire issue no matter what the patient initially presents. This requires talking about sex with patients with virtually every presenting problem, something many therapists and patients would rather not do.

There are two groups of features that generally accompany desire problems—functional and emotional.

Functional Co-Morbidity

Functional here refers to the body's mechanical functioning during the sexual response cycle. *Co-morbidity* refers to the common joint occurrence of two or more conditions. Following are the mechanical dysfunctions that commonly accompany desire problems.

1. Painful intercourse (dyspareunia)
2. Arousal and orgasmic problems
   Anorgasmia (inability to have orgasm)
   Rapid ejaculation
   Inhibited ejaculation
   Erectile dysfunction, female arousal disorder
3. Difficulties with conception
4. Medical illness and medication side effects

Conditions 1–3 above can *result* from desire problems: from being sexual when one doesn't want to be, wanting sex and feeling powerless to get it, feeling bad about the consequences of getting sex, and so on. On the other hand, Conditions 1–4 can *cause* desire problems by making sex unenjoyable or anxiety provoking.

Therefore, we have to ask patients about these conditions— not necessarily by name, but nevertheless explicitly: "In general, how's your sexual functioning? Do you have lubrication or erection difficulties? Can you have an orgasm? When you have sex, how often do you have an orgasm? Is it pretty easy? Pain-free?" This will put presented desire problems in context, or will provide clues to desire problems that may not have been presented.

Although it is quite possible to enjoy sex despite functional problems, most people have difficulty doing so. Thus, these conditions often reduce desire. Those patients who respond to a functional problem with a sense of desperation or compulsivity may find themselves engaging in increased sexual activity. However, this kind of "desire" is often an attempt to prove that they are functional or sexually adequate; it involves anxiety rather than a desire for pleasure and relatedness.

Functional problems can undermine desire not only for the person with the problem but also for his or her partner. For example, a man heavily invested in his partner's orgasm may find her anorgasmia so frustrating that he loses interest in sex with her, even though she remains enthusiastic. A woman whose partner has unreliable erections may initially remain interested in sex with him but lose her desire as he does.

Patients with fertility problems often have to have intercourse "on schedule" in order to conceive. This typically creates performance pressure; highlights any insecurity, inadequacy, or desire contrasts between partners; and forces people to have sex when they may not want to—a recipe for difficulty both during and after sex.

I have seen many patients who were successfully treated for erectile or female arousal problems who have gone on to develop desire problems. Whereas for many people successful therapy is a godsend, for others it can create unexpected problems. A man may want to use his now-functional penis all the time, oblivious to his partner's mood. A woman may start accusing her newly potent husband of infidelity. Couples may think that they "should" have a lot more sex, or "should" focus more on intercourse, now that they can have it reliably.

Emotional Co-Morbidity

Rapidly identifying which emotions are present in a desire disorder helps build the therapeutic alliance, and guides diagnosis and treatment as well. I have found that at least one of the following emotions accompanies virtually every desire problem: anger, shame, fear, or anxiety.

I say "accompany" because by the time people come to therapy, it is difficult to detect the direction of causality. Do the patients lose their desire because they are ashamed of their fantasies, or have they become ashamed that they don't desire their partner the way they think they should?

Discovering the actual relationship between a patient's emotions and desire problems can be slow, tedious work. It is not unusual for patients to deny the therapist's hypothesized link between their rage or anxiety and their reduced or restricted sexual desire.

Maybe a given patient is right to disagree with the therapist about this, and maybe not. As with other clinical topics, we may leave the subject and return later, or simply approach it from another direction. I frequently explain that just as strong emotions—conscious or otherwise—can interfere with digestion, sleep, and concentration, they also affect sexual desire. Thus, I invite patients to join me in looking for the strong emotions that are probably part of what is disrupting their sexual desire.

The emotions that attend desire problems may be connected to preferences or fantasies, events at any stage of life, the amount or kind of sex the patient usually has, the patient's body, and a variety of fertility issues.

The emotions that can manifest in loss of desire include the following:

- Anger—at self, partner, all men/women, sex
- Shame—regarding fantasies, passion, body, past experience, childhood sexual exploitation, one's first sexual experiences, date rape, rejection, parental humiliation, homoerotic encounter
- Fear—of fantasies, physical pain, becoming pregnant
- Anxiety—about performance, rejection, physical pain, responding appropriately

HOW ARE DESIRE PROBLEMS DIAGNOSED?

A diagnosis is a working hypothesis of what underlies a patient's presenting problem. It is only valuable if it effectively guides treatment. Because a diagnosis is a hypothesis rather than a fact (even after a patient's problem is "cured," there is no proof that our diagnosis was correct), and because we are continually collecting information about the patient, every diagnosis is subject to continuing revision and even rejection.

A good diagnosis guides treatment by keeping us focused on what needs to change in order for the patient's functioning to improve. A good diagnosis will guide our questions, sensitize us to details that we might otherwise overlook, and prepare us for likely avenues of resistance.

Ruling Out Medical Factors

With almost all sexual problems, the first diagnostic task is to rule out medical factors. This is important because medical factors require treatment that psychotherapists rarely offer. If a medical issue underlies a desire disorder, all the therapy in the world will not be sufficient. How do we proceed to rule out medical factors?

Medications. Ask patients about any medications or prescription drugs. "Do you take anything to help you sleep, wake up, relax, concentrate, digest better, increase your strength or reflexes, deal with pain, or feel less nervous? Have you taken any medications like this in the last few years?" In particular, antihypertensives such as Inderal and antidepressants such as Prozac are known to depress libido. Refer to Table 2.1 for a complete list of medications that can affect sexual function.

If a patient is taking a medication that commonly affects sexual functioning, or whose common side effects you don't know, you or the patient (or both of you) should talk with the prescribing physician. Get the drug's name, dosage, purpose, and length of prescription. You can also question your local pharmacist.

Street Drugs. Ask patients if they take any recreational drugs, "confidentially, of course." Get information on which drugs they use, how much, how frequently, and whether they use them in connection with sexual activity. Alcohol, cocaine, barbiturates, and marijuana are all known to depress sexual desire, especially with chronic use.

You should inform patients if the street drugs they take (particularly cocaine, amphetamines, alcohol, and barbiturates) are known to affect sexuality. Emphasize that your concern is not moral but pragmatic. Psychotherapy and sex counseling are of limited value when a patient periodically ingests chemicals that block sexual desire and response. If a patient seems to live or has lived in a subculture in which drug use is prevalent (for example, truck driver, artist, student at a high-pressure school, member of a youth gang, Vietnam veteran), directly ask why the patient hasn't found drugs compelling. This may uncover drug use (which can affect desire) that the patient is hesitant to discuss.

Depression. Patients frequently describe themselves as "depressed," and are often (though not always) correct. You can also look for common symptoms of depression: unusual patterns of sleeping, eating, isolation, fatigue, self-destructiveness, crying, or irritability. Depression can be expressed by withdrawal from sex or by a hostile insistence on sex that pushes a partner away. If appropriate, antidepressant medication or therapy should be a precursor to counseling for desire problems.

Menopause. Every woman between thirty-five and fifty should be asked about such common menopausal effects as hot flashes, headaches, irritability, weight changes, and depression. Ask these patients if they have discussed menopause with their physician and if they are under medical supervision.

Whether menopause is thought of as a quasi-illness or as a normal development stage, every woman in her forties should have a plan to deal with the inevitable symptoms, which can include changes in lubrication and desire. Refer patients to an enlightened medical practitioner and to such popular books as *The Pause*, by Lonnie Barbach, or *The Silent Passage*, by Gail Sheehy.

Illness or Chronic Pain. Ask whether patients are experiencing pain or have a medical illness, as either can stifle desire. If a patient waves the question off with "Oh, just the usual aches and pains," ask for more detail. Keep in mind that those in chronic pain often use alcohol or other drugs simply to get through the day; they should be asked about this in a nonjudgmental but straightforward way.

Taking a History

Our most critical diagnostic tool is the history. This refers to collecting information, in an organized way, about the patient's

- Family of origin
- Health status
- Relationship history
- Sexual history
- Current social nexus: job, family, friends, pets, and intimate relationship(s)
- Reason for coming to therapy, including the decision to do so *now*

You will probably recognize these as elements of the typical history you take on each new patient. It is helpful to remember that history taking is part of the patient's experience of being in therapy. That means that our vocabulary, responses, affect, and choice of questions are all part of therapy. We should not get so caught up in our early-session routine that we forget this. For example, if your patient visibly winces when you question her about masturbation, you should gently ask her about her comfort with discussing the topic before proceeding further.

Simply put, the goal of history taking is to get a clear picture of the patient's current situation. However, we therapists are inclined to make assumptions—either because a situation seems transparent, or because we're uncomfortable asking for certain details, or because we sympathize with a patient's obvious discomfort discussing sex. However, our assumptions prevent us from viewing the patient clearly, leading to diagnosing and treating with incomplete information.

For example, if our question is "How often do you have sex?" we don't know if a patient's answer refers to intercourse, passionate kissing, or cuddling; worse still, the patient may infer that our view of sex is rather limited. Similarly, "Are you monogamous now?" may elicit information about intercourse with others but miss the fact that the patient is talking sexually with one or more people on the telephone or the Internet.

A good desire-related history aims at collecting the following information, though not necessarily in this order:

- What sexual activities, experiences, or feelings do you desire?
- How often would you like these?
- How do you feel about what you want? How does your partner feel about it?
- How much do you like to masturbate? Has that changed recently?
- When do you desire sex more, and when less?
- What do you do to increase or decrease your desire?
- What have you learned to expect from sex with your current partner? Do you believe this can change?
- What, if anything, do you like about sex with your partner? What do you dislike? Have you discussed either?

Then we can look at the bigger picture, sexually and otherwise:

- Has your sexual situation changed recently? When?
- Are you satisfied with how your body responds sexually with your current partner, with other partners, and when you masturbate?
- Is your sexual relationship supposed to be exclusive? If so, do you have any sexual relationships outside this one?

- How would things change if desire were no longer a problem?
- Why are you seeking therapy now?
- What will happen if therapy doesn't work?
- Does your partner know you're here?
- What other life issues developed around the same time as this difficulty? Issues may be nonsexual (I lost my job, my son flunked out of school, I moved in with my boyfriend, I resumed using cocaine), health related (illness, surgery, or chronic pain), or sexual (someone caught me masturbating, I got pregnant unintentionally, I was raped, my husband discovered my affair).

Taking a desire-oriented history is similar to the history most therapists take with new patients. It requires sensitivity, intuition, the noticing and tracking of patterns, and the ability not to get distracted by content. There are other familiar aspects of the process:

- The patient is self-critical and wants to know what's normal.
- The patient tests our empathy and neutrality.
- The patient's entry into therapy with us is another iteration of his or her history and relationship patterns.
- How the patient conveys information, regardless of content, is itself important information.

Taking a sex-related history requires that we pay special attention. The need to establish a common, helpful language is more important than usual. We need some familiarity with anatomy, physiology, aging, hormones, and fertility. Patients often find it harder to trust a therapist when the content is sexual in nature; in fact, they are more prone to lie in early sessions (about extramarital sex and paraphilias, for example).

The final point to note about the sex-related history process is that our patients may reveal things that make *us* extremely uncomfortable. Some patients will say that sex disgusts them, whereas others will insist they can't get enough of it. Patients may describe fantasies or experiences with highly inappropriate partners, or beliefs about men or women that we find appalling. Patients may cross dress, enjoy being whipped, or have sex in semipublic places with the hope of being discovered. To be helpful, we must accept such things the way we accept everything else when listening to a patient—with calmness, compassion, and curiosity.

Veteran therapists know when material—sexual or otherwise—is beyond their tolerance. The responsible, mature, and ultimately career-affirming response is to refer the case elsewhere as early as possible.

Understanding Contexts and Situations

One crucial piece of information is how patients function sexually in a variety of situations. If a woman complains of low desire with her husband, for example, is she sexually apathetic with men she meets at work? Did she notice any attractive men as she walked from the parking lot to the office? Similarly, if a man (or his partner) complains that his desire depends on extremely narrow conditions—say, that his partner wear lingerie or speak to him sternly—is this true with every partner or just his primary one? Is it also true when he masturbates, or are his masturbatory fantasies far more flexible?

Such information can tell us if the patient's complaint is more a reflection of unacknowledged feelings about his or her current relationship than about sexuality per se. It also helps us decide if the preferred treatment modality is individual therapy or couple therapy.

To put it another way, we can see the patient's life as a series of natural experiments, and observe the varying results. Compare the life circumstances associated with the problematic results (the presenting problem) with those of better results (with this partner in the past, or with other partners). Codifying the similarities and differences leads to a diagnosis. For example, a woman who desires hours of uninhibited sex with casual acquaintances but desires only sporadic, "vanilla" sex in long-term relationships may have difficulties with intimacy and dependence.

As you collect information, try to get a feel for the power dynamics of the patient's relationships. Do you see control struggles? Distancer/pursuer dynamics? Sadomasochistic patterns? Low or narrow sexual desire, for example, is often the only way a person who feels powerless can exercise control in a relationship.

In addition, evaluate the stability of the relationship. The patient may be trying to separate from his or her partner, and developing a desire discrepancy may be an unconscious strategy to get the other person to leave.

The Medium Is the Message

Use your real-time experience of patients to feel who and what they are. Collect evidence that you can codify to back up that experience. Does a patient feel stingy to you? He may be a stingy lover. Does a patient seem meek to you? She may disempower herself in bed and blame the results on the "fact" that men are selfish.

One way or another, all patients tell us their vision of sex, relationships, and their eroticism. The challenge is to neutralize our own assumptions (*particularly* if they match the patients') and perceive this vision. We will then be able to see how patients create their own difficulties. For example, a woman who believes that men are selfish lovers will hesitate to trust a new sexual partner, which will make arousal difficult and orgasm impossible. In each relationship, she will eventually lose much of her desire, inevitably driving her partner away and proving herself right.

As another example, suppose we have a patient who believes that all sex is a performance. Such a patient will report on the previous week's sexual experience as if we will judge it; in fact, he will treat the therapy itself as a performance. We must accept his perspective without agreeing that this is the inescapable, natural way sex is. When he gets angry about others allegedly expecting him to perform, we can expect him to do the same with us. *Predicting* this iteration may be an effective intervention. Thus, we don't just consider how patients behave outside the office; we study how they behave with us. Our relationship is a handy laboratory.

The first things we see with a new patient are not deeply hidden. If we are not trapped in our own clinical routines, we can observe a great deal in surface details: how the patient dresses (seductively?), speaks (without eye contact?), looks at the office (surreptitiously?), asks about billing (defensively?), talks about others (sarcastically?). Do patients apologize or criticize a lot, seem far too acquiescent in setting the next appointment, express their eagerness for change by insisting they are passive objects in our hands? These are all clues. Formulating and refining the tentative meanings of such behaviors are the therapeutic tasks.

Finally, let us remember to diagnose people's strengths. These may include, say, an appreciation for beauty, a sense of humor, the willingness to tolerate ambiguity, the ability to control impulsiveness, and the desire to take responsibility for oneself. These will all come in handy in dealing with desire problems. And, of course, we should watch how patients deal with our mentioning or appreciating these strengths. Are they uncomfortable in the spotlight? Are they afraid that our appreciation is really expectation in disguise? Such an attitude is an additional obstacle to intimacy and relaxation during sex.

HOW ARE DESIRE PROBLEMS TREATED?

This section applies to patients for whom we have ruled out medical factors. Any issues of depression, medication, and street drugs (including alcohol) *must* be addressed before using psychotherapeutic techniques.

Myths and Incorrect Assumptions

Let us start by noting some common myths and incorrect assumptions about treating desire problems:

- *There is a right amount and type of desire.* As human beings, all therapists have an intuitive idea of how much and what kind of sexual desire is "normal" or right. You may feel masturbation is acceptable once or twice a week. You may believe that enjoying being blindfolded during sex is unhealthy. You may think that people who love each other should have sex at least several times per month, and that it should include intercourse.

   These values are not clinical facts, however. We must not take sides in desire disputes, nor affirm that what someone wants is either "kinky" or "average." Even if we think patients' sexuality is "kinky" or "average," we will serve them better if we interpret patients' *interest* in our opinion rather than *giving* our opinion.

- *We need to identify the low(er)- and high(er)-desire partner.* People with desire problems typically identify themselves as either the high-desire partner or the low-desire partner. These self-definitions are limited and misleading. So-called low-desire partners may be extremely desirous of sex that is different from what is currently available. So-called high-desire partners may be much less interested in sex if their partner suddenly starts initiating. Agreeing with patients' descriptions of themselves or each other draws us into their definition of their situation—a definition they have come to us to change.

- *Good sex should be a reinforcer.* The classic picture of people who don't want sex much is that they don't enjoy it. Many people who resist sex with their primary partner, however, function perfectly and know how to enjoy it. A good sexual experience does not motivate them to initiate or participate again soon thereafter because sex is an element in an intrapsychic conflict or in the couple's power struggle.

A patient who after good sex feels "Phew, got through that without being too inept" will not be motivated to have sex again soon, especially if she has no confidence that she will be able to repeat the "performance."

• *If we work out the intimacy issues, desire will rebound.* Desire is not always a function of intimacy. Many people in intimate relationships have sex that is boring or frustrating, which can increase or decrease desire dramatically. Conversely, there are couples who can maintain exciting sex as long as they don't get too intimate. If they happen to request counseling for a nonsexual problem, resolving it by enhancing their closeness and communication may unintentionally *reduce* their sexual comfort with and desire for each other.

Along with the public, we therapists tend to think that people who love each other should naturally desire each other sexually. This is often not the case. Clinicians rarely see loving couples who are satisfied with very little sex, which makes it difficult for our profession to expand its ideas to include this reality.

• *We should help couples reach a "compromise."* Frequently, the source of a desire discrepancy is not that the partners want contrasting amounts of sex but that they want contrasting types of sexual experiences—which they express as desiring contrasting amounts of sex. Thus, encouraging A to acquiesce to more sex, or B to tolerate less sex, misses the point—and will frustrate both while empowering neither.

• *We should increase the frequency of a low-desire couple's sex, even if the sex is mediocre.* We tend to think that increasing the frequency of sex between people who love each other is a good thing, regardless of the content of the sex. But if that sex is dull or frustrating, more of it won't energize the partners or make them feel closer. We should make sure we get agreement on the kind of sex we're going to help patients have more of.

- *Enhanced communication will increase desire.* If a partner's message is "I dislike your body" or "I don't trust you," communicating it more clearly may not increase sexual desire. Sometimes clear communication—whether verbal or behavioral—*is what has blocked* a sexual relationship.

- *Monogamy is healthier than non-monogamy.* This common idea is a cultural and professional value, not a clinically validated fact. Siding with one partner against another in a monogamy dispute is as inappropriate as taking sides in, say, a couple's financial dispute.

- *If people participate less in pornography, commercial sex, or masturbation, their desire for their partner will increase.* There is no clinical or other data to support this belief. The idea actually reflects our field's discomfort with these behaviors, and the belief that they are inferior to sex with an emotionally involved partner. As clinicians, we need to understand the meaning of these activities for our patients and to see them as legitimate forms of sexual expression. Only then can we help people design a satisfying sex life that best reflects their values.

  If someone prefers masturbating to lovemaking, taking away masturbation generally will not increase his or her desire for lovemaking. It will only reduce the options the person has for nurturing him- or herself. This can actually make people less able to approach their partners.

Goals and Strategies of Treatment

What, then, are appropriate goals for problems of desire? Our goals should be to help people to

- Identify the kind and amount of sex they'd like to have, under what conditions
- Clarify and communicate exactly what sexual contract they want with their partner(s)

- Identify and resolve what's keeping them from wanting what they want to want
- Identify and resolve what's keeping them from creating what they want, including current emotions and unfinished past relationship events
- Get more from the sex they have
- Get more from the nonsexual parts of their relationships, including things they thought they could get only from sex
- Change their relationship and relationship style so they generate fewer bad feelings in the present

To accomplish these goals, the following strategies are typically helpful:

- Redefining sex and promoting new sexual concepts
- Reducing the incidence of such anxiety-filled activities as initiating sex, requiring an erection, and expecting orgasm
- Normalizing the problem
- Identifying what makes patients want to initiate or resist sex
- Exploring how sex actually feels
- Exploring what patients want from sex, and what it means for them
- Discussing individuals' and couples' strengths, and exploring how to get people to apply those to their sexual relationships
- Discussing how sexual difficulties sometimes mirror other personal or relationship difficulties
- Correcting misinformation about sex
- Helping people individuate
- Finding productive ways for partners to discuss their pain with each other
- Helping people find ways to enjoy sex despite their current functional limitations

Misinformation

One of the most important things patients with desire problems need is accurate information about how their bodies function sexually. Even in our modern times, many people are still uninformed regarding, for example, the existence and location of the clitoris; the fact that sexual function continues regardless of age; how menopause affects sexuality; the fact that arousal does not have to culminate in orgasm every time for either men or women; and the fact that sexual fantasies are harmless and do not predict sexual behavior. Misinformation about these and other issues can directly undermine or distort sexual desire.

Similarly, many patients have beliefs about what men and women are "really" like sexually: that most women don't care about orgasm, whereas men must have one every time they get aroused; that men don't enjoy cuddling, or don't need touching to get erect; that men have higher sex drives than women, and so on. Challenging such incorrect beliefs about the genders can help reduce both anxiety and anger, and help people hear what their partners have been saying all along.

Finally, we can help support patients' desire by giving them a realistic picture of what they can reasonably expect from sex. If people don't have much spontaneity in their lives, they shouldn't expect to have spontaneous sex. If they don't devote languorous hours to various leisure pursuits, they probably won't do that with sex either. If they aren't unusually flexible and comfortable with their bodies in general, they probably won't have highly vigorous, artistic sex. And just as professional athletes have extremely atypical bodies that can accomplish unique feats, actors in porn films have abnormal bodies that can do unusual things most of us cannot.

Inhibited Desire As a Defense

For many people, inhibited or conditional sexual desire is a defense against the challenges to self-image raised by their sexuality. Consciously or not, allowing their sexual fantasies, desires, and energy to flow raises various uncomfortable feelings and self-perceptions. These include the following:

- I'm a slut
- I'm a pervert
- I'm terribly self-indulgent
- I'm afraid I'll destroy you or pervert you
- I'll be punished
- I'm being disloyal (to my antisex family, to one parent who suffered sexually at the hands of the other, to my antisex culture, and so on)
- I'm too vulnerable
- I'm too powerful

The loss of sexual desire "solves" such inner conflicts. The therapist's position, of course, is that such a strategy is rarely chosen consciously and with full understanding. We believe that bringing the decision to consciousness and helping patients accept the difficult emotions and situations behind it can lead to a more life-affirming decision and access to the resources needed to implement it.

Our job is not to argue that "being sexual doesn't make you a tramp" or that "your bisexuality won't contaminate your boyfriend." Rather it is to help patients examine how they came to such decisions, what the experiential implications have been, and what an alternative way of living might look and feel like.

SHERRY

I recall a patient named Sherry, a pleasant thirty-eight-year-old recently married to her high school sweetheart. She had been having sexual fantasies and dreams about women, which she found increasingly troubling. She thought they meant that she was, deep down, a lesbian. As she worried more and more about the fantasies, she desired sex with her husband less and less. Both the fantasies and her diminishing sexual desire seemed completely out of her control.

Our work together focused first on getting her to accept the fantasies and the possibility that they might reflect something other than homosexuality—or, for that matter, might reflect nothing at all.

The second aspect of our work examined her lost desire. It turned out that she had become afraid that the fantasies would increase, that she would be irresistibly drawn to sex with women, and that her husband would leave her—"and who could blame him?" she cried. For Sherry, losing desire was an unconscious attempt to desexualize herself to protect a relationship she treasured. This is exactly the kind of decision that, when brought to consciousness, can be evaluated—and challenged—by a patient who has the proper therapeutic support.

Inhibited or conditional desire can also be a defense against relationship experiences perceived as too painful or costly. The beliefs connected to these situations include the following:

- Good sex will make us too close.
- Good sex will make me too dependent on you.
- Good sex will make me vulnerable to being taken advantage of.

TOM

For example, Tom was a thirty-year-old man who had never had genital contact with a woman. He currently lived with his rather lusty girlfriend, Amy, who in previous relationships enjoyed sex many times each week. After two years of no sex with Tom, she had gotten frustrated and was threatening to leave. (Yes, we do wonder why a lusty woman would fall in love and move in with a twenty-nine-year-old virgin.) Tom was eager to overcome his sex phobia, and Amy seemed fairly supportive. I decided that working with Tom alone would be faster than working with the couple.

The therapy soon focused on two things: his extremely close attachment to his mother, and his perception of women and intimacy as rather alien and almost sinister. With his mother giving him lifelong messages about not abandoning her, Tom had developed a fear that any woman he cared for would try to steal him away and remake him in her own image—as his mother had subtly attempted to do for so long.

By helping Tom understand the role his sexual phobia played in "protecting" him, we were gradually able to reduce the phobia. An important part of the therapy was teaching Tom to tolerate Amy's disappointment and other emotions, which was critical if he was going to take tiny steps toward her. He had never learned to tolerate his mother's sadness, anxiety, or other emotional discomforts; this inability had put him at a serious disadvantage in dealing with women. It would have been inappropriate to dismantle Tom's sex phobia without teaching him how to tolerate the feelings his independence would raise in his partner.

Desire Problems Secondary to Functional Problems

As discussed previously, many desire problems are an expression of anxiety, anger, or shame resulting from functional problems (anorgasmia, rapid ejaculation, and so on). Our job in such cases is to sympathetically confront the common belief system underlying this dynamic: "I can't enjoy sex or satisfy my partner because of my functional problem."

Men and women *can* enjoy sex without a reliable erection, an ejaculation inside the vagina, an orgasm from intercourse, and the other elements of normative sex. Sometimes, the partner of the person with the functional limitation has been saying this for months or even years, to no avail. We can then ask why the partner's plaint has gone unheeded—an interesting relationship dynamic of its own.

"Working around" the patient's functional limitation to create the most satisfying sex possible will not only help resolve a patient's desire problem but also help resolve the functional problem as well.

PROMOTING NEW SEXUAL CONCEPTS

One of our therapeutic tasks with desire patients is restructuring their vocabulary and belief system about various aspects of sexuality. The following concepts, probably new to your patients, are important parts of this restructuring.

The Source of Arousal: Ourselves

Most of us who grow up in our overly romantic culture believe that someone else turns us on, that is, that our arousal is in the hands of our lover. If we aren't as aroused as we want to be (an important source of inhibited desire), we feel justified blaming this on our partner's deficiencies.

Therapists should promote, instead, the understanding that we turn ourselves on, whether we are conscious of it or not. We can choose to focus on what we like about our lover's body, or on its imperfections; on what we hope to enjoy in sex, or on what we probably won't get; on what we can ask for and perhaps get, or on the inconvenience of having to ask.

Furthermore, we can enjoy who the person is inside our lover's body, or we can compare that body to others that are younger or more shapely. We can look at ourselves and enjoy the sexuality we bring to an encounter, or we can feel self-conscious about our body, experience, and limitations.

It is our task, not our lover's, to create desire in us. Our lover's job is to support us in feeling the desire we want to feel. Lingerie, candles, and sweet words are nice, but they should not be the first step. They are the second—we ourselves provide the first. This perspective puts responsibility for desire on the shoulders of patients, where it belongs, and helps them realize that they are not passive objects in their lovers' hands (a lack of control that, unconsciously, can be very scary anyway).

The common passivity model allows people to blame their partner or relationship when the first blush of passion inevitably declines; the concept of responsibility makes this decline a normal developmental challenge that people must master if they wish to enjoy a sexual relationship past its initial stage. The concept also supports Partner A when Partner B says "You are too fat [or too inhibited, and so on] for me to desire."

Conditions for Good Sex

In his updated classic, *The New Male Sexuality*, Bernie Zilbergeld described how people have conditions for good sex. Expanding on this, we can note that these conditions fall into three categories: conditions about myself (for example, I like to be clean and feel healthy); about my partner (for example, I like her to feel trusting of me and be willing to talk during sex); and about the environment (for example, I like privacy, plenty of space, and the option of making lots of noise when I climax).

Each of us has a unique set of conditions that facilitate our desire, arousal, and satisfaction. Yet many people believe that their bodies and minds should be able to function sexually regardless of circumstances. By explaining how we all have conditions, and helping patients explore theirs, we can normalize their frustrating experiences and support them in creating sexual situations in which they will feel desire.

Communication

Under the sway of the popular idea that sex should be "natural and spontaneous," many people believe that sex should require little or no communication. If it does, these people believe they are with the wrong partner, or that love has declined, or that one or both of them are poor lovers.

For the vast majority of people, sex without communication—both in and out of bed—is unlikely to satisfy and in itself can create low desire. So can the fear of being judged for honestly sharing one's sexual preferences and needs.

We need to tell our patients that sexual communication is neither a burden nor an admission of inadequacy but rather an opportunity to energize a partnership and share information. The only kind of sex that is "natural and spontaneous" is strictly procreative—with no expectations of closeness, emotional satisfaction, or pleasure. Considering that the overwhelming majority of sex is done for nonprocreative reasons, we should approach it with appropriate expectations and skills. These include communicating what we want, how we feel, and any concerns we have about our adequacy or our partner's experience. Communication helps support desire in two ways: it makes the sex more enjoyable, and it helps people feel less isolated and anxious.

POWER DYNAMICS

Part of treating problems of desire is addressing the power dynamics in a relationship. Analogous to Gresham's law in economics (bad currency drives out good currency), the partner who is less interested in sex typically controls the frequency and content of the sexual relationship. This may be an unintended consequence of other factors, a conscious grab for power, or some of each.

Some people may play out this dynamic by deliberately withholding sex; a partner also may use sex to manipulate, guilt-trip, or barter for favors, forgiveness, or agreements. We can also see power dynamics at work when people try to use sex to deal with what's going on in the rest of the relationship.

PETER AND MARIA

One example was Peter and Maria, a nice couple in their late thirties. For much of their marriage, sex had been satisfactory. The trouble started, I realized, when Maria received a big promotion and salary increase at work. As Peter felt threatened, his desire waned. At the same time, Maria's desire increased. She was enjoying being powerful, and wanted to experiment in new areas of life, including sex. On the other hand, she bought into Peter's accusations that she wanted sex all the time, and in kinky ways, "like your new high-class friends." It was a dangerous combination, with sad results.

Therapy involved helping Peter acknowledge feeling resentful about Maria's success—which he didn't think he had a right to, because they needed the money Maria was now making—and helping Maria not rescue him by agreeing that her desire was wrong. She also had some guilt about her glee at finally "beating" him at the income game, which I normalized.

When they could deal with these feelings verbally, their sex life resumed in a cooperative, nurturing way. In fact, they were able to use sex to heal themselves—he to feel strong and valued, she to feel she could be strong and surrender at the same time. I helped Maria experience her sexual power as an asset of the couple, not as a problem; this helped reduce her guilt considerably.

We can often be helpful by reminding patients that the power games they play in bed do not necessarily reflect the power arrangements in the rest of their relationship. I recall one very loving couple fiercely devoted to their truly egalitarian relationship. They both enjoyed dominant-submissive games in bed— duke and maid, policeman and prostitute, coach and cheerleader—but were so worried about what the games "meant" that they tried to extinguish them. Doing so, unfortunately, took the heat right out of the sex for them.

I explained that these erotic power games could be perfectly harmless—that their bed was a sacred space in which they could do what they liked without affecting or expressing the rest of their "secular" lives. I could only do this, of course, because I was not caught up, as many therapists are, in the idea that there is some pathological "meaning" of consenting dominance-submission sexual games.

Our therapy included getting the couple to decide that they—not some political ideology or what the neighbors might think—were the final arbiters of the acceptability of their sexual relationship. Once we did this, their desire rebounded, and they completed therapy soon after.

Many patients are concerned that the flexible, sensual, self-referenced model of sexuality that we promote as an antidote to performance anxiety and inhibited desire is "immoral," un-Christian, and so on. Rather than shy away from or apologize about this, we should address this question directly.

I tell patients for whom this is an issue that "God made you sexual, and God wants you to have sex—Godly sex. That means sex that fits your ethical values—honest, responsible, caring, consenting. When God looks at human sexual behavior, God doesn't care what part of one person's body is inside what part of another person's body; God cares what you have in your heart when you're being sexual."

Note that this not only relieves anxiety about having "bad" sex but also empowers people to decide for themselves whether their sexual expression is wholesome, instead of giving the decision to outside authority.

Because of traditional religion's role in pathologizing healthy lust and sexual expression, we should ask all patients about their religious background and current practice. We should also remember that sexuality is a divine gift that was created for human satisfaction.

CLINICAL TECHNIQUES

At this point we have examined a variety of clinical strategies and approaches. There are a few other helpful techniques that deserve explicit discussion.

Ban on Intercourse or Other Sexual Expressions

One of the most common sources of inhibited desire in both men and women is performance anxiety. In particular, patients of both genders fear failing at intercourse. Men fear they will not get or keep an erection, or that they will ejaculate too quickly, before their partner can climax. Women fear they will not become aroused quickly enough and that their climax will take too long or not happen at all. Desire cannot bloom in such an arid environment.

When intercourse (or any other sexual activity, such as fellatio) is the focus of great sexual anxiety, temporarily eliminating it from people's sexual repertoire can help them quite a bit. It encourages them to try a broader range of sexual activities, which they can often enjoy with less anxiety. Thus, banning intercourse for a period of time can be very effective. Keep in mind the following:

- Don't begin the ban too early in the course of therapy; compliance requires patients' trust.

- Make sure patients know the ban is on *intercourse only*, not "sex" (this is the whole point).

- Make the ban long enough that the patient(s) would ordinarily have, or struggle about having, intercourse—usually six or more weeks.

- If you are working with a couple, have each partner take *100 percent* responsibility for the agreement, not 50 percent. This makes it less likely that one partner will push the other for intercourse; if he or she does, the other can refuse more easily.

- Make sure you process the ban in detail during each of the first few sessions after assigning it, and at least briefly each subsequent week.

- Remember that compliance is not the goal—learning about sex and relationship behavior is the goal. Noncompliance is not failure; indeed, with low-desire couples, it may be a paradoxical success.

Masturbation

Masturbation provides a wonderful opportunity to experiment with sex, including technique, fantasy, self-nurturing, and observing one's emotions. For people who simply refuse to make noise with a partner, masturbation provides a chance to experiment with vocalizing during arousal, which makes orgasm easier and more satisfying. For people who are embarrassed to be touched in particular places, masturbation can be an opportunity to explore those places and make new decisions. People can even experiment with giving a partner directions when they caress themselves alone.

Discuss the concept of masturbation with patients before giving home assignments that include it. Remind them that masturbation isn't a substitute for sex, it *is* sex. Give explicit permission to use toys—vibrators, lingerie, baths, erotica—and to take time. The heightened sensitivity and increased self-knowledge that usually result help support sexual desire for a partner.

Hand Massage

This couple exercise provides a controlled setting in which patients can experience initiating, surrender, giving and receiving verbal feedback, and sensual focus, as well as any discomfort that accompanies these activities. Each person agrees to initiate the homework once before the next session. During the assignment there should be no radio, TV, or music on, and phones should not be answered. The instructions are as follows:

> The person initiating invites the partner to do the homework now or at a specific time later. The partner either agrees to the initiator's time or suggests an alternative. At the agreed-upon time, the initiator puts a small amount of lotion on his hands, takes one of the partner's hands, and massages it for his *own* pleasure. He experiences the shape, color, textures, and so on and rubs in several different ways. The partner should not comment except if something hurts or tickles, in which case the initiator should change what he is doing.
>
> After two minutes of this, the initiator should switch to the partner's other hand, again applying a small amount of lotion. This time the partner should comment a great deal: "That feels good; that would feel better in the following way; that is uncomfortable"; and so on. The initiator should change what he is doing to accommodate the partner's feedback.
>
> After both of the partner's hands are done, both members of the couple should take a few deep breaths, shake out their hands, switch roles, and start over, repeating the process.
>
> After doing so, partners should tell each other one thing about their experience—something they liked, disliked, thought of, were surprised about, and so on.
>
> Sometime between that day and the next therapy session, the person who was asked to participate in the exercise switches roles and becomes the initiator. The exercise unfolds exactly as before, with the roles reversed.

You should make it clear that patients cannot "fail" this assignment: whether they enjoy it or not, understand it or not—in fact, do it or not—they will get value from it and have plenty to discuss at the next session. Be sure to process this at the start of the next session: Did you do it? What did you like and dislike about it? Were you more comfortable receiving the massage or giving it? Hearing the feedback, or giving it? Did you actually *experi-*

ence the activity in your hands, or were you mostly observing, thinking, and feeling? Therapist and patients can then draw parallels to the couple's sexual situation.

COUNTERTRANSFERENCE

As therapists, it is very important for us to monitor our own thoughts, fantasies, reactions, and inner experience when dealing with patients' sexuality, particularly with desire issues. Few of us feel completely secure about sexuality in our personal lives, making us vulnerable to projecting feelings or needs onto our patients.

We are probably having difficulty if we ask patients for unnecessary details of their sexual experiences or fantasies; if we criticize patients' choices because of moral rather than pragmatic considerations; if we take sides in couples' conflicts or consider one partner far more to blame than the other; if we feel enraged by the actions of patients, their partners, or their parents; and, of course, if we have *persistent* sexual fantasies about or make sexual comments to patients. Physical sexual contact with a patient in or out of session indicates extremely poor clinical judgment; the therapist has lost control of him- or herself, regardless of the patient's ostensible "needs." In many states, it is also illegal.

Similarly, we should observe how we deal with the issue of what is "normal." We should be extremely hesitant to define normality for patients in any arena—spending, neatness, recreation, and so on—and this is especially true for sexuality. Any eagerness to instruct patients in what is sexually normal is probably a reflection of our own anxiety or anger. If we have a good reason to present our sexual values or morality, we should clearly label them as our values, as distinct from facts. Any belief, for example, that oral sex is disgusting or that pornography degrades women should rarely, if ever, be shared with patients; if a belief is shared, it should be done as an example of self-disclosure, not of clinical expertise or objectivity.

Finally, can you use appropriate sexual words, and helpfully reflect patients' sexual words and ideas? Although we are not required to use or reflect words that are slang ("cock") or extremely hostile ("frigid bitch"), we should be able to communicate on a level that patients find friendly, comfortable, and knowledgeable. Just as we want to talk about money and parenting in patients' language, we should be able to say "come" or "butt" when appropriate. If we are more uncomfortable about sex and sexual words than about more "polite" clinical subjects, we should pursue supervision, therapy, or other supportive work.

WHAT IS THE PROGNOSIS FOR DESIRE PROBLEMS?

In general, the prognosis for desire problems is guarded. The reasons for this are that some percentage of each person's desire is biologically determined—and no one is sure exactly how much, or which parts; also, the dynamics behind changes in sexual desire include a variety of deep-seated fears (of intimacy, dependency, physical contact, loss of control, rejection, damnation, pregnancy, and so on). In many cases, therefore, changing the frequency, content, or object of desire is only possible through fundamental change in the patient's character or relationship. Many patients simply do not want to change the basic building blocks of their lives. When a patient is willing to work on such fundamental changes, therapy is usually long and involved. In discussing the prognosis of desire problems, I am considering therapy focused specifically on the sexual issues, which lasts between ten and thirty sessions. As a general rule, the prognosis for specific situations is as follows:

- *Desire discrepancy.* If the contrast appears constitutional to those involved (that is, the desire levels of the partners have *not* changed during the relationship) rather than situational (it started after a bankruptcy, birth of a baby, disclosure of an affair, and so on), the prognosis is *poor.* If it appears to be situational rather than constitutional, the prognosis is *better.*

• *Joint low desire.* If two partners have mutually lost their desire for each other (as opposed to only one partner changing), the prognosis ranges from *very poor* to *good,* depending on the underlying dynamics.

• *Inhibited desire.* The prognosis is highly variable, depending on the underlying dynamics. If patients have a great deal of underlying anger toward their partner, *and* can acknowledge it *and* are willing to work to resolve it, the prognosis is *medium.* A patient who cannot acknowledge this anger or doesn't want to let it go has a *very poor* prognosis. Inhibited desire sometimes reflects boredom with the current sexual relationship, boredom along with the assumption that nothing will change. At other times it represents what lay people call a lack of "chemistry" that has existed from a relationship's beginning. These are very different situations. The prognosis for the former is mixed and for the latter is *extremely poor.*

• *Panic/aversion.* For those who do not want to change but are in therapy at the demand of a partner or because they think they "should" be, the prognosis is *very poor.* For those who really want to overcome their sexual aversion, particularly if it can be traceable to a specific trauma, the prognosis is slightly *better.*

• *Hyperactive desire.* If this is accompanied by impaired reality-testing or deep rage, the prognosis is *poor.* If it is part of an alcoholic syndrome, the prognosis depends on confronting and reducing the alcohol abuse. If the hyperactive desire is an expression of mild forms of self-destructiveness that the patient can recognize, the prognosis is *good.*

໑ৄ

Working with sexual desire disorders is often difficult. It is also fascinating and rewarding. Sexual interaction is one of the joys of being human, and loss of desire is a loss of joy and the potential for relatedness on a deep and meaningful level. Helping patients to rediscover their desire for intimate and pleasurable sex is one of the great satisfactions of being a psychotherapist.

Let me close with four basic assumptions about sexuality that guide my understanding of sex and sex therapy:

1. Sex should always be consenting in the broadest sense; if it is, any nonmanipulative sexual activity is acceptable.
2. Sex is far more than intercourse.
3. Nonprocreative sex has its own value.
4. Men and women have a vast, life-affirming sexual potential.

NOTES

P. 201, *Some people leave marriages:* Schnarch, D. (1993). Personal communication.

P. 205, *Since the late 1980s, authors such as Patrick Carnes:* Carnes, P. (1989). *Contrary to love.* Minneapolis: Compcare.

P. 226, *In his updated classic, . . . Bernie Zilbergeld described:* Zilbergeld, B. (1992). *The new male sexuality.* New York: Bantam.

FOR FURTHER READING

Barbach, L. (1993). *The pause.* New York: Dutton.

Carnes, P. (1989). *Contrary to love.* Minneapolis: Compcare.

Sheehy, G. (1992). *The silent passage.* New York: Random House.

Zilbergeld, B. (1992). *The new male sexuality.* New York: Bantam.

8

TREATMENT OF AROUSAL AND ORGASMIC DISORDERS

Randolph S. Charlton and Faith W. Brigel

This chapter is designed to help you treat the spectrum of arousal and orgasmic disorders. We'll present a theoretical overview and a series of illustrative case examples. We encourage you to be honest with yourself and curious about what it's like to be in your patients' shoes.

ISSUES OF DIAGNOSIS

We've only been able to provide adequate treatment for disorders of arousal and orgasm for about the past twenty-five years—not a very long time, considering the centuries mankind has been getting turned on and off. In order to treat these disorders, you must first recognize and understand them.

Making a diagnosis of an arousal or orgasmic disorder may seem simple on the surface. If patients aren't becoming sexually excited, they have an arousal disorder. If they can't have an orgasm, they have an orgasmic disorder. This common sense is often accurate, but you'll inevitably come across situations in which the obvious isn't the answer.

Differentiation of Physical and Psychological Causes

In general, individuals who can successfully masturbate have their "plumbing and wiring" intact and are suffering from a psychologically based dysfunction. If a man is unable to maintain an erection during masturbation, there is significant likelihood that his problems involve some degree of physical impairment. Similarly, a woman who once masturbated pleasurably and successfully who loses the ability even though she is interested, may have a physical problem. Of note is the fact that individuals with organic causes of sexual difficulties often experience intermittent periods of better function. It's quite possible for a man with erectile problems secondary to multiple sclerosis, for example, to have periods when he gets and maintains a firm erection. Thus, brief periods of adequate function do not in themselves eliminate the possibility of a physically caused sexual disorder.

Differential Diagnosis: Desire, Arousal, or Orgasmic Disorder?

A number of patients with an arousal or orgasmic disorder present with a narrative focused on lack of desire. Your history is the key to understanding whether the problem began with lack of arousal, lack of orgasm, or lack of desire. Any sexual disorder can turn into lack of desire when an individual's patience and tolerance disappear. Thus a man with premature ejaculation may appear in your office complaining of impotence or lack of interest in sex. If his difficulties are of long enough duration he may have all but forgotten that it all began with his inability to control his ejaculatory reflex.

Unless disappointment and failure have resulted in depression and resignation—a situation that is more likely to happen the longer the symptoms are present—patients with arousal and orgasmic disorders are interested in sex. They will tell you that they'd like to have sex, or at the very least, they used to desire sex until they lost hope of enjoying the experience.

Once in a while, you may see a woman who is lubricating but for psychological reasons is disconnected from the subjective experience of arousal. Physiologically she does not have a sexual disorder, but psychologically she does. This kind of dissociation can be connected to previous abuse situations and is seen in borderline and hysterical personality disorders.

CAUSES OF AROUSAL AND ORGASMIC DISORDERS

A variety of medications and diseases can lead to an arousal or orgasmic disorder. You can refer to Chapters Two and Four, where these problems are reviewed. Other causes of arousal or orgasmic disorders include inadequate stimulation, myths and misinformation, interpersonal conflict, anxiety, and shame and guilt. We will discuss each of these in turn.

Inadequate Stimulation

Adequate sexual stimulation is a mix of physical sensation, mental imagery, and emotion. Such issues as sensitivity to touch, the kind of touch, and the length of the touching are the physical determinants of whether an experience is stimulating or not. A woman whose partner only touches her genitals for a few moments before proceeding to intercourse is not likely to become fully aroused. A man with premature ejaculation will likely tolerate less genital stimulation than the average. Some women can only reach orgasm with the particular focused touch of oral sex, others with the knowing caress of their own fingers. What's adequate stimulation for one individual might be too much or too little for another.

Sexual excitement occurs in psychical and emotional context. Sexual fantasy is a powerful aphrodisiac, and arousal can occur without any touch at all. The perfect touch by the wrong person will be exciting but distasteful, and even repulsive. The more you know about what your patient finds arousing, both in fantasy and in reality, the more you'll be able to understand how her sexual experience works.

Myths and Misinformation

Even in an age where sexual information is available at the local library, sex remains associated with sin and secrets. Some secrets are kept because of religious prohibition, some because of cultural power games, some because of shame and guilt. A few secrets, perhaps the most basic ones, are kept because sex, in order to work, requires at least a bit of mystery.

When sex, secrets, and power mix, sexual myths create pressures that can interfere with arousal and orgasm. Following is a list of the myths we hear most often:

- *Girls and women should not be sexual.* Alfred Kinsey is reputed to have said, "Ninety-eight percent of men in our study said they'd masturbated. The other two percent lied." There is ample evidence that the prevalence of masturbation among young women is increasing, but it is far below 98 percent. In our culture it's normal for a man to be sexual. Boys pursue girls. Girls have to defend themselves. A girl's virginity is "lost," even if she wasn't looking for it. Thus women are more vulnerable to being shamed about their sexual appetites than men.

- *A woman's sexual response should be like a man's.* Believing as our culture does—that the male sexual response is the more basic, perhaps more healthy one—women have been encouraged to judge their sexual experience based on a man's yardstick. When this happens, a woman is expected to become aroused more rapidly than her body will allow. When a woman does not become excited as quickly as her male partner, either the man, the woman, or both may feel disappointed and frustrated. This problem can be cured with patience, persistence, and communication, but often all three are lacking.

- *There are healthy vaginal orgasms and unhealthy clitoral orgasms.* Though it has generally lost credence, the myth of the vaginal orgasm still lurks in the corner of the cultural mind. Freud distinguished the vaginal from the clitoral orgasm, believing that the former was a sign of a healthy adult woman, the latter a sign of a psychological arrest in development. Research has dispelled the notion that there is a physiological basis for the distinction between orgasms, and for the most part women and men have abandoned their concerns about the issue.

• *A real man can have sex with anybody, anytime.* Some men believe they should be able to perform sexually regardless of the nature of the relationship. There are situations where it is not reasonable to open oneself up to sexual intimacy. A man who believes that he should be able to have intercourse no matter what will disregard the messages he receives from his feelings and forge ahead, sometimes to find himself unable to perform. This can result in an ever-deepening spiral of anxiety and sexual failure.

• *A real man is dominating, penetrating, and incisive.* A related notion about masculinity is that "real" men aren't passive, receptive, or unsure of themselves. Many men fear their own passive-receptive wishes, finding them feminine, unacceptable, and likely to bring ridicule and shame. Pseudo-homosexual panic is related to this phenomenon. It occurs when a man is afraid of the culturally nonmasculine aspects of his personality, and though he does not experience erotic attraction to members of his own sex, he fears that his feelings and behavior are indicative of weakness and "latent homosexuality."

• *There are right and wrong ways to be sexually aroused.* An individual is the only one who really knows what's exciting for her. Some women can't reach orgasm during intercourse without direct manual stimulation of their clitoris. This is not abnormal and only becomes a sexual problem when it is believed to be one. The same is true for a man who finds oral sex particularly exciting. There is no simple answer for the problems of sexual predilection, prejudice, and misinformation. Our general stance is that the more information an adult has about the nature and function of his own body, the more able he will be to make those sexual choices that are morally, emotionally, and physically right for him.

- *Sexual fantasies that are not about normal sex are abnormal.* There are legal and religious prohibitions about what is sexually normal, but normal sex is a myth all its own. In reality, sex is most "healthy" when it provides pleasure, minimizes displeasure, and doesn't injure anyone. This leaves a lot of room for fantasy and friction. We've spent years listening to people's sexual fantasies, and we can tell you that if it's possible to imagine it, someone, somewhere, is getting aroused by it. However, a woman who masturbates to images of rape does not necessarily want to be raped. In fact, that would be decidedly rare. A man who imagines being caught masturbating and becomes aroused by the idea does not necessarily want this to happen in real life. He would probably be terribly ashamed if it did.

Interpersonal Conflict

Anxiety, anger, shame, and guilt are powerful anti-aphrodisiacs. In situations where these conflicted feelings aren't present at the time an arousal problem begins, they often appear. Sex is one of the ways people have of sharing their bodies and feelings, of discharging anger and reconnecting in the face of life's pain. When sex isn't working well, one of the major communication lines between members of a couple isn't working either. Add to this the physiological and emotional frustration of a poor sex life, the propensity for both partners to blame the other, and the loss of self-esteem that inevitably tags along with sexual failure, and just about any couple is going to have trouble.

Women, in contrast to men, can have intercourse even if they are not aroused. The use of a vaginal lubricant allows a woman to participate in sex without the natural lubrication that would be produced were she to be aroused. Some men, unaware of or uncaring about this fact, ignore the possibility that their partner's use of a lubricant means that she is not becoming aroused.

Each partner's reactions are a vital link to the other's sexual response. There are times when a sexual problem is a function of a partner who is unable or unwilling to engage intimately.

MICHAEL AND CAROL WARNER

Michael, a forty-two-year-old physician, and his wife, Carol, came to therapy because Michael could no longer maintain an erection. He was able to masturbate and to become aroused when fantasizing about sex, but when he and Carol would get together, his erection would all but disappear.

Michael was perplexed. As far as he could tell, their relationship was pretty good. Their kids were doing well in high school. They had enough money. He liked his work. He loved Carol. The cause of the problem, when it eventually became apparent, was a shock to Michael. Carol's father had died in the last year, and she'd been understandably glum. Both she and Michael thought it was normal mourning, but secretly Carol feared there was more to it. She had become anxious about sex. She was embarrassed and scared and didn't want anyone, even Michael, to know that sexual images of her father were appearing in her mind's eye during sex. This had never happened to her before.

Sexual communication, especially in an intimate relationship, can be both subtle and powerful. In this case, Michael's penis "knew" more about the situation than Michael did. Carol was relieved to be able to talk about her fears, and Michael's understanding response helped her understand that he still loved her. Michael's sexual arousal problems abated when he understood Carol's struggle.

Anxiety

Anxiety leads to fight-or-flight reactions, to defense and protection, all of which are antithetical to sexual arousal. A parent worrying about a sick child coughing loudly in an adjacent bedroom is going to be distracted and less than usually interested in sexual play. A woman with a conscious fear that intercourse will be painful is going to have a difficult time remaining sexually aroused as the possibility of penetration nears. A man with deep-seated concerns about his inadequate masculinity may be totally unable to become sexually excited.

Anxiety can be mild, moderate, or severe, as these examples indicate. It can be situational, short lived, and easily forgotten, or it can be a constant and debilitating aspect of an individual's personality. There are as many causes of anxiety as there are things that can go wrong in an individual's life.

Many fears are generated in the outside world. They are the "stressors" of *DSM-IV*: financial worries, divorce, loss of a job, a sick child. Remember that positive experiences, such as a job promotion, buying a new house, and having a child, also generate stress. These nonsexual concerns are often the proximate cause of sexual difficulties; they should never be dismissed as irrelevant. Sometimes the best "sex therapy" involves helping a patient to manage a difficult life event that has little or nothing directly to do with sex.

Anxieties that are ascribed to the external world by a neurotic, conflicted personality can be irrational, deep seated, and generalized. General psychodynamic wisdom suggests that unconscious anxiety originates in childhood. Childhood fears—of separation, of dependency and autonomy, of power and control—can live on to affect the sexual life of an adult.

Sometimes it is sex itself that is the patient's major worry. Fears that sex will not work, for whatever reason, exist in almost all patients with arousal and orgasmic disorders, and it is important to address these apprehensions directly. What is it the patient *specifically* believes will not work? Her body? His penis? His feelings? A man who is convinced that he cannot please his partner may look the same on the outside as a man who is afraid he will not be able to obtain and maintain an erection because his body does not work properly. A woman who has intrusive thoughts about a previously traumatic sexual experience may have the same physiological problems becoming aroused as a woman who fears that her body is unattractive. The only way to know what's going on inside the patient is to talk about it.

Performance anxiety is a particular kind of distress that is often associated with sexual problems. It is, as the name suggests, a fear of not being able to perform adequately. Most often it is described in the literature as a rather superficial form of anxiety that can be alleviated by the removal of the pressure to perform, but in our experience, fears about performance can stem from any developmental level and can be mild, moderate, or severe. A useful way of thinking about performance anxiety is that it is what happens when a person can't trust that the natural sexual reactions of his body will work properly. Once a person loses trust in the natural function of the body, he inevitably loses touch with sexual arousal. The deeper and longer-lasting the lack of trust, the more severe the sexual problem.

Shame and Guilt

Unwanted but perhaps unavoidable intruders into everyone's sexual life, shame and guilt are particularly difficult: they not only generate their own brand of painful affect but also even the possibility of their appearance induces anxiety.

When a patient with an arousal or orgasmic disorder comes into your office, shame will come in with them. Feelings of not being normal, of not being a healthy man or woman, further distance sexual pleasure. Shame is inhibitory. It makes people want to hide, to disappear. There is no joy, no excitement in uncovering one's body if one is ashamed of it. Shame takes away the freedom to explore and enjoy sexuality.

Shame can be a response to a sexual dysfunction, or it can be the cause of one. Issues such as weight loss or gain, aging, and loss of hair or skin tone can invoke a shame in one's physical self, leading to an inability to enjoy sex. The shame need not come directly from one's own self-image. On more than a few occasions, we've seen the scornful criticism of a partner lead to a sexual problem.

Guilt, like shame, is a powerful anti-aphrodisiac. Whereas shame is a feeling that the self is defective, guilt involves a sense that the self needs to be punished. It is a response to the belief that one has done something wrong, transgressed some boundary, caused some harm that is against the person's moral code. The guilty person requires some form of punishment and will often find a way to enact it. Confession and atonement operate on this principle. How many Catholics first begin to think and talk about sex with the words, "Forgive me, Father, for I have sinned"?

A common form of guilt-induced self-punishment is to remove sexual pleasure from one's life. If this process is unconscious, then the individual only knows that she isn't enjoying sex, not that she requires herself not to enjoy it.

Sexual arousal requires a free and safe space in which to exist. When the four horsemen of sexual failure—Anxiety, Anger, Shame, and Guilt—appear on the scene, they create a negative feedback loop in which failure begets more failure.

TREATMENT STRATEGY

Strategy is a concept one might think is better suited to chess or the military, but it's also appropriate here. We conceptualize strategy as understanding the dynamics underlying the sexual problem and framing our interventions accordingly. The strategy behind all forms of treatment for sexual arousal and orgasmic disorders involves four general steps:

1. Remove or alleviate physical causative factors.
2. Remove or diminish the proximate cause of the dysfunction.
3. Remove or diminish the deep causes of the disorder.
4. Create successful sexual experiences.

To illustrate these four steps, let's return to the example of the Warners.

MICHAEL AND CAROL WARNER

First, the couple's history as well as physical and laboratory examinations told us that Michael and Carol's problems were psychological in origin, so there was no need in this case to deal with organic difficulties.

Second, the proximate cause of Carol's arousal disorder was the shame and anxiety generated by images of her father that appeared while she was making love. Carol bravely discussed her intrusive thoughts and distracting images in the initial therapy session. Michael expressed his support and love, and asked what he could do. Carol started crying, and he went over and held her.

Neither Michael nor Carol was ready to jump back into being sexual, but from that moment on, Carol never again had a distracting image of her father during sex. It's not always this easy, but discussion and sharing of anxiety can be a powerful source of reassurance and support. Genuine love and caring in a relationship has a healing effect far greater than anything a therapist can do. Had Carol's anxiety about the appearance of fantasies of her father continued, we would have considered several courses of action: (1) continue to examine the issues involved in couple/sex therapy, (2) refer Carol for individual therapy, or (3) use a very small dose of an anxiolytic medication (Inderal, Xanax, or Librium, for instance) before she engaged in sex.

Third, the deeper roots of Carol's sexual conflicts were addressed in the course of couple/sex therapy. She quickly made a connection between the loss of her father and her desire to be held and comforted by Michael. In her mind, Carol was mixing up soothing and sex, mixing up the past with the present, and finding that they didn't go together very well. Separating her needs and feelings for Michael from those that belonged with her father allowed Carol more freedom to love and be loved in her marriage.

For his part, Michael realized that his erectile difficulties were a manifestation of his connection to Carol. He'd never before understood how deeply he cared for her and how he'd made her "a part of himself." He also realized that he'd been operating unconsciously. Unable to separate his feelings from hers, his body was left holding the bag.

Michael resolved to become more conscious and more expressive of his feelings. Carol dedicated herself to being more open and honest with Michael. This was enough to resolve their sexual problem, because once their anxiety and fear were diminished, Carol and Michael were able to perform the fourth step—to create a slew of successful experiences—on their own.

Unfortunately, this isn't always the case. One of the more difficult aspects of therapy is helping your patients create successful sexual experiences for themselves. What is a successful sexual experience? Is sex successful if both partners reach orgasm? If they feel close and loving afterwards? Both? Is your therapy successful if an arousal disorder is eliminated and the couple decides to get a divorce? If a man's premature ejaculation is cured and he has promiscuous sex and gets AIDS?

Defining successful sex is not a simple endeavor. In fact, we don't think there is only one definition. A major aspect of every therapy for arousal and orgasm problems is helping your patients to find their own answer to the question of what is successful sex.

An Integrated Model

We began with the Masters and Johnson approach to treatment back when it was all shiny and new. It remains the foundation of much of what we do, but like Grandfather's ax, which has had three new handles and two new heads, our vision of sex therapy has changed a bit.

We've come to think of Masters and Johnson's paradigm as one that attempts to protect patients from themselves while they watch and feel what their bodies do with potentially adequate sexual stimulation. It's a romantic and optimistic view of sexual function in which the innate pleasure of sex is believed to be powerful enough to pull an individual toward a more healthy, more enjoyable relationship once the inhibitory forces of anxiety and ignorance are removed.

Our experience suggests a more complex view of human nature and sexual conflict. There are men who have held on to erectile difficulties because they were afraid not of failure but of success. We've seen women who can't become sexually aroused with their husbands but get excited just thinking about seducing a stranger. We've seen couples who have no problem having sex, but can't sit down and have an intimate conversation about what really matters to them. These patients have convinced us that performance anxiety and ignorance are not enough to explain such tenacious and self-destructive behaviors.

We're either eclectic therapists or thieves. We've borrowed from just about everybody. Masters and Johnson. Alan Wheelis and Stephen Levine. David Schnarch and Roy Schafer. Avodah Offit, Lonnie Barbach, Dr. Ruth, Anne Rice, and Erica Jong. Freud, Jung, Kohut, and Robert Stoller. Behaviorists Joseph LoPiccolo and Charles Lobitz. James Joyce, D. H. Lawrence, Vladimir Nabokov, the Marquis de Sade, and some Victorian fellow by the name of Anonymous.

It takes more work to understand, organize, and use a variety of therapeutic approaches, but in the end, we think this will allow you to work more effectively with a wider variety of patients.

We'll go over each aspect of the therapy of arousal and orgasmic disorders with you: beginning and framing the therapy, working with anxiety, using homework and other specific techniques, and dealing with countertransference. We provide case examples of each disorder.

BEGINNING AND FRAMING THERAPY

After your evaluation and decision to begin therapy, you must decide if you want to work with a set number of sessions or if you'll leave the issue open and figure out when to end therapy after you've had a chance to see how the work progresses.

Open-Ended Versus Time-Limited Therapy

Managed care contracts often limit a patient's length of treatment. We've been pressured to use time-limited therapy because of this, but we think it's vital to make your clinical decisions based on the good of your patients.

Some couples or individuals are reluctant to participate in an open-ended contract. The motivation for this varies—concern about finances, fear of dependency, or genuine desire and belief that a specific sexual problem can be resolved in a few months' time.

Twelve or fifteen sessions may be enough to resolve a patient's symptoms

- When anxiety is mild to moderate and limited to the sexual arena.
- When the patient exhibits no significant psychopathology.
- When the sexual symptoms are of recent inception. As a general rule, the longer a patient has suffered from impotence or an arousal disorder, the more difficult and protracted the treatment. Three or four months is a problem of short duration. Six months to a year, moderate duration. Over a year, we consider long-term.
- When rapid (premature) ejaculation exists as the only symptom. This obviously depends on the individual and his relationship, if any.
- When a psychologically healthy woman has an uncomplicated arousal or orgasmic disorder.

In our experience, retarded ejaculation and long-standing impotence (over a year's duration) cannot be treated in a handful of sessions. The treatment of these disorders is often more complex than for other sexual disorders. The directed, homework-oriented format of sex therapy is sometimes useful with these disorders, but we've found that it is almost always necessary to combine this with psychodynamic work on the patient's underlying conflicts.

If the number of sessions is determined before therapy begins, then patients know that they will have ten, fifteen, or twenty meetings to resolve their problems. Behavioral therapists suggest that this puts pressure on clients to work hard and take therapy seriously. A significant drawback to limiting the number of sessions is that it creates its own form of performance anxiety. When possible, we prefer to leave the number of sessions open.

Frequency of Sessions

Masters and Johnson saw people at their clinic in St. Louis. Their patients took two or three weeks off from their lives and went to therapy every day. Some therapists still ask couples to take time off from work and concentrate on therapy, but the majority see patients once or twice a week. There are significant benefits to having the couple continue the regular routine of their lives. In practical terms, it is not always possible for both partners to take a two-week vacation at the same time. When couples participate in sexual therapy while maintaining their usual level of activities, they get used to incorporating sexual experience into their daily routine, which makes for an easier transition once the program is terminated.

Therapy Guidelines

In general, most therapists ask couples to agree to the following guidelines:

- The couple will come to their therapy sessions or pay for missed sessions.

- The couple will find time to be together without the distractions of television, social visits, phone calls, overnight guests, and so on.

- The couple will do their best to be open and honest.

- The couple will work to understand each other's perspective as best they can.

- If homework will be part of the therapy, the couple will endeavor to do what is agreed on during their sessions and will be willing to discuss their experience in the ensuing therapy session.

- They will have no sexual interaction during the course of therapy except what is agreed on in each session.

These guidelines are set up in order to reduce performance anxiety, make it less likely for a couple to reach beyond their capacity and unwittingly create a failure situation, and give them a clear understanding of what will be required during the therapy. Some therapists have the guidelines already written up, and go over them explicitly with each couple. We find that a dialogue about how your therapy works and what will be expected of your patients offers more opportunity to observe patients' reactions and to set the stage for the process of therapy than does a written contract.

ASSIGNING HOMEWORK

Many therapists who treat disorders of arousal and orgasm rely on homework assignments as the mainstay of their therapy. Others, David Schnarch among them, do not use homework at all. Our own position lies somewhere in between.

For those therapists who espouse homework, the crux of each exercise is that it be specifically designed to create a series of successful experiences. After the first homework exercise, the structure of each session is relatively similar. The beginning is used to go over the previous homework, the middle to deal with what did or did not happen in the course of the homework, and the latter part of the session to determine the next homework assignment.

Some therapists who use homework listen to their patients, evaluate what the patients are able to accomplish successfully, and assign the homework like a teacher. Other therapists prefer to create the homework with the help of the patients. That is, the therapist or one member of the couple makes a suggestion, and it's discussed as part of the therapy hour. This allows the couple to be more a part of the process. It also allows the therapist to get an idea of how accurately he or she has gauged the likes, dislikes, and anxiety tolerance of the couple.

Masters and Johnson devised a specific form of homework they called the sensate focus exercise. Basically, they wanted to direct patients' attention toward their immediate sensations and away from a preconceived notion of sexual success. They hoped in this way to diminish performance anxiety and allow the natural pleasure of touching and sexuality to pull the patients forward into successful sexual interactions. Masters and Johnson's five levels of sensate focus are as follows:

1. *Nondemand caressing and touching of the partner's body, excluding the breasts and genitals.* Partners take turns giving and receiving, usually for equal amounts of time. *Nondemand* refers to the fact that the receiver concentrates on what the touch feels like and does not ask for anything specific. He or she may ask that something unpleasant not be done.

2. *Caressing of the body, including the breasts.* The specific way of touching can be left open or described in minute detail, depending on the dynamics and anxieties of the couple. A woman who dislikes having her breasts "manhandled" may find herself able to relax if she knows her usually aggressive husband

will touch her gently. On the other hand, a woman who enjoys vigorous, even slightly painful touching of her breasts, who is paired with a gentle, feathery man, might benefit from an exercise focused on more zealous fondling.

3.   *Caressing, including genitals.* This exercise is not specifically intended to induce sexual feelings, though that might happen. Patients are asked what the touching feels like, not to note their erotic response. This way, patients are complying with the intent of the assignment even if they say the touching doesn't feel like anything. There is a bit of a paradox in this, as most patients find it difficult not to feel something sexual. Of course, this usually works in the service of reversing the sexual symptom.

4.   *Quiet containment of the penis in the vagina.* This exercise too is not intended to be exclusively aimed at erotic feelings. One valuable aspect of this experience is that it gives each partner the chance to slow down and really feel what it's like to be joined together. Intercourse is for some couples an experience of sweat and friction. These couples can benefit from having enough space to see what else is going on. Some couples are able to use this exercise to talk to each other while they are sexually connected. Many have never had a conversation during intercourse and are amazed at how intimate and connected they feel.

5.   *Intercourse without orgasm.* Sex directed solely toward orgasm can be like wolfing down a gourmet meal. The subtle tastes of each course are lost in the helter-skelter desire to get to dessert. Having intercourse with the knowledge that a climax is not to be part of the experience is designed to remove performance anxiety. More than one couple has found themselves unable to control themselves, and they've rushed on to screaming orgasms. This is fine on one level, especially if they were an anorgasmic couple. However, if the exercise is seen as an opportunity for communication and communion, then a rush to orgasm may be counterproductive.

The idea behind homework is to increase arousal and enjoyment while eliminating as much anxiety and performance demand as possible. If you stop and think about it, what the sensate focus exercise is trying to do is allow patients to reexperience the natural progression of sexual learning without the usual pressures to perform. There is a reason why most teenagers kiss and caress before "going all the way." It allows them time to experience the newness of almost overwhelming sexual sensations while adjusting to the interpersonal matrix in which these sensations occur. This is also one reason why masturbation is a "training ground" for later sexual activity. By removing the interpersonal matrix there is significantly less to worry about, significantly less to try and to control, and significantly more room to do whatever feels good.

Originally, Masters and Johnson prescribed the full sequence of sensate focus exercises for most disorders. Although it can be helpful to progress through each level of exercise, even therapists who are very much in favor of using homework feel that it's usually unnecessary to go through each of the five steps.

There's nothing magic about these five steps. There are as many variations as a creative therapist and creative couple can devise: facial, hand, and foot message; bodily caresses done wearing sexy underwear or covered only by a silk scarf; a licking exercise, starting with fingers and progressing to the neck, breasts, and genitals. The variations are limited only by the patient's fears, desires, and conflicts.

Our experience suggests that homework can be a helpful adjunct to therapy of arousal and orgasmic disorders, but not for every couple and not in every situation. It's important to think through why you might or might not use homework. There are cases when it's helpful, and others when it actually gets in the way. Further, if you decide to go ahead and use homework as part of therapy, you must look at the specific dynamics of each couple in order to decide what kind of homework makes sense. If you simply run through Masters and Johnson's five levels of sensate focus exercises, you'll probably do pretty well in the beginning, but when you hit a rough spot, you'll be in trouble.

WORKING WITH ANXIETY

Perhaps your first task as a sex therapist is to watch the level of anxiety in your patients very carefully. When you see anxiety increasing in an individual or a couple with an arousal or orgasmic disorder, you must do something. What are your choices?

Observation, Confrontation, Interpretation

Your first choice is to address the anxiety directly. If you believe your patients can deal with a conflict verbally, then work with them to resolve the anxiety. This is the basic tenet of all good psychotherapy and is just as important in sex therapy.

PETER AND ELLEN TJARNBERG

Newlyweds Peter and Ellen came to therapy to deal with Peter's inability to maintain an erection once the possibility of intercourse approached. Peter could masturbate to orgasm without difficulty. He could become excited and get an erection by kissing and petting with Ellen. While they were dating, he'd had orgasms when she touched him through his pants. Once married, they discovered that as soon as they undressed, Peter would lose his erection and was unable to recreate it.

Peter, an electrician, was not psychologically minded, but he knew that the idea of intercourse made him terribly anxious. His initial understanding was that he was anxious because he was afraid he'd fail. He said he'd always felt that way. Although this made some sense and was certainly true, it did little to explain how the problem got started or what exactly to do about it.

The therapist watched Peter carefully as Peter discussed his sexual responses. As long as he was talking about failure, Peter seemed reasonably relaxed, but when asked to talk about the times he was able to keep his erection and reach an orgasm, he sat up straight and said he was never able to do that. The therapist reminded Peter that he could masturbate and could have an orgasm if Ellen touched him while he still had his pants on. Peter's face grew red. He started breathing faster. He stuttered. Anxiety had arrived in force.

The therapist acknowledged Peter's discomfort and asked him to talk, if he could, about what it was like to be anxious, what he felt like.

Peter said he felt like running out of the office. As he talked on, he gradually grew more comfortable. His comments and associations were not directly sexual. He spoke about his family upbringing, about his father who was a minister, about how scared he was as a little kid that he might accidentally sin and be damned to hell. He laughed nervously, saying that he didn't believe that anymore.

Ellen was supportive and concerned, but also curious. The two of them didn't reach any resolution during the session, and the therapist made no effort to come up with something for them to do before the next session other than talk together about their relationship. In this context, Peter told Ellen that he wasn't sure, but maybe he felt that his "seed" was dirty and that he shouldn't, couldn't, get it on her. Now that the subject was broached, Peter opened up and brought his sexual fears into therapy. He felt embarrassed doing this, but with Ellen's help he persevered. The therapist's job was made considerably easier by Ellen's help. She repeatedly reassured Peter that she did not feel that sex, his genitals, or his semen were dirty. She said straight out that she didn't mind touching his semen or getting it on or in her. As far as she was concerned, semen was natural, and if God made nature, then semen was OK with both her and God.

With a bit of support and information about what's in seminal fluid (basically, Peter needed to know that it's sterile and doesn't have any urine in it), they made up their own homework. With an understanding that there would be no orgasm, they went quickly from nongenital touching to genital caressing. Peter had no trouble obtaining an erection. If anything, he had trouble not having an orgasm.

They decided to try mutual masturbation. Peter was a bit anxious about this. He now knew with his mind that his semen was clean and that Ellen didn't mind getting it on her, but his feelings weren't so cooperative. The first time Peter had an orgasm with Ellen, she held a washcloth over his penis to catch the ejaculate. Then, with some trepidation, they looked at it together. Ellen touched it with her finger. He got pretty nervous when she brought her finger to her mouth and tasted it, but when she laughed and said it was salty, he relaxed a bit.

The therapist's job in working with anxiety in this case was twofold: (1) keep Peter and Ellen moving, and (2) make sure they didn't move too fast or in the wrong direction. You can probably see from the way Ellen and Peter were able to get past his situational arousal disorder that they continued to progress, both in the intimacy and openness in their relationship and in the sexual pleasure they shared.

Slowing Down

If you believe that your patients cannot tolerate a direct discussion of mounting anxiety, then you can help them slow down.

One of the biggest mistakes in treating arousal and orgasmic disorders is allowing patients to move too rapidly from one stage to another. They may want to skip the easy stuff and move on to something more exciting. One member of the couple may try to pressure the other to do something that person is neither capable of nor ready to do.

Do your best to help your patients solidify one level of intimacy and sexuality before moving on to the next level. There are several ways to conceptualize this process. Cynthia McReynolds and David Schnarch's discussion in Chapter Five of the struggles involved in moving from a fusion position to a differentiated stance are quite relevant to the problems of anxiety in sexually directed therapy. Schnarch's book, *Constructing the Sexual Crucible*, is a helpful resource for anyone wishing to treat arousal and orgasmic disorders in the context of helping patients create intimate and passionate lives.

Empathy

Anxious patients benefit from support and understanding. Your third choice when patients become overwhelmed with apprehension is to empathize with their plight and support their healthy aspirations. Anxiety is inevitable in intimate situations. If you can help patients tolerate the natural anxiety of togetherness by understanding and acknowledging their feelings, you're doing the right thing.

SPECIFIC DISORDERS

Let's look now at each of the arousal and orgasmic disorders. We'll use case examples to give you a better idea of how various techniques and therapeutic strategies are used in real life. We'll also comment on women's sexuality groups as a form of therapy for problems of arousal and orgasm.

Female Arousal Disorder

AMELIA MARPLAN

Amelia, a twenty-six-year-old school teacher, was rarely able to become sexually aroused. She and her husband were seen by a therapist who was accustomed to assigning homework with her patients. Amelia was particularly anxious about showing her naked body to her husband. Evaluation suggested that her discomfort was not because she felt her body was unattractive but because she had grown up in family with a seductive father and a hypersexual mother who often went about the house partially clothed. Both her mother and father had affairs that Amelia knew about as a child. She once came home from school to find her mother on the living room couch having intercourse with a stranger.

Amelia always undressed in the bathroom and went to bed covered head to toe with a flannel nightgown. Her apprehension made it difficult for her to become sexually aroused. She had never masturbated and had never had an orgasm. When she had sex—always at her husband's insistence—she made sure the lights were off, and she stayed under the covers.

Amelia's therapist realized that the first homework should not involve bodily caressing, for that would be too much exposure and anxiety. Instead, she suggested that Amelia go into the bedroom, close the door, and lie on her bed naked while her husband was in the other room. Even this seemingly safe assignment made Amelia anxious. Knowing that her husband was right outside the door made her nakedness sexual and reminded her of her promiscuous mother.

The therapist understood Amelia's anxiety and didn't push too hard. She worked with Amelia to help her feel in control of how much she could handle. It took ten weeks and eight steps for Amelia to feel safe enough to lie on the bed unclothed with her husband. The eight steps were:

1. Husband in the other room, door closed; Amelia on the bed in bra and panties
2. Husband in the other room, door open
3. Husband, dressed, in the room with Amelia in her bra and panties, lights off
4. Husband, dressed, across the room; Amelia naked but covered by a towel, in candlelight
5. Husband, dressed, across the room; Amelia lowers the towel when she feels safe, in candlelight
6. Husband, naked, across the room, towel as needed, in candlelight

7. Husband, naked, lying on the bed next to Amelia, towel as needed, in candlelight
8. Amelia and her husband on the bed together, towel as needed, begin Masters and Johnson sensate focus exercises with non-genital caressing

There was discussion during each therapy session about Amelia's guilt and fear, and about her husband's frustration and apprehension that he would come on too strong. Amelia's anxiety returned with each new step. The therapist taught Amelia breathing and relaxation exercises. That and her husband's reassurance helped Amelia to tolerate her anxiety and move toward a new level of comfort with her body and sexuality.

When therapy progressed to genital touching, Amelia's fear returned full force. The therapist responded with a suggestion that they give each other a bath. The idea of cleanliness and the warmth and relative protection of a bubble bath allowed Amelia to be naked in a safe and enjoyable way, and at her request they did the next few exercises in the bathtub. Amelia was soon able to return to the bedroom. Her comfort with nakedness gradually increased, and she found herself more able to become sexually aroused. After thirty therapy sessions, Amelia was able to have an orgasm with her husband's touch.

The therapist in this case worked flexibly. She dealt effectively with issues of intimacy and passion, anxiety and shame, sexual fear and sexual pleasure.

Amelia's therapy is an example of why you cannot expect all client's to be "cured" in ten or twenty sessions. The therapist in this case was sensitive to Amelia's anxiety, and she responded appropriately. Had she tried to push Amelia to complete her "homework" in fewer sessions, the therapy would not have worked.

The prognosis for reversal of a female arousal disorder is fair to good in relatively short-term therapy. Factors that influence a positive prognosis include the woman's motivation to become more sexual, good health, no history of sexual or physical abuse, a stable personality structure, and a flexible and healthy relationship.

Female Orgasmic Disorder

BETH BELTZER

Beth, a twenty-one-year-old college student with an orgasmic disorder, had never had a sexual relationship. As a teenager she'd tried stimulating herself manually and had once used a vibrator, but each time she started to feel "tingles," she stopped.

Beth had been in therapy for several months when her therapist, a thirty-five-year-old woman psychologist, came for supervision. Therapy had begun with an aim toward helping Beth reach orgasm, but as their work progressed, Beth became sexually attracted to the therapist. The psychologist was uncomfortable with Beth's increasingly detailed fantasies and wanted help deciding if she should refer Beth to someone else.

The supervisor realized that it would be narcissistically mortifying for Beth to be referred to someone else at this point. She would undoubtedly feel rejected, and it was likely that she would assume, correctly, that it was her sexual needs and feelings that were responsible for the abandonment. If Beth's sexuality was under wraps before, it would be under a lead blanket after such a forced termination. The supervisor suggested that unless the psychologist was quite sure she couldn't manage her discomfort, she should continue seeing Beth, using supervision to help her understand her countertransference so that she could work with Beth's sexual desires.

Strong sexual feelings are an expected part of successful therapy for arousal and orgasmic disorders. Most often these feelings are directed at someone in the patient's life, but in Beth's case, she didn't have anyone in her life. Beth had wondered during her adolescence whether or not she was a lesbian, but had suppressed the issue and only opened it up again in therapy.

The psychologist had worked with gay women before, but she had never been the object of their desire. She thought she should be neutral, but she didn't feel neutral. She didn't want to hear how much Beth wanted to kiss her and touch her breasts. She didn't want to know about Beth's masturbation fantasies. She wanted Beth to calm down or go away.

Working with a powerful erotic transference can be difficult for any therapist. It is sometimes made more difficult in the therapy of an arousal or orgasmic disorder when the therapist encourages and even prescribes sexual activities for a patient. Short of sending Beth to another therapist, the psychologist wanted to make sure Beth understood that there would be no physical or sexual interaction between them by informing her of the rules about touching in psychotherapy.

The supervisor asked if Beth had said or done anything that indicated she thought they might have sex or that she literally wanted sex.

"Not really," the psychologist said. "She's pretty embarrassed and scared. I don't think she quite knows what's happening to her. She has said more than once that if she didn't trust me, she'd never tell me what she was feeling."

With support, the psychologist continued to see Beth and did her best to sit quietly, if not always calmly, with Beth's feelings. If Beth were to ask her if they could be sexual, she could and should say no and explain why that wouldn't work as part of the therapy. If Beth continued to feel sexual, the psychologist should discuss what that was like for Beth and help her integrate her feelings and fantasies into her life.

Beth overcame her anorgasmia by masturbating to orgasm while imagining herself being held by her therapist. In therapy, she said that orgasm was pleasurable, terrifying, joyous, disappointing, wonderful, and sad—all at once.

The therapist's first (and defensive) response was that Beth was using her sexual experience to defend against something else. Anger, dependency, regression—she wasn't sure what.

Instead of dismissing Beth's experience as a substitute for something else, it makes more sense to consider exactly what function Beth's sexual enactment played in her inner world. After some discussion with her supervisor, the therapist realized that

1. It was only because Beth felt safe and understood that she was able to feel and communicate her sexual desires.
2. The erotic transference carried the potential for growth as well as regression.
3. Beth was frightened of being overwhelmed by her newly discovered sexuality.
4. The anxiety that Beth would become "inappropriate" was an expression of the therapist's discomfort about sex between women, her guilt about stimulating such strong sexual feelings in a patient, and her fear that she didn't know what in the world to do with such rampant sexuality.
5. Beth was not using sexuality to defend against anger or dependency—she was in fact expressing her dependency within the sexual experience.

The next stage of the work was the one the therapist thought could never happen—reaching out into the real world to make a relationship. In many ways, Beth's gradual separation was like that of an adolescent leaving home. She needed to do it, but it was sad and scary. As Beth accepted the fact that she was attracted to women, she made more women friends. She joined a booster club for her college basketball team and met a group of gay women. Erotic feelings for her therapist never disappeared, but they gradually faded as Beth found other meaningful connections.

When she finally did get into a sexual relationship, she was initially unable to reach orgasm. Beth's partner was understanding, and she knew as much about sexual techniques as most sex therapists. It didn't take long before Beth was able to be orgasmic in the context of an intimate relationship. Beth stopped therapy when she graduated from college and she and her lover moved to another city.

The prognosis for female orgasmic disorders is generally good. Factors that mitigate against a good prognosis are a history of physical or sexual abuse, sexual aversion or phobia, and chronic, severe psychosomatic preoccupation.

Women's Sexuality Groups

A variety of women with arousal and orgasmic disorders can be successfully treated in a group format. In a recent conversation, Lonnie Barbach, the therapist who originated the women's sexual group format in the 1970s, told us that though there are currently fewer women's groups being led by therapists, they are still the best therapeutic approach for many female sexual arousal problems. Lonnie believes that the group format will become more popular again in the future. As far as we are aware, only female therapists lead women's sexuality groups, which perhaps indicates that one factor in their formation and success is the safety and sanctity of a woman's space without a man present.

Women's sexuality groups are recommended for (1) women who have never had an orgasm (sometimes referred to as preorgasmic women), (2) women with situational arousal and inhibited orgasm, (3) women with uncomplicated vaginismus, and (4) some women with sexual anxieties either with or without a relationship.

Women's sexuality groups are not recommended for (1) women with sexual aversion disorder, schizoid or borderline personality disorder; or (2) women with significant psychopathology who will be group "outcasts."

Patient selection is an important variable in the success of this form of therapy. In general, younger women, women who have never had an orgasm, and women highly motivated toward self-expression seem to do the best. Additionally, some older women born in a time when sexual mores were less open have been able to use the experiences of the younger women in the group to great advantage.

The women's sexuality group is time limited and focused on the attainment of successful sexual experience. Goals are heightened sexual awareness, successful experience of arousal and orgasm, and more sexual satisfaction in a relationship. As a general format, five to eight women attend weekly two-hour meetings for about ten weeks.

Some therapists create separate groups for women who have never had an orgasm and women who have had periods of adequate sexual function but are presently experiencing difficulty. In the present climate in which there are fewer preorgasmic women and more pressure to see patients quickly, many therapists are combining the two diagnostic categories into a single group.

The group begins with a discussion of each woman's goals. If any of them are unrealistic, as is often the case, the therapist works to create goals that are more attainable. A common problematic expectation is to have an orgasm with sexual intercourse as the only stimulation. Although this is possible for many women, it is not possible for all. It's a lot more reasonable for a woman to expect that she will be able to become aroused and have an orgasm, one way or another, as a result of the group experience.

Homework is a central aspect of the women's group. The most common first "assignment" is to find one hour a day to do nothing but relax. Curiously, this is an assignment that meets with significant resistance.

Each week a different topic is discussed: the sexual response cycle, masturbation, orgasm, eroticism, sensuality, and sexual fantasies. For the most part, discussion of the women's partners is kept to a minimum until the later sessions. This encourages each woman to focus on herself and her own pleasure, something few of them are accustomed to doing.

Homework assignments are basically a form of systematic desensitization. They progress from experiences with little or no anxiety to ones with potentially greater degrees of anxiety. Each group member is asked to keep a journal of her reactions to the homework assignments, and to bring it to the group.

Assignments might include viewing your naked body in a full-length mirror; using a small mirror to view your genitals; touching your body except for breasts and genitals; viewing or reading explicit sexual material; buying clothes (underwear, lingerie) that feel particularly sensual; creating a sexual fantasy and discussing it with the group; taking a warm bath and pouring water over your genitals; and touching breasts and genitals.

Male Erectile Disorder

JOHN ANTONELLI

John had his first bout of impotence in his thirties. When he came to therapy, he was sixty-four, had been married three times, had raised two families, had made, lost, and then remade a fortune in Silicon Valley, and was now impotent with his forty-year-old girlfriend.

If John ever wrote a book about his life, it would be a fascinating tale: growing up in Chicago during Prohibition, palling around with Mafia hoods, getting shot at, losing his virginity to a prostitute, getting married at age eighteen because he "knocked up" his girlfriend, leaving his family's poverty to attend an Ivy League school on money he'd made in ways you don't want to know about.

John began in individual therapy because he didn't want to involve his girlfriend in what he saw as "his problem." John was a very independent individual and a perfectionist. He looked to his penis as a power gauge—when it was erect, so was he. When it wouldn't go up, he was down. There was no room in his world for doubts and insecurities. His business philosophy matched his sexual philosophy: "If you're not sure what to do, do it anyway." This credo got him into financial trouble, just as it got him into sexual difficulties.

John complained that he didn't even masturbate anymore. It wasn't that he didn't want to. Masturbation was fine by him. It was that he couldn't get it up when he tried. He was worried that his girlfriend would get tired of oral sex and leave him. He was also angry at fate or God or whoever the hell controlled things. It wasn't fair, he said. He figured that he deserved a certain number of orgasms in his life, and he hadn't gotten even close to that number yet.

John's medical examination was normal. NPT sleep laboratory testing was particularly helpful in determining whether his lack of waking erections was psychological or somehow physical in origin. John was both relieved and annoyed when he discovered that his nocturnal erections were perfectly sound. He didn't like the idea that his mind and body weren't under his control.

Several months of individual psychotherapy, twice a week, helped John see that he was trying to control just about everything in his life, from his penis, to his girlfriend, to his therapist. He was terribly afraid of getting older and losing his potency—not just his sexual potency but his attractiveness to women and his ability to do whatever he wanted, whenever he wanted. At sixty-four, he said proudly, he still lifted weights, played tennis, rode his Harley Davidson, and could out-drink anyone who worked for him.

In this last statement, John revealed a hidden aspect of his sexual problem. When initially asked about alcohol consumption, he said he didn't drink. In truth, when he was challenged or when he felt anxious, he'd drink himself under the table. Unfortunately, when he got together with his girlfriend, John felt both challenged and anxious, and he often ended up getting drunk. Although this wasn't the main cause of his erectile dysfunction, it was a contributing factor. Never one to back off from a challenge, John vowed not to take another drink.

Much of the individual work centered on what a Jungian would call John's anima, his feminine side. There had been little if any room for such a thing in John's conscious life. He'd been a rough-and-tumble father, an entrepreneur, a man's man. He didn't know the first thing about softness, vulnerability, emotional need, and letting nature take its course.

In many ways, John acted as if he himself were an erection. He was supposed to be able to stiffen up and take any problem in stride. When he was up, he enjoyed being noticed; he felt in charge and ready for anything. When he was down, he wanted to disappear, to slink off into a dark corner and hide.

The first inkling that John was beginning to understand and change came not in a sexual way but in the way he related to his girlfriend, Adrienne, when she was upset that he'd been unable to complete the lovemaking process. She told him she was disappointed, but not for the reasons he expected. Adrienne said she got more than enough sexual pleasure from his other ministrations, but she missed the closeness that intercourse would bring to their relationship. John was loath to admit it, but he teared up at that moment.

John's next big step in reversing his impotence was telling Adrienne about his therapy and asking her if she'd be willing to participate. She agreed, and John asked his therapist if he would see the two of them.

In most cases, we think it's inadvisable to switch between individual and couple therapy. It's very difficult to bring a new person into an established therapeutic relationship and not have someone's feelings hurt, not have someone feel left out, ganged up on, or rejected. The therapist in this case said as much to John, expecting him to respond with blustery outrage, or at the very least with a request for the name of someone who would see them together. But John grew sad and said he didn't know if he had it in him to start with someone else. This was the first open admission of vulnerability he'd uttered. After a few sessions spent going over the pros and cons of switching to couple therapy, John and Adrienne decided to try it on a trial basis. If either John or Adrienne felt that it wasn't a safe and workable arrangement, they'd stop and find someone else for them to see.

Adrienne was an energetic, intelligent, and attractive woman. She was understandably a bit uncomfortable, but quite able to voice her perceptions and concerns. The therapist met with her twice individually in order to understand something of her background and her needs in the relationship. Like John, she was hoping that the relationship would turn into a marriage and was willing to do whatever she could to help improve their communication and their sexual relationship.

In this case, therapy was conducted twice weekly. The therapist asked them what they thought it would it be like if they agreed not to have an orgasm until they decided together that it was time. Adrienne thought it would be OK, adding with a wry smile directed to John, "as long as it doesn't last longer than a year."

John didn't think that was funny. He said angrily, "I'm already missing out on orgasms, so what the hell good will it do not to have them?"

The therapist replied that it might help him slow down enough to feel whatever the hell it was he was feeling when he and Adrienne got together.

John couldn't stop himself from laughing at the imitation of his brusque style. "All right," he said after a moment's thought. "I'll try it, but no way for a year."

It was clear that giving John weekly homework would either create World War Three or the Berlin Wall. So the only specific guideline or homework was the prohibition on orgasm. Otherwise John and Adrienne could do anything they wanted. For the most part they talked about their sexual and emotional fears, desires, and needs, and used their sessions to decide how they wanted to be sexual.

It was a pitched battle for John to give up a position of power. When he began therapy, the only way he knew how to get an erection was to feel dominant, and that obviously wasn't working anymore. John could not differentiate being weak from being receptive. Any time Adrienne tried to give something to him, whether it was sexual or emotional, he felt momentarily emasculated. He was used to being the one who gave, even if on some deeper level he resented it.

Once Adrienne understood John's fear of passivity, she was able to be more forceful. She teased, cajoled, and pushed him into letting her please him sexually. When Adrienne all but forced John to let her stimulate him orally, his erections returned.

In the ensuing weeks, John learned to recognize his anxiety. He usually moved away from it so quickly into his "I'm in charge" stance that he didn't even feel it. For John to find a new kind of masculine potency, he had to find his feminine sensibilities. John and Adrienne were gradually able to change the underlying assumptions of their sexual life. In order to do this, John had to change his assumptions of what it meant to be a man. He came to understand that his attraction to Adrienne, a more open, honest, and independent woman than he'd been with before, was the beginning of his desire to change.

Aside from the suggestion about prohibiting orgasm, the therapist functioned to help both of them (1) know what they were feeling, (2) communicate their feelings and perceptions clearly, (3) recognize and confront the ways they avoided their own and the other's feelings, and (4) create a therapeutic space that was reliable and safe. The therapy ended not quite two years after John first appeared in the therapist's office. He and Adrienne had been able to have intercourse for almost eight months by that time, but they'd decided to continue therapy until they trusted that they'd be able to work out any difficulties that came along. A few months after their last session, the therapist received a wedding invitation. At the bottom John had written, "Hey Doc, never thought I'd ever feel like this. Thanks."

Prognosis for male erectile disorders is quite variable. Factors that suggest a good prognosis are good physical health, short duration of the symptom, no alcohol or other problematic medications, success in other areas of the patient's life, the ability to make and maintain a reasonably good relationship, motivation to improve the situation that goes beyond repairing a damaged sense of masculinity, and some flexibility in the patient's personality and defensive structure.

Male Orgasmic Disorder

MR. AND MRS. BROWNELL

The Brownells were introduced in Chapter Three. They came to therapy because Mr. Brownell was unable to have an orgasm during intercourse. Mr. Brownell had confessed to his retarded ejaculation after his wife went for a protracted infertility evaluation. His sexual symptom was primarily the result of a complicated posttraumatic stress reaction to his freezing up when his former fiancee fell through the ice on a skating pond and drowned—an event Mr. Brownell had never revealed to his wife and that he asked the therapist to keep secret. For her part, Mrs. Brownell had never had an orgasm and wanted to have both a baby and a better sex life.

Twice-weekly therapy was begun with the aim of alleviating the Brownells' sexual symptoms, improving their communication, and helping each of them to be more present in the relationship. Initially, Mrs. Brownell was nervous but also excited to have a forum to explore her sexual feelings. She soon experienced orgasm with self-stimulation, and then when being stimulated manually by Mr. Brownell.

The more difficult problem was finding a way for Mr. Brownell to open up and come alive within the relationship. His extraordinary guilt made any form of sexual pleasure difficult. As his wife became more excited and encouraged about their sexual potential, Mr. Brownell became openly depressed. They were more able to talk about feelings and sexuality, but the progress they made toward being together sexually was all one-sided. In fact, Mr. Brownell began to have difficulty maintaining an erection, and his desire and interest in sex all but disappeared.

In this context, a "terrible" thing happened. While discussing Mr. Brownell's depression and his new sexual difficulty, the therapist more or less said, "Well, isn't it understandable you can't let yourself enjoy sex with your wife, given what happened?"

Mr. Brownell looked as though he'd seen a ghost. He grew pale, stammered something, and got up and left the session. The therapist felt about as anxious and guilty as a therapist can feel. Mrs. Brownell, however, looked almost relieved. She asked what the therapist meant. The therapist didn't know what to say.

Mrs. Brownell saved him. Gently, she proclaimed that she knew what he meant. She went on to reveal that Mr. Brownell's mother had told her about the death of his fiancee, how it happened, even how he felt about it. Her mother-in-law made her promise never to tell. All this time, she'd known what had happened but had pretended that she didn't know!

Mr. Brownell returned for the next session. He accepted the therapist's apology and commented that maybe it was better the secret was out. At that moment, the pain and suffering they had endured in an effort to "protect" each other washed over the Brownells. Long-standing resentments surfaced. They argued. Sex was forgotten. In the next weeks, they reevaluated their commitment. They decided that they really did love each other and wanted to stay together. Slowly, they found ways to talk about what really mattered to each of them. Mr. Brownell was able to obtain and even enjoy having an erection with his wife, though he still couldn't have an orgasm in her presence.

The most common homework-oriented treatment method for male orgasmic disorder is to use whatever works and pair it with the patient's partner. This usually means having the man arouse himself in the presence of the partner. The trick is finding a way to include stimulation by the partner and have it be arousing enough to bring the patient to orgasm. In this case, Mr. Brownell could masturbate to orgasm when he was alone, but as mentioned, it was not a soothing or joyous experience for him at the best of times. Any connection between orgasm and their relationship inhibited Mr. Brownell completely. He was even unable to reach orgasm with self-stimulation when his wife was out shopping but knew what he was doing.

In spite of this, Mrs. Brownell was more able to enjoy sex than at any time in her life. Mr. Brownell even began to enjoy their sexual encounters. He still could not have an orgasm with her, but he could say what he was feeling and thinking, and he did begin to enjoy being held and touched. In this context, they decided that they didn't want to wait any longer to have a child, and turned to artificial insemination. Mr. Brownell understood the deep-seated nature of his withdrawal and his guilt-induced need for self punishment; he elected to go into individual therapy.

This is an example of a partially successful therapy. There is no doubt that the Brownells' relationship was improved, as was their sex life, but Mr. Brownell's predominant sexual symptom remained. We've found that the prognosis for male orgasmic disorder is often poor unless it's a response to the side effects of medication.

Rapid (Premature) Ejaculation

BEN KOONTZ

Ben, a twenty-four-year-old electronic engineer, came to therapy because he was "going nuts." No matter what he did, he couldn't control his "damn cock." As far as he was concerned, he said with some humor, it was "half-cocked."

Ben related a history that was similar to others we have heard from men who are unable to manage any control of their ejaculatory reflex. He grew up in a middle-class family, went to church, did quite well in school, and was liked by his friends. He was afraid of yet fascinated by girls, and didn't begin masturbating until he was eighteen and living away from home. He'd had a few sexual relationships with women, and each time he either came in his undershorts or long before he got inside a vagina. His inability to have intercourse left Ben embarrassed and led to the end of several otherwise good relationships.

Most men learn through experience how to vary their excitement. The average guy figures out how to alter the degree of penile stimulation in order to control the timing of his orgasm. Ben didn't know how to do this. In fact, he didn't even know how excited he was. The problem of uncontrolled ejaculation is one of nature's ironies. It appears on the surface that these men are feeling too much, when in fact they feel too little. Out of a fear of coming too fast, Ben was doing everything he could to avoid his excitement. He'd think about calculus, doing his taxes, anything to distract him from the urgent sensation in his groin.

One of the first things the therapist did was to suggest that Ben's attempt to solve his problem made a kind of sense but that it was exactly the wrong thing to do.

Back in 1956, urologist James Semans proposed a way for those men who hadn't yet figured out how to regulate their arousal to learn this important fact of sexual life. Semans was pragmatic and sensible. He suggested that a man lie comfortably on his back while his partner stimulated him manually. The man's job was simply to pay attention to his arousal and tell the partner to stop when he felt himself getting anywhere close to an orgasm. Three or four successful pauses were to be followed by stimulation to orgasm. Masters and Johnson altered Dr. Semans simple procedure with what they called the "squeeze technique." It is the same as the stop-start method, but when the man finds himself approaching orgasm, the partner uses thumb and forefinger to squeeze the penis just below the glans. We've had excellent success with the stop-start method, and don't see much reason to complicate matters with squeezes where most men would rather not be squeezed.

The learning curve for the stop-start process varies, but most men will gradually find that they are able to both feel their arousal and obtain some control of how far it is going to go. After the initial process can be done successfully, it can be varied by adding a lubricant and allowing the man to reach orgasm after an agreed-upon number of stop-starts.

The next stage is to perform the stop-start with vaginal penetration. Again, it seems to work best with the man on his back and the partner on top. Once this is mastered, the couple can move to a side-to-side position, and then to the man on top. Finally, once the man feels that he is aware of his level of arousal (this is the most important aspect of treating a rapid ejaculator), he can vary the speed with which he thrusts from slow to fast to stop.

Ben was quite willing to see if the stop-start technique would help him, but he had a big problem. He didn't have a partner to do it with. It was Ben's idea to see if he could do it himself. He rented several pornographic movies and followed Dr. Semans's advice.

I think most teenage boys use a less formal version of Ben's variation on Dr. Semans's procedure. Perhaps they use *Playboy* magazine or their imagination instead of a videotape, but the idea is pretty much the same. Ben mastered the self-administered stop-start experience in a relatively short period of time, and was ready to move on to more fertile ground.

When he did connect with a new girlfriend, he was understandably more nervous than usual. He didn't know how well his home training program was going to work, and he wasn't sure how to ask a woman if she'd do the stop-start exercises with him. As it happened, when it became clear that they both wanted to be sexual, Ben discussed his problem with his girlfriend. She was quite willing to help. In fact, she thought up a bunch of ways the exercise would be fun and exciting, and asked Ben if he'd do the same for her. The two of them became experts on sexual arousal—exactly what the man with rapid ejaculation needs.

Sex therapists used to say that premature ejaculation was 100 percent reversible. That was perhaps more true for those patients who sought out sex therapy in the 1970s. Experience suggests that the prognosis for altering this symptom remains good, but there are intractable and difficult cases. We've also found that many men with this symptom find that the problem recurs in times of stress or anxiety: at the beginning of a new relationship, during periods of marital or financial difficulty, with the birth of a child, and so on. However, if the stop-start method worked well before, it will usually work well again.

GENERAL COMMENTS ON OUTCOME

Reports, both anecdotal and controlled, of the outcome of therapy for sexual disorders vary significantly from paper to paper and therapist to therapist. Problems exist in that therapy has been conducted using different therapeutic methods, a variety of outcome measures, and variable populations.

Masters and Johnson reported their highly successful results as far back as the early 1970s (see Table 8.1). All couples were treated intensively for two consecutive weeks at Masters and Johnson's facility. Success was measured by reversal of the presenting symptom.

You can probably see why these results created such a stir. An overall success rate of 81 percent was remarkable. You can also see that there is some variation in Masters and Johnson's results: primary impotence was the most difficult disorder to reverse, and vaginismus and premature ejaculation were the easiest.

Table 8.1
Outcome Results for Masters and Johnson (1970)

Disorder	N	Success rate (%)	Relapse rate, 5 year number reporting %	
Primary impotence	32	59.4	0/7	0
Secondary impotence	213	73.7	10/90	11.1
Premature ejaculation	186	97.8	1/74	1.5
Retarded ejaculation	17	82.4	0/5	0
Vaginismus	29	100	no report	
Primary anorgasmia	193	83.4	2/77	2.6
Situational anorgasmia	148	77.2	3/60	5
Overall results	*790*	*81.1*	*16/313*	*5.1*

Source: Adapted from Wright, J., Perreault, R., Mathieu, M. (1977). The treatment of sexual dysfunction: A review. *Archives of General Psychiatry, 34,* 881–890.

Other studies found significantly lower success rates. The most important difference in results appears to be related to patient selection. When patients with psychopathology outside of the sexual arena were treated, the outcome was not as good as the patients who were motivated and able to spend two weeks in St. Louis at Masters and Johnson's clinic.

Where does this leave today's therapist? Patients who are coming for consultation today have more complex disorders and psychopathology. It's very unlikely that any of us will be able to approach the success rates seen in Masters and Johnson's selected population. Further, we think that our work today is aimed at a broader spectrum of issues in our patients' lives. Success is certainly measured in terms of symptom reversal, but it is also measured by the improvement in subjective enjoyment of sexuality, by the ability to communicate within a sexual relationship, and by the ability to form and maintain an intimate relationship.

∽

We hope you now have a pretty good idea of how to treat arousal and orgasmic disorders. If you apply the basic principles we've discussed to your individual cases, you will be able to make sensible clinical decisions that will guide the therapy.

One of the joys of working with these sexual problems is seeing the symptoms change and patients' reactions to the way in which their lives open up and become more than they were before. Sex therapy was one of the first areas in which it became abundantly clear that diminishing or removing a troublesome symptom and replacing it with a pleasurable experience can be enough to change people's outlook on life, their sense of self-esteem, and their ability to relate in an intimate and meaningful manner.

Notes

P. 241, *Freud distinguished:* Freud, S. (1953). Three essays on the theory of sexuality. In J. Strachey (Ed.), *The standard edition of the complete psychological works of Sigmund Freud* (Vol. 8). London: Hogarth Press. (Original work published 1905)

P. 241, *Research has dispelled:* Masters, W., & Johnson, V. (1966). *Human sexual response.* Boston: Little, Brown; Fink, P. J., Murphy, R. S., Fischer, S., deMoya, A. deMoya, D., Diamond, M., & Gray, M. J. (1973). What is the basis for the distinction many patients make between vaginal and clitoral orgasms? *Medical Aspects of Human Sexuality, 7*(11), 84–103.

P. 275, *urologist James Semans:* Semans, J. H. (1956). Premature ejaculation: A new approach. *Southern Medical Journal, 49,* 353–357.

P. 277, *Masters and Johnson reported:* Masters, W., & Johnson, V. (1970). *Human sexual inadequacy.* Boston: Little, Brown.

P. 278, *Other studies found:* Studies reported in Wright, J., Perreault, R., Mathieu, M. (1977). The treatment of sexual dysfunction: A review. *Archives of General Psychiatry, 34,* 881–890.

FOR FURTHER READING

Barbach, L. (1980). Group treatment of anorgasmic women. In S. R. Lieblum & L. A. Pervin (Eds.), *Principles and practices of sex therapy.* New York: Guilford Press.

Barbach, L. (1982). *For yourself.* New York: Doubleday.

Kaplan, H. S. (1974). *The new sex therapy.* New York: Brunner/Mazel.

Kaplan, H. S. (1975). *The illustrated manual of sex therapy.* New York: Quadrangle.

Levine, S. B. (1992). *Sexual life: A clinician's guide.* New York: Plenum.

Lobitz, C., & LoPiccolo, J. (1972). New methods in the behavioral treatment of sexual dysfunction. *Journal of Behavior Therapy and Experimental Psychiatry, 3,* 265–271.

LoPiccolo, J., & Lobitz, W. (1972). The role of masturbation in the treatment of orgasmic inhibition. *Archives of Sexual Behavior, 2,* 163–171.

LoPiccolo, J., & Stock, W. (1988). Treatment of sexual dysfunction. *Journal of Consulting and Clinical Psychology, 54,* 158–167.

Masters, W., & Johnson, V. (1966). *Human sexual response.* Boston: Little, Brown.

Masters, W., & Johnson, V. (1970). *Human sexual inadequacy.* Boston: Little, Brown.

Offit, A. (1977). *The sexual self.* Philadelphia: Lippincott.

Offit, A. (1995). *Night thoughts: Reflections of a sex therapist.* Northvale, NJ: Jason Aronson.

Schafer, R. (1983). *The analytic attitude.* New York: Basic Books.

Schnarch, D. (1991). *Constructing the sexual crucible: An integration of sexual and marital therapy.* New York: Norton.

Semans, J. H. (1956). Premature ejaculation: A new approach. *Southern Medical Journal, 49,* 353–357.

Wright, J., Perreault, R., Mathieu, M. (1977). The treatment of sexual dysfunction: A review. *Archives of General Psychiatry, 34,* 881–890.

CHAPTER

9

TREATMENT OF PARAPHILIAS

Randolph S. Charlton

The word *paraphilia* describes a variety of sexually intense experiences that run counter to what is considered normal. Formed by the prefix *para* (meaning "beside" or "alongside of" or "abnormal") and *philia* ("love"), a paraphilia then was originally conceived of as a sexual act or fantasy lying "alongside" (or "outside") the normal experience of love.

When we talk about paraphilias, most of us are speaking of sexual perversions. The word *perversion* has come to be associated with a set of moral judgments, and an effort has been made to replace it with the less familiar, more scientific sounding, and, one hopes, less judgmental term *paraphilia*.

Altering a descriptive word does not change the social and psychological dynamics behind a concept. Perverse sexual acts are behaviors considered abnormal by the arbiters in a given society. What is normal in any given epoch changes, but the sense of shame and wrongdoing woven into the concept of perversion remains, regardless of what we call the specific sexual behaviors. Perverse sex means sex that breaks the rules. Shame and guilt are central aspects of the paraphilias. For this reason, I use the term *perversion* as a synonym for paraphilia.

A CLINICAL DEFINITION

The most recent *Diagnostic and Statistical Manual (DSM-IV)* considers a paraphilia to have three basic characteristics:

1. An intense, recurrent sexual experience existing for at least six months that involves fantasy, urges, or behavior.

2. A particular object of the sexual experience—nonhuman things, individuals who suffer or are humiliated, children or other nonconsenting persons.

3. A particular result of the sexual experience—clinically significant distress or significant impairment in social, occupational, or other important areas of function.

Thus perversions aren't confined to actions. A man who masturbates several times a day to images of a woman being whipped has a perverse sexual orientation. He has a diagnosable paraphilia if this experience has been recurring for six months or more, leaves him depressed and ashamed, and caused him to lose his job because he missed too many business meetings.

The *DSM-IV* classifies perversions into eight categories:

1. *Exhibitionism.* The exhibitionist is usually thought of as a man who exposes his genitals to a stranger. It is unusual for an exhibitionist to do more than show himself and perhaps masturbate. Most men anticipate the viewer's shocked response, though some imagine that the surprised woman will find them sexually desirable. In general, exhibitionists are younger men who began their activity prior to the age of eighteen.

We intuitively make a legal and psychological distinction between a man revealing his genitals and a woman doing the same thing. However, a woman who reveals her body can be sexually stimulated by the act. She can be ashamed and yet drawn to do it. Her need to show herself can cause social and interpersonal problems. Though we tend to think about it differently, women can be exhibitionists.

2. *Fetishism*. When I think of a fetish, I picture a small black onyx bear carved by a Zuni Indian. When a person with a paraphilia pictures a fetish, visions of women's panties, bras, shoes, or stockings dance in their head. Leather and rubber clothing are sometimes used as fetishes. Men more often use nonliving objects for sexual arousal than do women. The fetishist's most common sexual activity is masturbation. These individuals do not often come to the attention of either the police or the therapist unless they are troubled by their sexual interest or the inevitable loneliness that goes along with it.

Objects that are specifically made for the purpose of sexual arousal (vibrators, for instance) are not fetish objects. A fetish is an object that represents a person. It is the symbolic energy the fetish contains that imbues it with sexual power, not two AA batteries.

3. *Frotteurism*. If I'd never lived in New York City, I might not believe that frotteurism was real. However, having traveled the length and breadth of Manhattan on the subway, I can assure you that the practice of rubbing up against a stranger in a crowded place in order to obtain sexual gratification does happen. Although I've never seen a case in therapy, I can tell you that the individual who does it is male and usually younger than twenty-five.

4. *Pedophilia*. Sexual interest in children is perhaps the most problematic and destructive of the paraphilias. To leave room for adolescent sexuality, the diagnosis is not made unless the perpetrator is sixteen years or older and is at least five years older than the victim. A child is generally considered to be anyone age thirteen or younger.

Statistically, more pedophiles are interested in girls than boys, but those who are interested in boys are twice as likely to return to their sexual behavior after legal action or psychiatric treatment.

Pedophilia by its very nature involves the victimization of another. Some pedophiles rationalize their behavior by saying that the children enjoy it, or that they provoked it, or that they will learn from it. Our recent awareness of the prevalence of incest and sexual molestation within a family or stepfamily suggests that the incidence of pedophilia is perhaps much higher than we've imagined. Some pedophiles are also sexual sadists. The horror of their activities leads us all to consider the problem of evil in human actions.

5. *Masochism.* True sexual masochism involves sexual excitement generated by one's own humiliation, pain, or suffering. It can involve being spanked, whipped, tied up, or made to say humiliating things. Sexual asphyxiation, a form of masochism that involves becoming oxygen deprived—often by a rope around the neck—is a particularly dangerous form of sexual arousal that leads to a number of deaths in the United States each year.

In 1953, Kinsey reported that one quarter of both males and females in his survey found that they had an erotic response to being bitten during sex. In a 1974 survey, 10 percent of unmarried women and a little over 6 percent of unmarried men acknowledged that some kinds of pain were sexually stimulating.

When masochism exists in fantasy, images of rape, sexual torture, slavery, being spanked, and of being forced to have sex are used for masturbation. Sexual arousal at such images usually occurs fairly early in life and remains a lifelong pattern. Some sexual masochists are able to maintain fairly stable relationships to consenting partners, whereas others' need for stronger stimulation gradually increases.

6. *Sadism.* Sadism exists in a spectrum from mild fantasies of dominance all the way to lust murder. The sadist is more likely to be a man, is likely to have known about his predilection as an adolescent or young adult, and is likely to maintain this form of sexual interest for many years.

Sadism can be combined with any of the other sexual perversions, including masochism. In a sample of almost three thousand individuals, 14 percent of men and 11 percent of women said that they'd had sadomasochistic experiences. The authors of *Sex in America: A Definitive Study* found that 3 percent of a carefully randomized sample of men acknowledged that they were excited about the idea of forcing a woman to have sex. A separate and perhaps overlapping 3 percent of men admitted to having actually done it.

The sadist who selects a nonconsenting individual is committing a crime. Obscene phone calls are motivated by sadistic impulses that usually go no further than masturbation. Sexual fascination with urination (sometimes called golden showers) and feces are specific forms of sadomasochism.

7. *Transvestic fetishism.* A man who wears women's clothes because he believes he is a woman in a man's body is a transsexual. A man who wears women's clothes because he gets sexually aroused while doing it is a transvestic fetishist. This disorder is limited to males, most of whom are heterosexual, though some may report homosexual experiences. Their preferred sexual release is masturbation, and their desire is stimulated by the clothes they wear. A gender identity disorder (transsexualism) may appear in these individuals depending on their degree of satisfaction with their maleness. The diagnosis and treatment of such situations are complex. Fewer and fewer centers are performing sexual reassignment surgery. Individuals desiring an alteration of their physical habitus from one sex to another often exhibit severe personality disorders and are best evaluated psychiatrically.

8. *Voyeurism.* A voyeur is someone who seeks out situations where he can secretly observe another person undressing, naked, or engaging in sexual activity. The voyeur masturbates while peeking, or afterwards while the memory is still fresh. Interest in sexual looking begins in early adolescence and to some extent is both normal and supported by our culture. It becomes a paraphilia when it persists, becomes an individual's main form of

286 Treating Sexual Disorders

sexual gratification, and causes him distress or leads to social problems, the most common of which is getting caught.

∽

In order to treat a patient with a sexual predilection that lies "alongside" our personal and cultural norms of what is desired, expected, or tolerated, a therapist will inevitably experience a variety of difficult emotions; prominent among them are fear, guilt, shame, disgust, and contempt. Here lies our first problem in the treatment of these disorders.

COUNTERTRANSFERENCE AVERSION

It's been known for centuries that the best way to understand why another person would think, feel, or act in a particular way is to put yourself in that person's shoes. With many patients, this poses only moderately difficult problems for the therapist. Empathizing with a woman dying of breast cancer is perhaps difficult, but not impossible. Allowing ourselves to feel what it's like to be impotent, or depressed, or terminally lonely is close enough to our experience as human beings that most therapists can make the leap without too much trouble. But what happens when a therapist tries to experience what it's like to be a sexual sadist? What would happen to you if you tried to immerse yourself in a pedophile's emotional and psychological point of view?

You might legitimately ask, "How can you expect me to feel what a sexual sadist feels?" Or you might understandably protest, "If I try to know what it's like to be sexually aroused by children, I not only won't be able to do it but I'll be so disgusted I'll want to get as far away from that patient as possible."

Most clinicians' primary identification is with the victims of pedophiles, voyeurs, exhibitionists, sadists, and the like. In a recent discussion about a pedophilic patient, three quarters of a class of graduate students (all the women and two of the men) wanted to either castrate the bastard or kill him outright. These sentiments are certainly understandable.

Gender Differences

Gender is definitely an issue in regard to paraphilias. The majority of perverse individuals are male. Those who are likely to harm other people are mostly men, and their victims are usually women or children. Perverse sexual orientation is certainly not limited to men, but the majority of women who fall into this category do not overtly victimize others. If a woman reveals her body in public, she is perhaps an exhibitionist, but it's unlikely the police will be called. If a man exhibits himself, it is a frightening experience for anyone who sees it, and it is considered a crime. Rapists are men. Sexual sadists are for the most part men. Women who enjoy sexually dominating men usually find consenting partners or paying customers.

An exception to this general rule is the female pedophile. Sexual abuse by a mother, a woman teacher, or a baby-sitter has the same potential to harm a young child as that done by a man.

Male therapists are somewhat more comfortable than female therapists when treating paraphiliacs. This may be so because men are less likely to be intimidated or frightened by the possibility of rape. Further, male therapists are somewhat more likely to defend against identification with the victims of these patients, and may have an easier time listening to perverse fantasies.

Many female therapists are understandably frightened of being alone in the same room with a sexual sadist who has exhibited violent sexual behavior toward women, or who has powerful, intrusive fantasies of raping or otherwise harming women. Male patients with less overtly violent behaviors and fantasies can also be quite frightening. There are times when it is prudent for a therapist to be apprehensive. I do not think a therapist should see any patient who makes her feel physically unsafe, or who frightens her so much that she cannot function professionally. If you end up having to evaluate such a patient in an emergency room, clinic, or private office, do your best to take care of yourself. If you can, bring someone into the room with you. Do not put the patient between yourself and the door.

Countertransference and Empathy

Fear, anger, disgust, and revulsion in the therapist all make it difficult, if not impossible, to treat perverse patients even if there is no immediate physical danger. Some therapists, often those who have known victimization themselves, have such strong reactions to these patients that they simply can't treat them. The tension between the victimizer and the victim, even when it exists only in a patient's fantasy life, is simply too strong and creates too much anxiety in these therapists for them to think and act objectively.

Therapists who take a punitive point of view toward perverse patients—but treat them anyway—are prone to strong countertransference reactions. They may try to stop the patient's "deviant" behavior regardless of the cost. They may repeatedly shame the patient, or inappropriately use guilty admonitions to stop the patient from revealing his sexual fantasies. Alternatively, anxious, uncomfortable therapists might react against their own punitive impulses by being too understanding and trustful of the patient. Either way, there are problems.

This chapter offers an answer to some of the perplexing and difficult problems in the evaluation and treatment of perverse patients. I'll help you decide which patients can and cannot be treated psychotherapeutically; you will better understand the dynamics lying behind all of the paraphilias and how best to conduct psychotherapy in those situations where it's indicated.

SUITABILITY FOR TREATMENT

Let me offer you three suggestions to help you organize your thoughts about how to deal with sexual perversions.

First, begin your evaluation by considering a perverse patient's potential to act out his sexual impulses, his potential for harming another person, and his degree of truthfulness.

Second, understand the psychodynamics of perversion. If you can see beyond the surface of a patient's sexual fantasy or enactment, you will be more likely to see a whole person and not simply a sexual misfit or deviant.

Third, be able to separate your countertransference reaction from an empathic connection to the perverse patient. Empathy is a trial identification. It is time limited, and it does not mean that you become the other person or that you have to feel everything he feels. Understanding a perverse patient does not mean that you must lose yourself in his sexual urges and desires, but it does mean that you must be able to tolerate and understand the motivations and feelings that drive the individual toward his particular form of sexual excitement.

Evaluation of perverse patients is difficult. This is so because most of us are unfamiliar with the treatment of these patients, because we are uncomfortable with the blatant sexual material that makes up so much of their inner and outer experience, and because we are unfamiliar and uncomfortable with asking penetrating, investigative questions.

Let's go over the factors that indicate whether psychotherapeutic treatment is indicated for a particular paraphiliac patient.

Violence

Perverse sexuality exists along a spectrum that ranges from individuals with relatively harmless sexual fantasies who have never acted them out, to individuals whose sexual urges have led them to rape and murder. In between are those individuals who find partners whose sexual excitement is complementary—the sadist and the sexual masochist, the voyeur and the exhibitionist.

Paraphiliacs become sex offenders when they inflict their sexual urges on innocent victims. They are responsible for child abuse, incest, rape, and exhibitionism, the sexual acts that are criminal and prosecutable. For the most part, these individuals do not come to the attention of a therapist. When they do, it is often at the behest of the court. The intensity of repeatedly enacted sexual violence is indirectly correlated with the likelihood that the paraphiliac will do well in psychotherapy; in other words, the more violent the act, the less likely that psychotherapy will be helpful. There can be a significant difference between those individuals who actually rape and those who imagine rape and are sexually aroused by it. It's important to determine how much pressure the patient is under to act on his fantasies. Patients whose impulses are barely controlled do best with medication, support, and supervision.

Motivation for Change

The most important criterion you can use to judge the potential value of psychotherapy for perverse patients is their motivation to change and to engage in therapy.

Those individuals who have little or no desire to give up their perverse excitements do not come to therapy unless forced to by the court or an upset partner. When you see a patient only after his nonconsensual acts have been discovered by family or police, and this is the only reason he is being evaluated, the likelihood that any form of psychotherapy will alter the nature of his sexual predilections is poor.

Patients involved with the legal system are notoriously difficult to evaluate and treat. I would advise you to leave their therapy to those experienced in this work until you've had a chance to treat and evaluate a number of patients with paraphilias who are not under legal sanction to attend therapy. In general, the kinds of therapy that have been used to treat individuals with violent, antisocial perversions are group therapy, medications, and various forms of behavioral therapy.

There *are* perverse patients who are motivated to change. Some perverse patients are uncomfortable with their sexual behavior itself. They come to therapy with a specific desire to change how they feel about sex. However, it is much more likely that a patient will be motivated to change not because of the specifics of their perverse sexual orientation but because of the emotional syndromes that are often associated with perverse sexuality. In my experience, the most common presenting complaint for these patients is depression of one sort or another.

VIVIAN KOCH

Vivian, a twenty-nine-year-old photographic model, came to see me when her marriage dissolved. She had been depressed in the marriage but was feeling even worse now that she was on her own. Vivian was bright, creative, well read, beautiful, and unhappy. Her modeling career had stalled, and she wasn't sure she liked it anyway. She'd recently agreed to do some "cheesecake" photos and found herself ashamed and wishing she'd never agreed to it.

Vivian initially reported that her sexual life within the marriage was empty. She'd had two affairs in the course of six years, but neither had made her happy. It was only after we'd worked together for several months that Vivian felt safe enough to tell me more about her sexual life. Basically, she was a masochist. One of the reasons her marital sex life was boring was that her husband was turned off by her desire to be slapped, spanked, and made to do sexual things. She was able to become aroused with him only because she would fantasize about these events when they had sex.

Vivian was not particularly motivated to alter her experience of sexual excitement, but she was determined to rid herself of her depression. In her case, therapy for the depression involved understanding and dealing with her sexual needs. In the course of two years, Vivian's depression improved considerably. Concurrently, her sexual fantasies changed from scenes of violence and humiliation to those of surrender and passion. Her masochistic preference did not disappear, but the degree of punishment she needed to become aroused decreased significantly.

I'll go into the relationship between depression and paraphilias later in this chapter, but for now, suffice it to say that paraphiliac patients who come to therapy voluntarily have a prognosis that varies from fair to good depending on the severity of their underlying conflicts. For the most part they have borderline, narcissistic, schizoid, and depressive personality organizations.

Suffering

A useful criterion for evaluating the potential effectiveness of therapy is the patient's degree of suffering. Obviously, this is related to motivation, but it is somewhat different.

Perverse sexual behavior and fantasy function to defend against a variety of unpleasurable feelings: shame and its near relatives, humiliation, mortification, and embarrassment prominent among them. If the defense is "working," the person experiences less suffering and less motivation to enter any form of therapy or alter the sexual status quo.

I've seen perverse patients whose reasons to come to therapy were highly intellectualized. One man said matter-of-factly, "I don't like knowing that I get off on hurting women." Another spent twenty minutes speaking about his success in law school, and with nary a blink went on to tell me, "I want to be a lawyer, and good lawyers don't go around wearing women's underwear beneath their suits." Obviously, these words could be uttered with great emotion, but in these cases they weren't. These men were not good candidates for therapy.

In general, perverse patients who are suffering, either because their underlying depression is leaking out or because they are ashamed, remorseful, or guilty about their sexual practices, are good candidates for psychotherapy.

Psychological Mindedness

Patients with some degree of psychological mindedness, who can look inside themselves and realize that their sexual actions are a sign of something happening within, are more likely to become successfully engaged in therapy.

In general, perverse patients are not particularly able to focus on their inner world. Sexual fantasy and arousal fill up much of their mental space, leaving little room for insight.

Social factors influence the definition of what is or isn't sexually perverse. If an individual conceptualizes his sadomasochism entirely in terms of a reaction to social constraints, he is unlikely to ever arrive in your office, and if he does, it's unlikely that he'll be there with an aim toward changing his sexual style.

Attachment

The ability of a paraphiliac to form lasting and meaningful relationships is an indication that psychodynamic psychotherapy has the potential to be helpful.

Many perverse individuals are more attached to the behavior they engage in than to the people with whom they engage in it. Perversions are disorders in the ability to love. The nature of perverse patients' attachments to others is an indication of their underlying personality structure. Isolation, avoidance of emotional experience, and paranoia all have a negative impact on the prognosis. The transference relationship is particularly relevant to understanding these patients' ability to form and maintain a relationship.

Severe Personality Disorders

Disorganized personalities with paraphilias are less amenable to treatment. Patients with paranoid schizophrenia, severe borderline personality disorder, major depression, or manic-depressive disorder may present with perverse sexual issues. It's important to deal with these patients' underlying psychopathology before attempting to treat the perverse aspects of their personality.

Dual-Diagnosis Patients

Paraphiliac patients who are actively using drugs or alcohol are poor candidates for all forms of psychotherapy. If a patient reports that he is actively drinking or abusing drugs, those issues must be dealt with first. Often an inpatient program will be the best setting for these individuals. Medication and group therapy are useful in the treatment of a variety of "hard core" perverse patients. Therapeutic models based on drug addiction treatment have some degree of efficacy in stopping these patients from acting out their fantasies. I've found that alcoholic patients with perverse sexual problems can do very well in twelve-step programs, especially if they're willing to discuss both their alcoholism and their sexual conflicts.

BREAKING THE FRAME: THE LEGAL RESPONSIBILITY TO REPORT

As a therapist, you have a moral and, sometimes, legal responsibility to protect the patient's victims; this obligation can be a significant problem in the treatment of those individuals whose fantasies or actions involve nonconsensual sexual activity.

Perverse individuals don't always look for a consenting partner. In fact, some perverse behaviors are based on finding a nonconsensual partner. This is a major factor in exhibitionism, frotteurism, voyeurism, pedophilia, and forms of sexual sadism. Although rape, sexual torture, and abuse are not listed specifically under the paraphilias, they all come under the heading of sexual sadism. The hostility in these perverse enactments is obvious—so obvious that many consider them crimes of hostility first, sexuality second.

All states have laws requiring psychotherapists, regardless of their degree, to report an incident of sexual or physical abuse of a minor. This means that the psychotherapy of the pedophile always involves the intersection of legal, moral, and psychotherapeutic issues. In most states, any "reasonable suspicion" of child molestation must be reported. Thus, if a patient tells you that they have sexually abused, seduced, or otherwise been sexual with a minor at any time in the past, you must report the incident either to the police or the local child protection service. Therapists who in good faith report suspected child molestation and abuse are immune to liability in most states, even if their suspicion turns out to be wrong. On the other hand, therapists who have failed to make a report when it was reasonable to deduce that a child was being abused have been subjected to legal censure.

The issue of mandated reporting is under debate in both local and federal forums. As Congress considers an overarching crime bill, witnesses are testifying on the benefits and drawbacks of the legal requirement to report. You should make sure that you know the laws of your particular state and that you keep abreast of any changes in federal reporting laws.

Management of Potentially Reportable Situations

If a patient tells you that he has been sexually involved with a child before you have told the patient of your legal responsibility, either because it wasn't mentioned in the initial informed consent procedure or because you didn't suspect the possibility, it's best to inform the patient that you will be making a report and discuss the consequences with him.

Patients who reveal that they've been involved with a child often know or suspect that you will have to make a report of the incident.

For example, a male patient asked his psychiatrist, "If I tell you things, is there any reason you would have to reveal them to someone outside this office?"

The psychiatrist answered honestly. She did not say, "Why do you ask?" or "Who do you think I'd tell?" She said that aside from a threat to kill or harm another person, a threat to kill himself, or a suspicion that he'd had a sexual relationship with a child, whatever he said in the office was confidential.

This particular patient chose to go ahead and talk about his sexual interest in his teenage daughter. He had not acted on his feelings and was more afraid of his impulses than of the authorities. He was motivated to control his sexual desires because he understood the potential damage to his daughter. Not all individuals will be as caring, direct, or honest. Some will already have been involved sexually and will put you in the position of having to make a report.

I suggest that you straightforwardly tell any patient whom you discover to have sexual interest in children that if he tells you he has had sexual contact with a minor you will have to inform the authorities. You should reveal this information to patients as soon as you know of their pedophilic desires.

I have supervised therapists who have been so shocked to have to deal with this problem when doing intake interviews in a general psychiatry clinic that they have let the patient leave without discussing the fact that they'd be making a report. Knowing ahead of time how you'll handle this difficult circumstance can help you stay on track.

Telling a patient of your legal responsibility creates a strain in the formation of a therapeutic alliance. Some patients will become angry and be unwilling to see you again. If the individual continues to work with you, the issue of confidentiality and trust will be central to the success or failure of your work.

Some patients will come to you consciously or unconsciously wishing to stop enacting pedophilic impulses, and will use therapy to confront the consequences of their behavior. In this case, it is your legal responsibility to report any involvements they may have had. There are a few times when the court and the therapist can work together with a motivated patient to contain the patient's perverse impulses while working toward some form of resolution in therapy.

Therapy of Sex Offenders

The majority of violent sex offenders are best dealt with by the penal system. All paraphiliac patients feel some pressure to act out their sexual impulses. Those individuals who are unable to incorporate moral and ethical judgment into their choice of action have severe impulse disorders. The great majority of these individuals are not suited to dynamic psychotherapy.

I have not worked with the penal system, and the information I present in the next few paragraphs comes from my reading, not my experience.

The question as to whether criminal paraphiliacs might benefit from behavioral or group psychotherapy or medication is a difficult one best left to experts in the evaluation of violent and sociopathic individuals.

As you would guess, group therapy for rapists, pedophiles, and sexual sadists has most often been conducted within the prison or parole system. Such groups focus on the sharing of strategies to cope with sexual impulses, discussion of the difficulty of competing and feeling adequate in the world of work and social relationships, and encouragement and support to move masturbatory fantasy to images of nonviolent adult interaction. Success rates for such groups are difficult to obtain, but anecdotal reports suggest that the treatment is not especially effective.

Castration was used as a "treatment" for sexual deviancy as far back as 1889. As late as the 1960s, electroshock therapy was used to treat pedophilia. Chemical castration using the injection of medication has been used to decrease sexual desire in sexually violent offenders and pedophiles. Estrogen and antiandrogens such as Depo-Provera significantly decrease sexually perverse behavior. In one study, John Money reported that all eight men who received the injections lost their interest in sexually perverse excitement.

Behavior therapy has been used to treat a variety of perversions. It operates on three basic levels:

1. The perverse individual is afraid of adult sexual relationships. This is especially true for the pedophile. Treatment of this sector of the patient's problem involves desensitization procedures, which use relaxation techniques paired with sexual images or experiences with adults.

2.   Perverse individuals do not know how to operate successfully on an adult level. Coping skills and strategies are taught using role play, videotape, and interaction with a therapist.

3.   Alteration of the perversion requires elimination of the perverse pattern of sexual arousal. This can be treated by the techniques of aversion therapy. In one example, ten pedophilic men were shown twenty photographs. Five were of naked adults, ten were of naked children, and five were sexually neutral. Electrical shocks were administered during the presentation of 80 percent of the slides of children. Each man showed a definite decrease in his sexual response to viewing pictures of children.

UNDERSTANDING THE
PSYCHODYNAMICS OF PERVERSION

In order to treat paraphilias you must first understand them. Let's move now into the dynamics that underlie all of the sexual fantasies and behaviors we're considering so that you'll have a better idea of how to work with those patients who are amenable to psychotherapy.

Sigmund Freud's View of Perversion

Freud thought a perversion was the "inverse of a neurosis." To understand his vision, we must understand neurosis. A neurotic symptom is the result of a compromise between a wish and the anxiety that the wish generates. The symptom, for example impotence, serves to hide knowledge and expression of a forbidden thought or action. We can say that the symptom expresses the wish and the fear simultaneously, and does this while keeping both out of the awareness of the individual with the symptom. Thus, a neurotic symptom is the mixing together of a wish and a fear. It is a displaced, often symbolized expression of a forbidden sexual or aggressive wish.

In a perversion this situation is reversed. Instead of feeling threatened by the open expression of forbidden desires, the perverse individual clings to them, is excited by them, wishes to enact them. Instead of the disgust or anxiety most of us would feel when confronted with the fantasy of being sexual with a child, the pedophile finds the notion arousing. Thus, the perverse individual enacts a forbidden sexual wish in fantasy and perhaps reality.

In a healthy individual, anxiety functions as a signal that some desires are unacceptable because they will cause trouble either in reality or in the inner world of prohibitions against incestuous, rapacious desires. The signal is recognized, and behavior is inhibited, rerouted. Defenses come into play to manage the impulse. Healthy defenses allow the energy behind the impulse to be used in socially acceptable, positive ways.

In the neurotic, defenses also come into play, but they are less adequate to the task. Instead of rerouting behavior into positive channels, a neurotic symptom appears. The man who (unconsciously) wants women to admire his erect penis is unable to speak in public. The woman who (unconsciously) desires to seduce the thirteen-year-old boy who lives next door is unable to go over and borrow a cup of sugar.

Freud noticed that children naturally enjoy and do many of the things we think of as perverse. However, as the child grows up and matures he leaves behind "polymorphous perverse" sexuality and replaces it with adult, genital sexuality. The perverse individual is neither concerned with giving speeches nor unable to borrow sugar. Instead, he puts on an old raincoat and heads for town, already hard in anticipation of revealing himself to the first young woman he sees. Instead, she makes sure the neighbor kid's parents are away, takes off her bra, puts on a filmy silk blouse, and heads next door to borrow some sugar.

The perverse sexual act serves to protect an individual from the anxieties involved in separating and individuating. In a sense, Freud was suggesting that perverse patients are desperately holding on to sexualized, childhood ways of experiencing and feeling and are unable to grow up and face the realities of adult sexual life.

The modern therapist who has most influenced my thinking about perversion is the late Robert Stoller. He began his work with a study of gender identity and transsexuality, and his researches led him to consider the nature of perversion. Stoller became interested in the fact that there was very little understanding of the psychological aspects of human sexual excitement. Masters and Johnson had published their studies of the physiological aspects of arousal and orgasm, but, Stoller wondered, what about the factors that make one fantasy exciting and another boring?

Robert Stoller's Model of
Perverse Sexual Excitement

Most people have something erotic in mind when they masturbate. Perhaps men use sexual fantasies more than women, but if what our patients tell us in psychotherapy is true, women are no strangers to exciting erotic fantasy. The question of why one person is turned on to mental images of gently making love on a Polynesian beach, another to rape, and a third to being spanked led Stoller to explore masturbation fantasies and pornography. It was a small step from there to consider why people enact sexual fantasies involving humiliation, children, high-heeled shoes, and looking in women's bedroom windows.

Stoller concluded that a particular kind of hostility drives all forms of sexually exciting fantasy. The more hostility, the more perverse the fantasy or action. Stoller wrote: ". . . hostility, overt or hidden, is what generates and enhances sexual excitement, and its absence leads to sexual indifference and boredom. This dominance of hostility in eroticism attempts to undo childhood traumas and frustrations that threaten the development of masculinity and femininity (gender identity). The same sort of dynamics, though in different mixes and degrees, are found in almost everyone, those labeled perverse and those not so labeled."

What does this mean? It means there is a spectrum of childhood trauma ranging from minor and unavoidable to severe and unusual sexual, physical, and emotional abuse. It means that when the child experiences these traumas as aimed at his or her developing sexual self, the child attempts to cope with the threat by the creation of fantasy stories that are sexualized. The themes of these stories eventually coalesce to form a core masturbation fantasy, which becomes the center around which adult sexual experiences are organized.

On the mild end of the traumatic spectrum might be a young boy's experience of seeing his father's penis. Children are small. To them, adults are giants. One man in therapy recalled that he noticed at age four how much larger his father's penis was than his. He decided that his dad must have two penises instead of one. If this had been all that ever happened, perhaps he would have grown up to have no more than the average degree of sexual conflict.

However, let's imagine that this boy's father was punitive. When the boy misbehaved he was made to wait in the bathroom, naked, until his father appeared and whipped him with a belt. Now the boy experiences himself not only as small in relation to his father but also as his father's victim. His sense of "boyness" will be damaged. The boy's humiliation and physical pain occurs in relation to his burgeoning sense of maleness.

What would happen then? We'd move from the mild end of the traumatic spectrum to a position between moderate and severe. This was the case for a patient, with whom I worked for several years. He was left with a need to prove his masculinity over and over again as he grew up. He was an athlete on the field and in the bedroom. He found the idea of spanking a woman to be his most exciting fantasy. He masturbated to it, watched movies of it, and wondered if he'd do it, given the chance. Therapy for this man involved the confrontation of several painful issues: (1) his own hostility, now sexualized and directed toward doing to a woman what was done to him; (2) his own sense that he was less than an adequate man; and (3) the rage that lay deep in his heart toward his father for beating him and toward his mother for allowing it to happen. Sexual fantasy and imagery were at the center of the therapeutic process. As he reexperienced his childhood trauma and understood the ways in which he'd been trying to cope with it, the pressure to return to his sexual fantasies in order to prove his masculinity diminished. As the content of his fantasies changed, so did his rage and his underlying depressive sense of hopelessness.

Although this man's early experiences were very difficult, there are worse. Some children experience repeated, intrusive sexual, physical, and emotional abuse. These unfortunate individuals experience real, not imagined, hostility and must do their best to cope with it.

Many victims of child abuse are so overwhelmed that they avoid sexual experience all together, but some are perversely drawn to it. It is a well-known fact that individuals who sexually abuse have often been sexually abused. I've found that a variation of this is also true for the majority of patients who act out violent, sexually perverse scenarios. If they have not been sexually or physically molested, they have been subjected to repeated hostile, humiliating emotional abuse that was experienced as an attack on their gender identity.

Stoller suggests that in order to contend with childhood traumatic events directed at our burgeoning sexuality, we write stories in our heads—fantasy stories that use elements of our actual experience but usually disguise the characters and always alter the outcome of the traumatic experience. Instead of reexperiencing the fear, loss of control, pain, and humiliation of early traumatic event(s), we rewrite history. What was once a painful and overwhelming experience is turned into an experience of mastery. Passive trauma is converted to active mastery: trauma becomes triumph.

Hostility appears as a desire for revenge following the *talion law of the unconscious:* from the Latin *Lex Talionis,* this term refers to the principal of retribution, for example, an eye for an eye and a tooth for a tooth. What was once done to the individual is turned around and done to a figure representing the original perpetrator of the trauma.

Stoller is suggesting that anger, rage, and revenge are innately human and that they motivate our actions, especially our sexually exciting actions. Perverse patients are drawn to revisit sexual trauma over and over again. The more violent, hostile, and damaging the original experience, the more violent, hostile, and damaging the perverse sexuality. Perverse sexual fantasy and action are attempts to change the past in order to prove to the individual that he is no longer the small, powerless, frightened little person that he once was.

TREATMENT

Let's begin our examination of psychotherapy for these patients by looking at an example of how fantasy and perverse sexuality go together.

LORI SUMMERSBY

Lori, an attractive thirty-two-year-old college administrator, came into therapy because she was having difficulty making and maintaining a relationship with a man.

Lori's sexual arousal focused on being looked at by men she didn't know. She would often go to a dance club in a sheer blouse and short skirt without any underwear. The idea that she was being seen and desired was the most exciting thing in her life.

In therapy, Lori disclosed that she'd used a variation of the same fantasy each time she masturbated ever since adolescence. In the fantasy, she's a secretary or some other lowly employee who is called into the corporate conference room. She's terribly nervous. Inside she finds a group of executives: all men, all older, all dignified and obviously self-satisfied. Lori is told to sit in a low chair, all alone at one end of the table. She's asked some trivial question related to her work. In the course of her response she either bends forward exposing her breasts or accidentally reveals her thighs as she crosses her legs. The room goes quiet. She can tell the men are all staring at her body. This is the point in the fantasy when Lori begins to touch herself. She's already lubricated and quite excited.

She continues the fantasy by teasing the men. She knows of their interest and she exposes her body little by little. Eventually, the chairman of the board begs her to get on the table and strip completely. The climax of the story, literally and figuratively, comes when Lori bends over and spreads her legs for the men, all of whom have forsaken their controlled demeanor and are masturbating madly.

What do Lori's exhibitionism and fantasy life say about her experience, past and present? The first thing that comes to mind is that power dynamics are very important in Lori's sexual excitement. She's a lowly secretary dealing with the chairman of the board. She's a single woman dealing with a group of ten men. She's a nervous employee called in to give some minor details to the leaders of the company. Lori's little, they're big.

The creative power of Lori's imagination allows her not only to survive the ordeal but to triumph. Her story ends with her being in charge and the men being completely and utterly out of control. She's big; they're little. This is also true in Lori's experience at the dance club. It didn't matter that men at the club conducted themselves in a civilized manner. For Lori it was the illusion that was sexually real. When she went home at night and masturbated, as far as she was concerned, the men who'd been looking at her were doing the same thing while wanting (and not having) her.

Lori is fascinated with the sexual potential of looking and revealing. In her fantasy, no one ever touches anyone but themselves. In her sexual world, it's the eyes that have the power. Lori's power over men comes when she shows them the sexual parts of her body. They lose control and are overwhelmed with desire.

Another aspect of Lori's fantasy concerns position, literally. When she first comes into the boardroom, Lori sits in a chair that is lower than those of the men. By the end of the fantasy she is standing on the table, above the men. Position here refers both to physical size and to relative power. To be lower is to be humiliated. To be above is to be triumphantly dominant.

How does Lori fabricate a stimulating erotic scene? She creates a situation, either of actual exhibitionism or in sexual fantasy, that involves the risk of repeating previous trauma directed toward her developing sexual self. She then reverses that trauma by (1) turning any hostility away from herself, (2) exacting revenge by doing to the men what was once done to her, and (3) creating safety factors that ensure that the situation does not become overwhelming (does not repeat the original trauma). One safety factor in Lori's fantasy is her choice of civilized men who beg her to undress, who are rooted to their chairs, and who prefer masturbation to rape. She also situates the scene in an office, with a secretary outside.

The value of looking at fantasies and sexual behaviors through the lens of early trauma, hostility, and reversal is not so much to recreate what might have happened in the past but to understand the dynamics of what's going on in the present. In order to alter a perverse sexual organization, a patient must be able to see beneath her sexual preoccupation to the pain that lies inside. A primary aim of any therapy designed to help the perverse patient is to help her tolerate and move beyond that pain.

Lori came to individual psychotherapy once a week for a period of twenty-six months. Initially, she was completely unaware of any anger or hostility in her sexual life. She experienced herself far more as the victim than the victimizer.

My first step in working with sexual masochism is to empathize with the patient's sense of victimization. When Lori felt that this aspect of her experience was understood, she was more able to acknowledge her disappointment in men. Because she trusted the therapeutic relationship, she was able to relate the specifics of her sexual fantasies. She began to understand the ways in which she opted for control and reversal and how she did the same thing in her "real" life.

A spiral of understanding led Lori to the ways in which she had actually been victimized in her childhood. Once this began, she was able to give up what might be seen as a form of false suffering and face the real suffering that was part of her life. As Lori had less need to enact the past, less need to protect herself from feelings of disappointment and failure, the power differential between Lori and the men she was drawn to decreased. She felt better about herself, more equal, more able to ask for what she wanted. When she decided to stop therapy she was in a relationship with a man who genuinely cared for her, and she was able to enjoy sex without needing a masochistic fantasy.

Creating a Therapeutic Alliance

Creating and maintaining a working alliance with paraphiliac patients can be a major stumbling block. These patients have particular vulnerabilities that make it difficult for them to trust that psychotherapy will be helpful and that any particular psychotherapist has their best interest at heart. Many who find themselves aroused by perverse sex consider therapists to be agents of society. Their expectation is that you will encourage or even force them to give up their "aberrant" sexual excitement. Furthermore, all perverse individuals deal with issues of shame and lack of self-esteem. It takes only one wide-eyed gaze from the therapist for them to conclude that therapy is neither helpful nor safe.

What can you do to make an alliance with these patients? Once you've decided that a particular patient would best be treated by individual therapy and that you can deal with his sexual feelings, do your best to *create a nonjudgmental environment* that will permit the patient to relate in as free a manner as possible.

Unless you find that he is in danger of harming himself or harming someone else, do your best to remain emotionally balanced between neutrality and concern. Obviously, issues of sexual abuse and child molestation require the definitive and clear approach outlined earlier in this chapter. It may not always be easy to remain objective, especially if a patient reveals the details of his sexual experiences. If you can remember that the sexual actions of a perversion are the tip of an iceberg that goes down into the very core of a patient's personality, you'll be less likely to mistake the tip for the entire problem.

The second important way to forge an alliance with a patient is to *understand the patient's initial motivation for therapy*. A case example illustrates this idea.

HENRY DENNISON

A therapist I supervise came to me gravely concerned for a new patient. She wanted to know if she should tell him that he had to stop his sexual "acting out" or she would stop the therapy. Henry, a young lawyer, was involved in a sadomasochistic homosexual affair, and the therapist was worried about both his physical well-being and what might happen if his colleagues found out that he spent his weekends in a leather bar wearing a leash and doing whatever his "master" demanded of him. Henry was quite aware of the dangers inherent in his behavior. He and his partner practiced safe sex, and the risk of HIV infection was not significant. He also knew that the lawyers in his firm might be uncomfortable with his sexual choices, but he was not willing to give the choices up for that reason.

The most important single question the therapist needed to answer was why had the patient come to therapy? What did he want? Henry was depressed, not about his means to sexual excitement but about the fact that the man he loved was not faithful to him. He was in therapy to work on his relationship, and he was quite willing to address his sexuality as it pertained to it.

The therapist calmed down and began to work on the patient's agenda as Henry himself saw it. At first he thought that perhaps he wasn't a good enough sexual slave—that was why his partner was unfaithful. As Henry saw more clearly the ways in which his own needs were not getting met, he reversed this opinion and decided that he needed to see what would happen in the relationship if he were less submissive.

In the end, both Henry and the therapist were happy with the results of therapy. The therapist felt that she had a better understanding of how perverse sexuality works and that she'd been able to help her patient. Henry left his relationship and found another man who was committed to him. Did his sexual preference change? A little. He was still excited by being made to submit sexually, but in his new relationship the interaction was much more playful, and there was considerably more room for the expression of caring and connection.

Recognizing Sexualized Hostility

If there is a spectrum of sexual arousal along which we all operate, then those fantasies and actions with the most hostility would be the most perverse. A man who uses a fantasy of killing a woman to become sexually excited is deeply and obviously involved with hostility. A man who actually carries out such terrible acts is all but lost in sexual hostility. A woman who imagines tenderly making love to her husband has very little, if any, need for hostility to drive her erotic daydreams. Lori Summersby's fantasy of sexual abandon involved a mild degree of hostility experienced as the tension between being controlled and in control, between being small and being big.

We must learn to recognize the hostility in our perverse patients' fantasies and actions. A perversion works just like a sexual fantasy. The idea of degrees of hostility in perversions helps to expand our therapeutic definition. One way to think of a perversion is as the sexual expression of hostility. Stoller succinctly calls perversion "the erotic form of hatred."

In sadism, the hostility is obvious. In masochism, exhibitionism, fetishism, sexualized cross dressing, and voyeurism, it is less so. In the latter cases hostility remains under the surface, known to the individual in a secret and private place but hidden to the outside observer.

One hostile element of a masochist's, voyeur's, fetishist's, or transvestite's desire is to turn another person into an object—an insensitive, inhuman thing. Stoller termed this *dehumanization;*

he saw it as the way the individual damages the other by taking away his or her humanity.

If you've had a truly sexually masochistic client, perhaps they've told you about who is actually in charge in a consensual sadomasochistic sexual relationship. Contrary to surface appearances, the masochist is almost always in charge. The sadist looks for cues to know what the masochist wants and can tolerate. This is not likely to be the case in the sadist's fantasy, but it's common knowledge among those who are involved in the consensual practice of S&M. Masochists do get themselves into difficulty, however, when they misjudge the degree of hostility in a partner, or when their provocative, risk-taking behavior leads to accidental injury or even death. Cases of accidental asphyxiation in masochists who find the delirium induced by lack of oxygen sexually arousing are not exactly common, but they occur more often than most people might imagine.

It is the matching of complementary fantasies that allows the sadist and masochist to come together (pun intended). According to Stoller, it's the pairing of complementary fantasies that gets most of us together with a sexual partner. We each need someone who is a "good enough" fit for the sexual drama we carry in our heads. Good enough generally involves looks, size, dress, demeanor, and, most important, the means to sexual excitement. A masochist will not find a man who abhors aggression a very good partner. A man with a penchant for a passive woman will most likely not marry an Amazon.

Recognizing hostility also means identifying the depth and degree of the patient's hostility. Stephen Levine has commented that working closely with paraphiliacs involves a confrontation with the nature of evil. I find it no accident that the most feared villain in modern fiction is not the witch or the zombie but the serial rapist-killer. The popularity of such books as *The Silence of the Lambs* and *The Red Dragon* by Thomas Harris, *Along Came a Spider* by James Patterson, and *Gone, But Not Forgotten* by Philip Margolin attest to our culture's fascination with the evil inherent in perverse sexuality.

Using Sexual Fantasy As a Window

People's sexual fantasies and actions are windows into the dynamics underlying their eroticism. The ways in which patients find fantasized or perverse sexual excitement can alert you to their psychological wounds and the ways in which they manage them.

Therapeutically, it is helpful to realize that the patient who imagines or enacts a perverse scenario is motivated by psychological pain. The perversion, be it in fantasy or behavior, is a significant form of defense against that pain. This is one reason why a perverse patient is notoriously so difficult to treat. Giving up the perversion means forsaking the barrier between the patient and his psychic pain.

When patients with perversions enter therapy, their perversion is usually more egosyntonic than not. That is, even if they are ashamed or guilty or scared, they desire to maintain their perverse behavior. Many of these patients arrive in therapy at the behest of someone else: the court, a partner, a parent. As we have discussed, one of the most difficult aspects of their therapy is the construction of a working alliance. From the perspective of the patient, what's in it for them? Giving up the only way they know how to enjoy sexual feelings? Letting go of the major way they protect themselves from painful memories and an injured self-image?

Working with Shame

Some perverse patients will come to you with intense feelings of shame. It's important to evaluate the basis of the shame. For many of these patients it will be quite external. They will say that society is making them feel bad about their sexual style. If society would just leave them alone, they would be fine. As perverse behavior is a protection against deeper shame, the patient cannot access his internal experience until therapy progresses.

Shame makes people want to disappear. We often have no words to speak of our shame. This is especially true of the paraphiliac who is defending against deep shame with a denial of it. Many forms of paraphilia involve the actual reversal of shame: what would be shameful for most of us—say, exposing our genitals in public—becomes sexually arousing for the paraphiliac. What is shameful is used as a defense against a deeper shame.

The first step in working with shame is to give it a name. If you can help your patient to see where and when he is ashamed or embarrassed, you've accomplished an important first step.

For many perverse patients, shame does not initially appear in the sexual arena. It comes when the patient is criticized, slighted, ignored, or belittled. Let's look at a case example that will underscore this point.

RICHARD NORTH

Richard was required to be evaluated for therapy when he was arrested for exhibiting his erect penis to a young woman on the street.

In contrast to what you or I might feel, Richard was embarrassed by his arrest, but not terribly so. What might be a risk for one person isn't necessarily a risk for another person.

What was the most significant risk in Richard's perversion? Not the shame of getting caught. Not the guilt of having a young woman become frightened by his erect penis. No, the risk was of being ignored.

Richard's deep-seated fear was that he wasn't an adequate, sexual man. This was manifest in other aspects of his life—his fear that his boss would fire him, his anxiety about public speaking, his inability to urinate in a public bathroom—but nowhere was it as strong as in his sexual life. Richard was compelled to exhibit himself in order to temporarily repair his damaged sense of masculinity by demeaning and frightening a woman. In this way, he proved to himself that she was not more powerful and dominant than he.

Police officers advise women that the best way to discourage a flasher is to ignore him—just keep walking as though nothing unusual is happening. There's an old joke: a woman was walking in the park when a man jumped out from behind a tree and wiggled his erect penis at her. She paused, put her finger to her cheek and said, "Gee, what's that? It looks like a penis but it's much smaller."

Both the advice and the off-color joke show the way beneath the exhibitionist's fantasized story of terrible, hostile male potency. They each reverse Richard's dream of potency. They turn the exhibitionist into a little boy with a little penis, humiliated and ignored by the adult world.

Getting caught was a hidden part of Richard's fantasy. Look at all the fuss that was created by his erection. It's obviously self-destructive in one sense, but if we are thinking of Richard's wounded sexual self, having the police after him for showing his penis makes him a formidable man indeed.

Richard's motivation for therapy wasn't to stop exhibiting himself. Other than the court mandate, he was ready to leave therapy the moment he walked in. The crux of the therapy was whether or not it would begin.

Once I understood where Richard's shame lay, I addressed it. We discussed his fears of failure, and how he felt when a woman looked at his erect penis with fear. He could see that his shame was diametrically opposed to the sense of power he felt when exposing himself, but this didn't stop him from wanting to enact his fantasy. The only reason to stop his sexual behavior that he could come up with was that he didn't want to lose his job. Richard was able to stop his paraphiliac behavior while we were meeting. When he could trust me a bit more, he told me that he was depressed a lot of the time.

I eventually concluded that Richard was not able to form a strong enough therapeutic alliance with me to delve deeper into his emotional life. No matter how hard I tried, Richard was in my office because the conditions of his probation necessitated it. I started him on Prozac, an antidepressant that would both help his underlying depression and decrease his sexual drive, something that he thought was a good idea. The medication helped, and Richard agreed to join a group specifically for exhibitionists.

Working with Shame in the Transference

What about those patients who are able to dig deeper and work more effectively with their shameful wounds? Unlike Richard, some perverse patients are able to form a working alliance. When that happens, you the therapist begin "to matter." As treatment progresses, the patient cares what you say, what you think, and what you do.

In many cases, patients will find that they are less pressured to enact or fantasize as long as the therapeutic relationship is present. The sexualization that was so prominent in their lives often diminishes, and there is an initial period in which you might think they are "getting better." Self psychologists have described this situation as involving a particular kind of transference in which the patient uses the therapeutic relationship to shore up his flagging sense of self. Whether he sees you as a mirror of his experience, as a special person who is everything he wishes to be, or as someone who is uniquely like him, you offer the patient the potential to feel valued, understood, and connected—something he deeply needs, but doesn't trust will actually happen.

Sometimes patients become particularly sensitive to any disappointments or disruptions in treatment. Misunderstandings, empathic failures, those days when you're tired, sick, or unable to get to the office are inevitable sources of hurt and disappointment for all your patients. Some patients are able to take these experiences in stride. They can express their reactions, digest them, and go forward. Others, many paraphiliacs among them, are not only unable to move forward after these experiences but unable to hold themselves together. They fall into a particular kind of depression. Varieties of shame appear, and their sexual symptoms return or even increase. When disappointed or let down, the narcissistically damaged individuals we're considering go back to what they know—perverse sexual fantasy or enactment.

In general, psychodynamic therapists are taught to "analyze" transference. That is, if a patient is using loving and caring feelings toward me to hide anger or disappointment, I point out this defensive use of the relationship. The positive transference is "analyzed." These insights and observations can be *genetic*, referring to repetitions of the patient's past experience, or *functional*, referring to the ways he uses the relationship in the present moment to manage immediate conflicts.

The kind of transference we're talking about here, called a *selfobject* transference, requires a different kind of management. Instead of analyzing it away, we must allow it to exist.

Allowing a patient to depend on you in an especially deep way does not mean inactivity. You must watch carefully for the ways in which the patient's connection to you is broken or shattered.

ANDY KLIEG

Andy, a forty-one-year-old successful engineer, was able to stop making obscene phone calls as his therapy took hold. As our relationship solidified, Andy told me that he wanted to go to medical school to become a psychiatrist.

How would you react?

With horror that someone who had been arrested for calling teenage girls wanted to be a physician? With confusion as to why a middle-aged man with an advanced degree in mechanical engineering and a yearly salary well over $100,000 a year would even imagine going to medical school?

Both of these reactions are understandable, but they miss the point. Andy was able to stop his phone calls because he had become invested in therapy. His desire to attend medical school was a sign that he looked up to me as an ego ideal. He wanted to be like me and to be liked by me. He was trying, albeit unconsciously, to reverse and heal his shame.

The most helpful thing I could do was to discuss Andy's interest and excitement without commenting on the likelihood that he would in fact go to medical school. I did not point out that he only wanted to be like me because he felt bad about who he was. This would have left him crestfallen and less trustful of my help. I didn't say that Andy was acting as though I was some kind of hero. This was true, but baldly saying it would leave Andy with the feeling that I wanted him to stop seeing me this way. His interest in becoming a therapist was an indication of a newfound source of ambition and values. For the moment, in the context of therapy, Andy felt more whole, more able to have a direction and a sense of self-esteem. This was an integral and positive aspect of the therapy.

The problem in Andy's therapy came later when I failed to live up to his image of me. Andy was doing well. He felt stronger, more competent in his job, more in control, quite able to resist the urge to make obscene calls and masturbate. He'd even begun to date a woman he found attractive. Our recent discussions centered on his hopes and fears that the relationship could become sexual. In this climate of success, I told Andy that I would be away from the office for several days, beginning in a few weeks. Andy spent that evening on the phone, talking to women and masturbating!

Knowing the kind of dynamic we were addressing, I had expected that something might happen. So when Andy came in for his next appointment looking distant and cold, I asked him what he was feeling.

"Nothing's happening," he said.

In this he was correct. At least nothing good was happening. I pointed out that he looked depressed and asked him what might have made him upset.

If looks could kill, I wouldn't be writing this chapter. A look may be worth a thousand words, but it was words that I was hoping for from Andy.

"No. I'm not angry. Upset at myself maybe, but not angry."

"What are you upset about?"

He told me about the phone calls. His fantasy while he was on the phone was that if the woman on the other end only knew what he was doing, she'd scream and drop the phone. It was particularly gratifying to imagine her fear, Andy said.

In the ensuing sessions, Andy and I worked to understand what was going on. Andy said he was just horny. I did my best to gently suggest that it might not be a coincidence that the pressure to call and masturbate returned on the night I told him I'd be going away.

I'd like to say that Andy got it, felt better, and stopped getting off on scaring women even if they didn't know it, but that's not what happened. He continued to make obscene phone calls and continued to masturbate. As far as he was concerned, his actions had no connection to me.

As my vacation approached, Andy became less involved in therapy. He said he didn't feel anything. His work deteriorated. He began to feel depressed.

Pornographic movies had not been of particular interest to Andy, but he started to watch them. Not surprisingly, he was drawn to movies in which the woman was frightened or surprised by a man. He liked it best when the man shamed the woman, forcing her to admit that she liked sex. Andy's depression disappeared into his new sexual obsession.

On the day before my vacation, Andy looked a little sad. He said he'd received an erotic tape in the mail the previous day, but for some reason didn't bother to watch it. He didn't know what was wrong with him. "Maybe," he said, "I'm coming down with a virus."

I didn't protest, but nodded sympathetically.

"Why don't you get mad at me?" Andy then protested.

That was the beginning of a definite change in our work and in Andy's experience of himself. He opened up, expressed his sadness at my leaving, and even hinted that he was angry at me. He wasn't sure, but maybe I was right that his sexual preoccupation had returned because I was leaving.

Therapeutic progress in this circumstance required that our empathic connection be reestablished. We worked long and hard, and Andy was able to see how he used his connection to me.

Self psychologist Arnold Goldberg has emphasized the import of sexualizations that occur around vacations and empathic disruptions.

The reestablishment of an empathic connection is the first step in helping these patients begin to empathize with themselves. It was the process of empathic understanding and the insightful explanation of how Andy fell apart when I told him I was leaving that reestablished our therapeutic relationship.

We dealt with Andy's relationship to me slowly, in digestible bites. Each time that we were able to reestablish our connection and look at the reasons for its dissolution, Andy understood the process a little better. The next time I looked inattentive, or misunderstood him, or told him I was going to leave for a vacation, Andy managed a little better. Much like lifting weights to make a muscle stronger, Andy gradually began to bear the weight of his own inner world.

In order for this process to work, the trauma must be experienced as bearable by the patient. To stay with the athletic metaphor, asking a new member of the health club to pick up three hundred pounds on his first effort is doomed to failure. Therapy reflects normal personality development in that innumerable, small, minimally traumatic disappointments lead to internalization of care-taking of the self. There are such things as too much and too little frustration. What works best in therapy, as in childhood development, is an optimal level of frustration. In childhood this might include appropriately protective parental prohibitions, admonitions, and constructive criticisms. In concert with parental responsiveness, approval, and mirroring, a child can develop a secure sense of self. In therapy, this means that you need to recognize and point out those moments when your patient is withdrawing or returning to sexual acting out in response to a sense of narcissistic injury.

Working with Anger Directed at the Therapist

Let me repeat that perverse patients react to shame, disappointment, and failure with sexualized defenses. The patient's hurt, rage, and disappointment in the therapist are often dispersed in withdrawal from the therapeutic relationship and in sexual acting out that serves to (1) discharge rage, (2) revitalize the patient's wounded self, and (3) distance and defend against dependence on the primary object, in this case the therapist. This process is essentially similar in relation to all those people who function as selfobjects for the patient—parents, siblings, husbands, wives, bosses, heroes, mentors, friends, and lovers.

Open and direct expression of anger and rage toward you after an alliance has been established can be an important event in the therapy of paraphilias. In many cases, sexualization is the only way these patients have been able to deal with disappointment and shame. The direct expression of hurt and anger is a statement that they have taken you in as a significant, even vital aspect of their developing self.

When this happens, your job is to

- Tolerate the patient's anger.
- Discover where and when an empathic disruption has occurred.
- Nondefensively accept your part in the misunderstanding, separation, or therapeutic error.
- Carefully track through the experience: illuminate the injury; the patient's usual response to it (perverse enactment or fantasy), which may be present to a greater or lesser degree; and the importance and positive significance of the patient's new-found ability to confront, discuss, and be angry.

It's no easy task to accomplish all this. No one can do it all at once, or the first time it happens. These four elements will help your patient experience anger and feel significant and potent without having to resort to perverse sexualization. Many such experiences strengthen the damaged aspects of the patient's self. He will be more able to experience a range of intense affect: not only hurt and rage but also joy and gratitude.

Working with Perversion As a Defense Against Depression

This idea, slightly altered in form, has become a central aspect of self psychology. It was put forward in relation to masochism over thirty years ago by Albert Lubin. He suggested that there is a continuum that runs between pure depression and pure masochism. Lubin wrote: "Broadly speaking, the depressive suffers and the masochist exhibits suffering." Lubin noted that masochists, and by extension patients with any of the perversions, minimize their depression when they are engaged in their chosen behavior.

Depression is a state of hopelessness. A perversion is an attempt to preserve hope and seek out the possibility of love. At one end of Lubin's continuum, the depressive withdraws and gives up on attachment. On the other, the perverse individual desperately holds on to attachment through sexual enactments.

Attachment

Bernhard Berliner wrote several fascinating articles about the nature of sexual and moral masochism. He related these perverse styles to the depressive character. His thesis was that children who grow up in situations in which they are not treated with love and respect will come to experience how they are treated as the coin of exchange in the world of attachment. That is, a child who is hated, mistreated, or abused will find that the intensity of that experience is what binds him to other people. Given the choice between nothing and mistreatment, mistreatment will win out.

Many patients who have found a way to integrate their sexual styles into their lives will tell you that their experience is not simply one of pain. A young woman who was sexually stimulated by being tied up, humiliated verbally ("You're a slut, aren't you!"), and tortured physically until she would admit that she was bad, explained that when her nipples were pinched it hurt but also felt good—good physically, because it felt good emotionally. She knew exactly what kind of pain she would tolerate and exactly how much of it. If her partner did not stay within the bounds of her needs, she would "fall out of the illusion" and demand to be untied.

Because her intuition was excellent, this woman was able to find a man whose needs were complements to hers. Between the two of them they were able to enact a "scene" in which she was gratified by being forced to undress and become aroused "against her will." Simultaneously, her partner was enacting a scene in which he was able to make a beautiful young woman strip and perform all sorts of salacious sexual acts for his pleasure.

The young woman was very clear in her feeling that she felt loved and cared for by her paramour. She was attached to him precisely because he could enact her fantasy seamlessly.

How could a person feel that someone who was sexually humiliating her was doing it out of love? Berliner suggests that children who have known abuse, punishment, sexual mistreatment, and neglect experience hostility as love. What most of us would consider hurtful, even hateful, action is perceived by the perverse individual as love. More than one perverse patient in therapy has remarked that when they first entered into what most of us would term a more loving relationship, they were bored. One man said, "It was like cotton candy. Nothing was happening."

Psychic Pain

In a classic paper, Mashud Khan suggested that perversions are substitutes. The false pain that is created in a sexual perversion is an attempt to avoid a genuine pain that lies beneath the patient's consciousness. Again, you can see that this is an idea we have examined in our clinical discussions. Khan's description of a woman patient who eventually uncovers the genesis of her sexual perversion is quite fascinating.

The idea that perverse sexuality reflects a deeper layer of psychic pain is also predominant in the writings of several Jungian analysts. Rosemary Gordon, for instance, takes on masochism as a perversion not of sexuality but of the need for surrender. The perverse individual is someone who is unable and unwilling to suffer the anxiety of genuine surrender yet who yearns for its receptive potential. Because masochists, and any other perverse patients, structure a sexual situation so that they remain in control, even if it doesn't look that way, they are refusing to acknowledge their need for ministration from another, all the while acting out this need.

∾

Working with sexually charged situations is rarely easy. It is particularly difficult when sexual excitement involves pain of one kind or another. Paraphilias lie alongside of normal love because they are infused with painful injury and vengeful hostility.

To treat perverse sexuality, we as therapists must not only tolerate the patient's injury but also our own. I'd go so far as to say that someplace inside, we all know about sexual perversions. We've all been children. We've all been hurt, frightened, and disappointed. We all use a little sexualization—well, most of us.

Making love is perhaps our best opportunity to let go of the moment and join with something greater than ourselves. When it works, we are each male and female, giver and receiver, passive and active. For a brief shining moment we can melt out of our individual cocoons into something larger. I believe that there is a place in that experience for injury, hostility, and revenge, but when sex works, these destructive forces are subsumed by caring, mutuality, and love.

Therapy can help motivated perverse patients to bridge the gap between rage and love, between injury and healing, in a deep and significant way. I've concentrated on individual psychotherapy both because it's what I know and because I think that the paraphiliac's deep-seated early wounds can be truly healed only in a deeply personal, deeply honest relationship.

NOTES

P. 282, *The most recent* Diagnostic and Statistical Manual: American Psychiatric Association. (1994). Paraphilias. In *Diagnostic and statistical manual of mental disorders* (4th ed., pp. 522–532). Washington, DC: Author.

P. 284, *In 1953, Kinsey reported:* Kinsey, A. C., & Pomeroy, W. B., (1953). *Sexual behavior in the human female.* Philadelphia: Saunders.

P. 284, *In a 1974 survey:* Hunt, M. M. (1974). *Sexual behavior in the 1970's.* Chicago: Playboy Press.

P. 284, *In a sample of almost three thousand:* Janus, S. S., & Janus, C. L. (1993). *The Janus report* (pp. 114–115). New York: Wiley.

P. 285, *The authors of* Sex in America: Michael, R. T., Gagnon, J. H., Laumann, E. O., & Kolata, G. (1994). *Sex in America: A definitive survey* (p. 227). Boston: Little, Brown.

P. 297, *the information I present:* Tollison, C. D., & Adams, H. E. (1979). *Sexual disorders: Treatment, theory and research.* New York: Gardner Press.

P. 297, *John Money reported:* Money, J. (1970). Use of an androgen-depleting hormone in the treatment of male sex offenders. *Journal of Sex Research, 6,* 165–172.

P. 298, *In one example, ten pedophilic men:* Quinsey, V. L., Bergersen, S. G., & Steinman, C. M. (1976). Changes in physiological and verbal responses of child molesters during aversion therapy. *Canadian Journal of Behavioral Science, 8,* 202–212.

P. 298, *Freud thought a perversion:* Freud, S. (1957). Three essays on sexuality. In J. Strachey (Ed. and Trans.), *The standard edition of the complete psychological works of Sigmund Freud* (Vol. 7, p. 231). London: Hogarth Press. (Original work published 1905)

P. 300, *Stoller wrote: "hostility:* Stoller, R. (1978). Sexual excitement. *Archives of General Psychiatry, 33,* 903.

P. 302, *Stoller suggests:* Stoller, R. (1975). *Perversion: The erotic form of hatred.* New York: Pantheon.

P. 308, *Stoller succinctly calls perversion:* Stoller, R. (1975). *ibid.*

P. 308, *Stoller termed this* dehumanization: Stoller, R. (1975). *ibid.,* pp. 132–134.

P. 309, *According to Stoller, it's the pairing:* Stoller, R. (1978). Sexual excitement. *Archives of General Psychiatry, 33,* p. 908.

P. 309, *Stephen Levine has commented:* Levine, S. B. (1992). *Sexual life: A clinician's guide.* New York: Plenum.

P. 313, *Self psychologists have described:* Kohut, J. (1971). *The analysis of the self.* New York: International Universities Press.

P. 316, *Self psychologist Arnold Goldberg has emphasized:* Goldberg, A. (1995). *The problem of perversion: The view from self psychology.* New Haven, CT: Yale University Press.

P. 319, *Lubin wrote: "Broadly:* Lubin, A. (1966). Discussion of the psychodynamics of the depressive character. *The Psychoanalytic Forum, 1,* 254.

P. 319, *Bernhard Berliner wrote:* Berliner, B. (1958). The role of object relations in moral masochism. *The Psychoanalytic Quarterly, 27;* Berliner, B. (1942). The concept of masochism. *Psychoanalytic Review, 29.*

P. 320, *Berliner suggests that children:* Berliner, B. (1966). Psychodynamics of the depressive character. *The Psychoanalytic Forum, 1,* 244–251.

P. 320, *Mashud Khan suggested:* Khan, M. (1979). *Alienation in the perversions.* New York: Routledge.

P. 320, *Rosemary Gordon, for instance:* Gordon, R. (1987). Masochism: The shadow side of the archetypal need to venerate and worship. *The Journal of Analytical Psychology, 32*(3).

FOR FURTHER READING

Benjamin, J. (1988). *The bonds of love.* New York: Pantheon.

Coen, S. J. (1992). *The misuse of persons: Analyzing pathological dependency.* Hillsdale, NJ: Analytic Press.

Friday, N. (1980). *Men in love: Men's sexual fantasies: The triumph of love over rage.* New York: Delacorte Press.

Harris, T. (1981). *The red dragon.* New York: Putnam.

Harris, T. (1988). *The silence of the lambs.* New York: St. Martins.

Khan, M. (1979). *Alienation in the perversions.* New York: Routledge.

Levine, S. B. (1992). *Sexual life: A clinician's guide.* New York: Plenum.

Margolin, P. (1993). *Gone, but not forgotten.* New York: Doubleday.

May, R. (1980). *Sex and fantasy.* New York: Norton.

Patterson, J. (1993). *Along came a spider.* Boston: Little, Brown.

Stoller, R. (1975). *Perversion.* New York: Pantheon Books.

ABOUT THE AUTHORS

Claire Appelmans, NP, RNC, is on the faculty of the Women's Health Care Nurse Practitioner Program at Education Programs Associates in Campbell, California. She received her B.S.N. from the University of Pennsylvania School of Nursing and a certificate from the Planned Parenthood Federation of America Ob/Gyn Nurse Practitioner Program in Philadelphia. She has taught at various medical schools in California and Philadelphia.

Bonnie Bernell, Ph.D., has been a licensed psychologist for twenty-three years, and is an adjunct professor at Santa Clara University and at the Institute of Transpersonal Psychology. She is a certified Imago™ therapist and a national workshop presenter. Her workshop offerings currently include workshops for stress in and out of the workplace and for developing communication skills, and intensive weekend workshops for couples and women. Bernell has a private practice in San Jose and Palo Alto, California.

Sandra Borrelli-Kerner, MFCC, is a licensed marriage and family counselor. As a psychiatric nurse twenty-five years ago, she was offered an opportunity to develop her interest in couple therapy by training in a Masters and Johnson–style approach at the Stanford Sexual Dysfunction Clinic. She practices psychotherapy with individuals and couples in Mountain View and Morgan Hill, California.

Faith W. Brigel, LCSW, received her degree from McGill University in Canada. She is a member of the Society of Clinical Social Workers and the American Association of Marital, Family and Child Counselors. She studied the techniques of sex therapy at the University of California Medical Center in San

Francisco. She has maintained a private practice of psychotherapy for the past twenty-two years in Palo Alto, California. She does individual, group, and marital therapy, and has recently started to work with the problems of infertility.

Randolph S. Charlton, M.D., is clinical professor of psychiatry and the behavioral sciences at Stanford University School of Medicine. He is a fellow of the American Academy of Psychoanalysis, a supervising and training analyst at the C. G. Jung Institute of Northern California, and a member of the Alpha Omega Alpha Honorary Medical Society. He is the author of articles and book chapters on clinical issues in psychoanalysis, psychotherapy, and sexual behavior. He has twice received the award for outstanding teaching in the Department of Psychiatry at Stanford for his courses on human sexuality and dream analysis. Dr. Charlton has lectured throughout the United States, and conducts a private practice of psychotherapy, psychoanalysis, and sex therapy in Palo Alto, California.

Alex Clerk, M.D., completed his residency training in psychiatry at Loma Linda School of Medicine. He is presently acting assistant professor of psychiatry and the behavioral sciences at the Stanford University School of Medicine, where he is the director of the Sleep Medicine Clinic.

Harcharan Gill, M.D., was born in Kenya and received his medical degree from the University of Nairobi. He trained at the British Institute of Urology in London and had a fellowship at the University of Pennsylvania. He is presently an assistant professor of surgery at Stanford University School of Medicine, where he specializes in urological oncology.

Marty Klein, Ph.D., MFCC, is a licensed marriage and family counselor and sex therapist in Palo Alto, California. In addition to training physicians, psychologists, and clergy, he is the author of several books, including *Ask Me Anything: A Sex Therapist Answers the Most Important Questions for the '90s.*

Cynthia McReynolds, M.A., is a licensed marriage, family, and child counselor in private practice in Palo Alto, California. She specializes in couples therapy and is an associate of the Couples Resource Center, where she trains other professionals and facilitates groups for couples. She leads ongoing groups and workshops for women, and has developed course materials in women's spirituality for the Institute of Transpersonal Psychology. She is co-director of A Foundation for Interdependence, which offers group experiences that explore the interconnection between personal and cultural dynamics.

Teri Quatman, Ph.D., is an assistant professor of counseling psychology in Santa Clara University's marriage and family counseling master's program, and teaches courses in human sexuality and the psychology of relationships. Her clinical specialty is object relations, which she employs in the treatment of individuals and couples as a licensed psychologist in private practice. She holds separate master's degrees in counseling and guidance, educational psychology, and psychology; her doctorate is in counseling psychology.

David Schnarch, Ph.D., is a licensed clinical psychologist and author of *Constructing the Sexual Crucible: An Integration of Sexual and Marital Therapy.* He is director of the Marriage and Family Health Center in Evergreen, Colorado. From 1977 to 1994 he was associate professor of psychiatry and urology at Louisiana State University School of Medicine in New Orleans. He is a clinical member of the American Association of Marriage and Family Therapy (AAMFT), and is certified by the American Association of Sex Educators, Counselors, and Therapists (AASECT) as a sex therapist and sex therapy supervisor. He served for eight years on the AASECT board of directors, during which time he chaired the professional education committee. His work has been featured on television and in print media both in the United States and abroad.

Vincent Zarcone, M.D., is professor of psychiatry and the behavioral sciences (clinical) at Stanford University School of Medicine. He is presently a staff psychiatrist at the Palo Alto Veterans Administration Health Services Center. Dr. Zarcone has served as associate director of the Stanford Sleep Laboratory and is presently director of the sleep laboratory at the Palo Alto Veterans Medical Science Center. He has written extensively about sleep disorders. In addition, Dr. Zarcone is a pioneer in the milieu treatment of drug-addicted veterans.

INDEX

chotic disorders, 63–64; and referral for medical evaluation, 73–75, 99–100, 111–112, 169; and referral for psychological testing, 72–73, 75–76, 169; resources about, 94; structure of, 61–69; tack and timing in, 62; therapist attributes needed for, 59; timeliness of, 61; typical format of full, 61–62. *See also* Diagnosis; Medical evaluation

Excitement phase: in Kaplan's triphasic model, 49; in Masters and Johnson's model, 42, 43, 46. *See also* Arousal

Exhibitionism, 59; clinical definition of, 282; *DSM-IV* definition of, 80; treatment of, in case example ("Lori"), 303–306; treatment of, in case example ("Richard"), 311–312. *See also* Paraphilias

Exposure therapies, 20–21

Extramarital experiences: and couple therapy, 177–180; and differential performance, 74

F

Family systems approaches: to differentiation, 128–139; to relationship dynamics, 139–147; in Schnarch's quantum model, 54–57. *See also* Differentiation; Emotional fusion; Relationship

Famotidine (Pepcid), 38

Fantasies, sexual: for arousal, 239–240, 242; in erotic transference, 263–264; normal, 242; and paraphilias, 282, 300–306, 308–309, 310; therapeutic use of, for bypassing anxiety, 50, 51, 52

Fear, and desire disorders, 208. *See also* Anxiety

Female Arousal Disorder, 59; *DSM-IV* definition of, 78; prognosis for, 262; versus sexual pain disorders, 79; treatment of, in case example ("Amelia"), 259–261.

See also Arousal disorders

Female Orgasmic Disorder, 59; diagnosis of, in case example ("Brownells"), 86–91; *DSM-IV* definition of, 78; prognosis for, 265; treatment of, in case example ("Beth"), 262–265; treatment of, in women's sexuality groups, 265–267. *See also* Orgasmic disorders

Fenfluramine (Pondimin), 38

Fertility problems, and desire problems, 206, 207

Fetishism, 59, 308–309; clinical definition of, 283; *DSM-IV* definition of, 80. *See also* Paraphilias

Fibrosis, penile, 115, 125

Fictitious disorders, psychological testing for, 75–76

Firepersons, 26–27

Fluoxetine (Prozac), 35, 38, 209

Fluphenazine (Prolixin), 38

Focused sex therapy: for arousal/orgasmic disorders, 250–251; books for client reading in, 181–182; couple therapy versus, 166–167; time limit of, advantages of, 170–171; using techniques of, in couple therapy context, 180–190; when to use, in couple therapy, 168. *See also* Arousal disorders treatment; Behavior therapy approaches; Desire disorders treatment; Homework assignments; Orgasmic disorders treatment; Therapy

For Yourself (Barbach), 181–182

Foreskin contraction, 115

Freud, S., 51, 56, 241, 249, 298–300

Friday, N., 323

Fromm, E., 198

Frotteurism, 59; clinical definition of, 283; *DSM-IV* definition of, 80. *See also* Paraphilias

Functional co-morbidity, with desire disorders, 206–207, 224–225

Fungal infection, 34

K

Kaplan, H. S., 48–52, 60, 92, 94, 199, 279
Keeping the Love You Find (Hendrix), 182
Kerr, M., 163
Ketoconazole (Nizoral), 39
Khan, M., 320, 323
Kinsey, A., 240, 284
Klein, M., 201–236
"Kleins" case example, 91–93
Kohut, H., 5, 249
Kolata, G., 94
Kolodny, R., 94

L

L-arginine, 117
Labia, and physiology of sexual response, 32
Lactation, 74
Language: evocative, 71–72; "I," for couple communication, 176, 185–186; for talking about sex, 71–72, 184–185, 234
Laumann, E. D., 94
Lawrence, D. H., 249
Legal responsibility to report, and paraphilias treatment, 294–296
"Leo and Shelley" case example, 128–129
Levine, S. B., 249, 279, 309, 323
Levodopa (Dopar), 39
Librium, 36
Lifestyle, and erectile dysfunction, 121–122
Lithium (Eskalith), 39
Lobitz, C., 249, 279
LoPiccolo, J., 60, 249, 279
Lorazepam (Ativan), 36, 39
"Lori" case example, 303–306, 308
Love, P., 182, 199
Lubin, A., 319
Lubricant, artificial, 181; and arousal, 242

M

Mahler, M., 56
Male Erectile Disorder, 59; *DSM-IV* definition of, 78; and multiple sclerosis, 74; prognosis for, 271; treatment of, in case example ("John"), 267–271. *See also* Arousal disorders; Erectile dysfunction; Impotence
Male Orgasmic Disorder, 59; diagnosis of, in case example ("Brownells"), 86–91; diagnosis of, in case example ("Kleins"), 91–93; *DSM-IV* definition of, 78; prognosis for, 274; treatment of, in case example ("Brownells"), 271–274; treatment outcomes for, 277. *See also* Orgasmic disorders; Premature ejaculation
Managed care, 56, 60, 98–99, 186, 250
Mania, evaluation of, 63–64, 76
Maprotiline (Ludiomil), 39
Margolin, P., 309, 323
"Mariah and Evan" case example, 191–193
Marital therapy approaches, in Schnarch's quantum model, 54–57. *See also* Conjoint therapy; Couple therapy; Family systems approaches
Mars and Venus in the Bedroom (Gray), 182
Masculinity: myths/fears about, 241, 268–271; and paraphilias, 301–302
Masochism, 59, 308–309; attachment and, 319–320; in case example ("Henry"), 307–308; in case example ("Lori"), 305–306; in case example ("Vivian"), 291; clinical definition of, 284; as defense against depression, 318–319; *DSM-IV* definition of, 81; and psychic pain, 320–321. *See also* Paraphilias
Masters, W., 20, 41–48, 60–61, 94,

Prozac (fluoxetine), 35, 38

Psoriasis, 34

Psychiatric disorders: and differential diagnosis, 76, 239; and evaluation, 63–66, 75–76; and paraphilias, 293–294. *See also* Depression; Personality disorders; Psychogenic versus organic causes; Psychosis; Sexual disorders

Psychoanalysis, 60

Psychodynamic approaches: in evaluation, 60–61; in Kaplan's triphasic model, 49–52; in Schnarch's quantum model, 54–57; and self psychology, 313–319; to transference, 313–314; to treating paraphilias, 303–321; to understanding paraphilias, 298–303. *See also* Emotional conflict

Psychogenic versus organic causes: of desire disorders, 209–211; of erectile dysfunction, 113–114, 124–125; of sexual pain disorders in women, 108–109. *See also* Evaluation; Medical causes; Medical evaluation; Psychiatric disorders; Psychological testing

Psychological testing: determining the necessity of, 75–76; referral for, 72–73, 169

Psychosis: evaluation of, 63–64, 169; and paraphilias, 293

Puberty: and cultural neurosis, 7; discussion questions about, 11–12; male versus female, 23–24

Q

Quantum model of sexual response, 52–57; clinical insights of, 54–55; clinical problems of, 55–56; clinical techniques in, 56–57; overview of, 52–54; physiological and psychological stimuli and, 52–54

Quatman, T., 1–28, 29–58

Quodoushka tradition, 26–27

R

Ranitidine (Zantac), 40

"Raul and Alison" case example, 129–139

Readings: about arousal disorders, 279–280; about couple therapy, 198–199; for couple therapy client reading, 181–182; about desire disorders, 236; about orgasmic disorders, 279–280; about paraphilias, 323; about sexual disorders evaluation, 94

Rectal cancer, 108, 120

Rectovaginal exam, 108

Red Dragon, The (Harris), 309

Reflective choice, 135–138

Reflective listening, 185–186

Reflex arc, 31

Reflex centers, 31

Reflex process, 31

Refractory period, 43, 44, 46

Relationship: anxiety in, 157–161; differentiation in, 128–139; dynamics of, 139–147; evaluation of, in gynecological evaluation, 104; nature of, and dynamic formulation, 82–86; passion in, 129–130, 147–152, 162–163; safety in, 155–156; Sexual Crucible model of, 152–162; and sexuality, 127–147; togetherness versus individuality drives in, 139–142. *See also* Couple relationship; Couple therapy; Differentiation; Intimacy

Relationship conflict: addressing of, before sexual evaluation, 67–68; and arousal disorders, 242–243; and desire disorders, 223–224; and differentiation, 128–139; and orgasmic disorders, 242–243; unresolved, 175–176. *See also* Couple relationship; Couple therapy; Relationship

Religious differences: and arousal disorders, 246; and desire disorders

ment; Diagnosis; Differentiation; Evaluation; Focused sex therapy; Medical treatment; Orgasmic disorders treatment; Paraphilias treatment; Therapists
Thiazide diuretics, 36, 40
Thioridazine (Mellaril), 40
Thiothixene (Navane), 40
Throxin, 33
Thyroid disease, 114
Togetherness versus individuality drives, 139–142
Touching: anxieties about, 20; nonsexual, homework assignment for, 187–188; in sensate focus exercise, 253–256; sexual, homework assignment for, 189–190
"Trace and Cal" case example, 177, 189–190
Tranquilizers, 36
Transference: anger directed at therapist in, 317–318; erotic, and countertransference, 262–265; and evaluation, 62; in paraphilias treatment, 293, 313–319; selfobject, 313–319
Transitions, 176–177
Transsexualism, 285
Transvestic fetishism, 59, 308–309; clinical definition of, 285; *DSM-IV* definition of, 81. *See also* Paraphilias
Tranylcypromine (Parnate), 40
Trauma. *See* Sexual/physical trauma
Trazodone (Desyrel), 41, 117
Trifluoperazine (Stelazine), 41
Triphasic model of sexual response, 48–52; clinical insights of, 49–51; clinical problems with, 51; clinical techniques in, 51–52
Trust, in relationship, 156

U

Uniqueness, 154–155
Urethra, 32
Urinary tract infection, 74
Urological evaluation, 110–122; case

examples of, 120–122; of erectile dysfunction, 112–119; referral for, determination of, 111–112; of retrograde ejaculation, 111–112
Urological treatment, 117–119
Urologists, 75, 110–111
U.S. Congress, 295

V

Vacuum erection device, 118
Vagina, and physiology of sexual response, 32
Vaginal infections, 107
Vaginal lubrication: artificial, 181, 242; insufficient, medical causes of, 74; physiology of, 32, 45
Vaginal muscle tone, 108
Vaginal scar tissue, 74
Vaginismus, 59; diagnosis of, in case example ("Kleins"), 91–93; *DSM-IV* definition of, 79; evaluation of, 74, 106–107; treatment of, in couple therapy, 195–196; treatment outcomes for, 277. *See also* Sexual pain disorders
Validation, self- versus other-, 142–147
Vascular surgery, 119
Vasodilan, 117
Venous leak, 121
Violence, 289–290. *See also* Abusive relationships; Paraphilias; Sexual/physical trauma
"Vivian Koch" case example, 291
Voyeurism, 59, 308–309; clinical definition of, 285–286; *DSM-IV* definition of, 81. *See also* Paraphilias
Vulva, and physiology of sexual response, 32

W

"Warner's" case example, 243, 247–248
Westfall, A., 199
Wheelis, A., 249
Winnicott, D. W., 5